THE BALTIC NATIONS AND EUROPE

THE BALTIC NATIONS AND EUROPE

Estonia, Latvia and Lithuania in the Twentieth Century

WITHDRAWN

John Hiden and Patrick Salmon

Longman
London and New York

LONGMAN GROUP UK LIMITED
Longman House, Burnt Mill, Harlow,
Essex CM20 2JE, England
and Associated Companies throughout the world

Published in the United States of America
by Longman Inc., New York

First published 1991

British Library Cataloguing in Publication Data
Hiden, John
The Baltic nations and Europe: Estonia, Latvia and Lithuania in the twentieth century.
I. Title II. Salmon, Patrick
947.08
ISBN 0-582-08246-3
ISBN 0-582-08245-5 pbk

Library of Congress Cataloging in Publication Data
Hiden, John
   The Baltic nations and Europe : Estonia, Latvia, and Lithuania in
   the twentieth century / John Hiden and Patrick Salmon.
      p.   cm.
   Includes bibliographical references and index.
   ISBN 0-582-08246-3 (csd). -- ISBN 0-582-08245-5 (ppr)
   1. Baltic States--Politics and government. 2. Soviet Union-
   -History--Autonomy and independence movements. I. Salmon, Patrick,
   1952–   . II. Title.
   DK502.7.H54 1991
   947'.4084--dc20   91-2401
                                                              CIP

Set in 10/12 Bembo

Produced by Longman Singapore Publishers (Pte) Ltd.
Printed in Singapore

Contents

List of maps and charts

Preface

Historians currently venturing to write about the Baltic republics and their recent past need all the help they can get. Recognition of the sheer scale of the task was what prompted us to join forces in the first place. This decision has been vindicated by the very obvious fact that we have completed the book. The plain truth is that we could not have done so, however, without much additional support, material and moral. It is a pleasure to acknowledge our many debts.

Our thanks go first to Longman for encouraging our project so enthusiastically.

For essential financial support we are grateful to the following: the British Academy; the British Council; the small grants committees of the Universities of Bradford and Newcastle upon Tyne; the History Department of Newcastle University; finally, the Baltic Research Unit at Bradford.

During our work we have been fortunate to have enjoyed the hospitality of a number of individuals and institutions. They include: Richard Langhorne and the Fellows of St John's College, Cambridge; Tony Badger of the History Department at Newcastle; Rolf Ahmann, of the German Historical Institute in London; Erwin Oberländer, Professor of East European History, University of Mainz; the Department of European Studies, University of Bradford; the Estonian Academy of Sciences; the Estonian Institute in Tallinn; Dr Arvo Kuddo, Estonian Minister of Social Affairs; members of the Tallinn Chamber of Commerce; Rein Helme, of the Estonian National Archive; Juri Bojars, member of the Latvian parliament and of the Congress of People's Deputies, as well as Professor of International Law at Riga University; Professor Aleksander Loit and the members of his Centre for Baltic studies, University of Stockholm.

For technical help in preparing the graphs and tables we are indebted to George Kazamias, of the Department of European Studies at Bradford University.

Inevitably, we have made free use of the expertise, time and attention of archivists and librarians. Among these, we would particularly like to thank Henry Gillett of the Bank of England archive. Thanks are also due to the staff of the Foreign Office Library, London; the Public Record Office, London; Bundesarchiv, Koblenz; Politisches Archiv des Auswärtigen Amtes, Bonn; Deutsches Zentralarchiv, Potsdam; the Estonian National Archive, Tallinn; Centre for Baltic Studies, Stockholm University.

It is much more difficult to acknowledge the very considerable debt we owe to Baltic specialists – in both the academic world and in those of government and commerce. We also have longstanding interests in Scandinavian and German history. Here too our contacts have been invaluable. We must single out the members of the Nordic History Group in the United Kingdom, for their helpful comments on papers that we have given to the group. The ideas of two historians have been particularly valuable: David Kirby of the School of Slavonic and East European Studies, University of London, and Merja-Liisa Hinkkanen, who is currently Visiting Research Fellow at the Baltic Research Unit in the University of Bradford. David Saunders, at Newcastle University, has shared with us his knowledge of Soviet nationality problems. Since 1985 we have both been involved in seminars and conferences at Stockholm's Centre for Baltic Studies. During these years we have been fortunate enough to talk with many academic visitors from Estonia, Latvia and Lithuania. Another great benefit following from our work in Stockholm has been the contact it has brought with a number of prominent American Baltic specialists. Many of them of Baltic origin, these scholars have perhaps done more than any other group to promote the study of modern Baltic history. Particular thanks are due to the late Edgar Anderson, who, as Professor of Baltic History at San José University, gave us very generous encouragement.

Since the Baltic Research Unit was set up at Bradford in the autumn of 1988 there has been a constant interchange of people and ideas with the Baltic republics. Academic, political and business leaders have taken part in Bradford's academic and business conferences in Britain; we in turn have been able to make visits to the Baltic. This has given us a unique opportunity to keep up to date with current events as well as the chance to discuss recent Baltic history. At this point it is appropriate to thank the Estonian, Latvian and Lithuanian communities of Bradford, who have done so much to welcome visitors from the Baltic republics.

We would also like to acknowledge the interest and support of the Baltic Council, whose London office has provided us with a valuable flow of information and arranged for members of the Baltic Research Unit to have a discussion with Estonian Foreign Minister Lennart Meri on 6 November 1990, at the Royal Institute of International Affairs.

Finally we turn, as ever, to our families. The writing of this book demanded repeated absences. The Hiden children have reached the age where the absence of a parent is something to celebrate; the Salmon children are still at the stage where they are pleased to see their father return. On the subject of our wives' views we dare not speculate. We thank them none the less for their patience.

John Hiden and Patrick Salmon
25 November 1990

For Jessica, Katie, Jessica, Hugo, Karen, Juliet

Introduction

In 1940 Estonia, Latvia and Lithuania lost their independence. Few would have predicted that the three republics would be celebrating the 50th anniversary of that event by making declarations of independence from the Soviet Union. How they arrived at such a momentous juncture can be explained only in part by reference to the changed conditions of perestroika and glasnost. These provided a foothold but the drive to win freedom from Soviet control comes exclusively from the Baltic peoples themselves. They have attempted to wrest an acknowledgement of their right to statehood from the central Soviet authorities. They have also fought to convince the outside world. For the Baltic peoples such daunting tasks are nothing new. Their present struggle is sustained by their history. The current Baltic 're-awakening' consciously echoes the national awakening of the nineteenth century; unlike the other Soviet nationalities the three republics draw on the achievements of twenty years of independent statehood between the First and Second World Wars; they take comfort too from the preservation of their national identities through fifty years of Soviet rule.

As historians we cannot help being struck by the extraordinary parallels between the present and past predicaments of the Baltic peoples. In 1990, in the ruins of the Soviet empire, they face challenges very similar to those their predecessors faced in 1920 in the ruins of the tsarist empire. No understanding of the current situation in the Baltic republics is possible without a knowledge of their history. On this conviction is founded our decision to write the book and the form it has finally taken.

In the first section we have attempted to convey something of the diversity of Baltic history from the middle ages to the end of the First

World War. Such a perspective demonstrates the tenacity with which the Estonians, Latvians and Lithuanians have held on to their small corner of Europe. It also underlines the fact that throughout their history the Baltic peoples have had to share their lands with other races, some of whom dominated them for centuries. Without this background, no reader will appreciate the way in which national identities were forged and preserved even under the rule of others. In 1918 the collapse of Russia and Germany gave the Baltic peoples the opportunity to seize control of their own destinies.

'Seize' is the operative word. The mere collapse of the great European empires was not a sufficient condition for Baltic statehood. The work of state building lay ahead, under the most adverse conditions. The second section of our book is therefore devoted to the period of Baltic independence. We try to show first that the societies constructed in the Baltic republics, though not perfect, were as viable as almost any other – and more than many – in the interwar period. Unlike some, the Baltic republics were not brought down by internal collapse but were destroyed by the actions of outsiders.

The international environment after 1918 was of paramount importance for the independent Baltic republics. This justifies the large amount of space devoted to it in the book. The Baltic perspective on international relations between the wars is an unfamiliar one. The insights to be gained from exploring it are all the more valuable. Important clues are provided to the way in which 'small states' have to operate in the international system. Although it is easy to assume that the lesser powers are merely passive members of the international community, closer examination of the Baltic reveals a more complex picture. It is more helpful to think of *interaction* between the Baltic states and the major European powers. The elimination even of a small state leaves the international system more vulnerable. It generates destabilising effects on the other members of the system, who are made more fearful by it. More unexpectedly, perhaps, the brutal treatment of weaker states has a habit of rebounding on the perpetrators. Nothing demonstrated the force of this argument more clearly than the extraordinary reverberations, in 1989, of the Nazi–Soviet pact of 1939. An unforgettable history lesson was dispensed by those citizens who joined hands to form a human chain stretching across the territories of the three Baltic republics on 23 August, the anniversary of the Molotov–Ribbentrop pact.

The emphasis on the international system between the wars has contemporary significance in another sense. Since the Baltic states fell victim to external aggression rather than internal collapse, the prospects for Baltic independence must be improved by global détente and the end of the Cold War in Europe. This is all the more likely in so far as there has always been a close connection between Baltic security and a flourishing East–West trade. Between the wars, ironically, the Baltic states were forced by Soviet policy to turn more towards the West. An ideal scenario for them would have been to function as economic bridges in a period of intensified trade between western Europe and the Soviet Union. Under Stalin, this vision disappeared. It has reappeared under Gorbachev, precisely because the USSR is now fixated on economic relations with the capitalist world. Western Europe for its part is integrated economically and to an increasing extent politically. There is no longer any threat to Soviet security from the West. The preconditions for Baltic prosperity, security and independence now exist.

Between the insecurities of the interwar period and the hopeful prospects of the present day lie fifty of the bleakest years ever experienced by the Baltic peoples. In the third part of the book the focus is on sheer survival. The catastrophes of war and occupation by both the Soviet Union and Nazi Germany were followed by decades of sovietisation from which there seemed until recently to be no escape. This was not compensated by the modernisation pushed through under Soviet auspices, even though the Baltic republics were among the most prosperous in the Soviet Union. The problem was that Soviet-style economic growth wrought profound demographic, social and environmental damage in Baltic society. Pollution provided in the end a crucial stimulus to the political reawakening of the Baltic republics.

In the final part of the book we undertake the difficult task of analysing events since the mid-1980s. We have been impressed once again by the way in which history provides clues to the present day. In a real sense, however, this part can never be finished. At the time of writing (November 1990) the Baltic republics are engaged in a fitful dialogue with Moscow as the Soviet Union plunges into a deepening economic, social and constitutional crisis. What can be said with certainty is that the Baltic republics are no longer so exposed to the threat of retribution as more and more republics follow their path towards greater autonomy.

Leaving aside the problem of interpreting contemporary events, the challenges of writing about the Baltic past are formidable. At this stage we should therefore offer our credentials. Our most obvious qualification is that we have been studying the Baltic area for many years. Our researches long pre-date the upsurge of interest in the Baltic republics which followed Gorbachev's reforms. This has given us a considerable advantage in comparison with many Soviet specialists. Understandably, many if not most of these were preoccupied until recently with trying to penetrate the mysteries of the Soviet system and took little interest in the Baltic perspective. On the other hand many Baltic specialists have taken too little account of the world within which the Baltic republics have had to live. Their work has been invaluable in tracing the history of the individual Baltic republics, as well as their culture and language. However, they have given relatively little attention to the international environment. As a result the work they have done has not reached the wider audience it deserves.

We have presumed to write this book precisely because of our conviction that a broader vista is required. We bring to the subject an expertise in the international relations of the period between the two World Wars. More specifically, we have written extensively on British and German foreign and trade policies, especially in relation to Scandinavia and the Baltic region. We have also taken a considerable interest in the nationality problems of the Baltic area, in particular those created by the once dominant German minorities of Latvia and Estonia. In addition, through our work with the Baltic Research Unit at Bradford we have become heavily involved in current Baltic affairs, engaging in a dialogue with political and academic figures in all three republics.

There are many who can claim with justice to have a detailed knowledge of the events unfolding in the Baltic in the 1980s. Many also have a knowledge of the more distant past. We are fortunate enough to have something of both and luckier still to find ourselves living in a part of Britain where Baltic émigré groups are still active and on whose resources we have been able to draw. Almost by accident, we have been placed in an ideal position to carry out our present work. We felt, moreover, that we had to do this work. Our belief is that history holds many of the most important keys to an understanding of the often bewildering course of events in eastern Europe today.

This makes us no less aware of our shortcomings. We do not have a mastery of any of the three Baltic languages. Yet if Estonia, Latvia and Lithuania were to rely solely on native Baltic speakers to interpret their past, this would compound the isolation from the mainstream which we have already noted. Nevertheless between us we have read widely in a number of languages, including German, French, Russian and the Scandinavian languages. We have also researched in many of the archives of those European powers most concerned with the Baltic area, especially those of Great Britain and Germany, where some of the fullest analyses of Baltic affairs are to be found. We have even been fortunate enough to penetrate the Estonian National Archive in Tallinn. Like all Baltic specialists, we have also been able to draw on a vast literature written by émigré historians, much of which has been remarkably objective under the circumstances.

We therefore feel as well qualified as anyone to tackle our themes. To repeat, we have been sustained above all by the conviction that study of the Baltic republics must be internationalised. More immediately it must be Europeanised if the Baltic nations are to take their full place in the future 'European home'.

It is not by chance that for much of the twentieth century Baltic leaders have sought above all to advance their nations by international-ising their cause. We shall be more than happy if we have contributed in the smallest way towards this goal.

PART ONE
Awakening

CHAPTER ONE
Against the Odds

The native inhabitants of the three present-day republics of Estonia, Latvia and Lithuania are directly descended from the tribes who settled on the eastern shores of the Baltic some 4,000 years ago.[1] They have lived there far longer than any of the peoples who have ruled over them since the middle ages – whether Scandinavians, Germans, Poles or Russians. 'The kernel of the historical awareness of the Baltic peoples is the fact that they are directly descended from the original inhabitants of their countries.'[2] Both the Lithuanians and the Latvians belong to the Indo-European race (Lithuanian, as nineteenth-century philologists were delighted to discover, is the closest living language to Sanskrit) while the Estonians are, like the Finns and Hungarians, of Finno-Ugric stock. Closely related to the Estonians are the Livs, a few thousand of whom are still to be found in northern Latvia. The Baltic peoples have never expanded beyond their native homelands. These, however, they have clung to tenaciously.

Their achievement is all the more remarkable in that the three races have been subjected over the centuries to the ebb and flow of war and conquest. The geographical position of the Baltic lands, at the point where East meets West, has made them a battleground for a succession of races and states striving for economic and political mastery in the region. By the time they became the victims of other peoples' ambitions in the early middle ages, the Baltic races had evolved viable pagan tribal societies which fought and traded successfully with their

---

1 Gimbutas *Th Balts* Londo 1963 43.
2 G von Pistohlkors, Die historischen Voraussetzungen für die Entstehung der drei baltischen Staaten. In B Meissner (ed), *Die baltischen Nationen: Estland, Lettland, Litauen*, Cologne 1990, p 11.

neighbours across the sea and in the interior of eastern Europe.[3] 'Many praiseworthy things could be said about these peoples with respect to their morals', wrote Adam of Bremen around 1075, 'if only they had the faith of Christ whose missionaries they cruelly persecute.'[4] Already, however, geography had transcended distinctions of race to separate the Estonians and Latvians in the north from the Lithuanians further south. Whereas the latter lived in impenetrable forests, isolated from the sea, the territories of the Estonians and Latvians, 'the tiny outlet of a zone stretching half-way across Asia', were important staging posts for trade between the interior of Russia and the western world.[5] In Estonian territory, Tallinn (Reval) on the coast and Tartu (Dorpat/Iurev) inland emerged as centres where furs, wax and slaves from the Russian hinterland were exchanged for salt, textiles and weapons.[6] The principal routes into the interior were, however, the rivers. Of the great rivers of eastern Europe only one, the Daugava (Düna/Dvina), ran through territories inhabited by the Baltic peoples. On its banks lived the Latvian tribes: Lettigallians to the north and Semigallians to the south. Another major river, the Nemunas (Memel/Nemen/Niemen), skirted the lands of the Lithuanians further south but was less important as a trading artery.

The Baltic peoples could coexist with their European neighbours as long as all lived at roughly the same economic, social and technological level. By the twelfth century at the latest these conditions no longer existed. Both the Scandinavians and Germans to the west and the Slav states of the east were becoming better organised and better armed. They were also showing an increasing interest in the Baltic lands. Those coming from the west had the advantage, however, in that they were infused by an aggressive Catholicism which enabled them to combine missionary zeal and material advantage.

The imprint of foreign domination, at first Swedish and Danish and later German, was most marked on the two most northerly peoples, the Estonians and the Latvians. Unlike the Lithuanians, they were

---

3 E Christiansen, *The Northern Crusades: The Baltic an th Catholi Frontie 1100–1525* Londo 1980 p 34–41.

4 Cited in Gimbutas, *The Balts*, p 25.

5 J Buchan (ed), *Baltic and Caucasian States*, London n.d. (*c.* 1923), p 122.

6 The names of Baltic places and geographical features present formidable problems. There may be as many as four different names: those used by the indigenous peoples (Estonian, Latvian or Lithuanian), as well as German, Russian and Polish, which in many cases are more familiar to non-Baltic readers. In this book we generally use the modern indigenous names, except in the case of names which have passed out of use (e.g. Livonia, Courland), but the first appearance of a name is followed in parentheses by its equivalents in other languages.

brought into the medieval Catholic world by conquest and forcible conversion – a brutal process which lasted for the whole of the thirteenth century. Thereafter they were subject almost continuously to political, social and economic domination by others. The provinces into which they were divided by their medieval conquerors corresponded only partially to ethnic divisions. The province of Estonia (Estland) comprised most of present-day Estonia, but Livonia (Livland) was carved out of the territories of the Estonians and Livs further south, and those of the Latvian tribes. A third province, Courland (Kurland), was detached from Livonia in the sixteenth century.

In the late twelfth century the German crusading orders, thwarted in the Holy Land, turned their attention to the pagan tribes of the eastern Baltic. While the Teutonic Order subdued the 'Old Prussians', the most westerly of the Baltic tribes, and absorbed them into a German colonial system, further north the Brotherhood of the Sword established a Christian, military state in Livonia. Its chief religious and commercial centre was the city of Riga at the mouth of the Daugava, founded in 1201 – after Lübeck the earliest German foundation on the Baltic Sea.[7] In 1346 a weakened Danish crown sold its right to Estonia, which had been subjugated by the Danes in the thirteenth century, and both Estonia and Livonia came under the rule of the Teutonic Order. The military monks established a German social, political and economic ascendancy which was to survive the dissolution of the Order and the secularisation of its lands during the Reformation of the sixteenth century. The rule of German landowners over a native Baltic peasantry, and the dominance of German merchants in commercial centres such as Riga and Tallinn persisted through the ensuing centuries of Swedish, Polish-Lithuanian and Russian rule.

In the sixteenth and seventeenth centuries the political geography of the Baltic provinces was subjected to further contortions as the region's great powers sought to succeed to the patrimony of the Teutonic Knights. As the Swedes established themselves in Estonia and fought the Russians for control of Livonia, the Lithuanians and their Polish allies created the Duchy of Courland out of the territory of southern Livonia. Then, in the seventeenth century, the eastern part of Livonia, Latgale, came under the direct control of Lithuania. The Latvians, formerly divided between two provinces, were now divided among three. To these political divisions were added religious ones as

---

7 R Wittram, *Baltische Geschichte: Die Ostseelande Livland Estland Kurlan 1180–1918* Munic 1954 19.

Livonia and Courland remained Lutheran while the position of Roman Catholicism was consolidated in Latgale, along with the rest of Lithuania.

With the Treaty of Nystad of 1721, marking the formal absorption of Estonia and Livonia into the Russian empire, Peter the Great confirmed the privileged position of the Baltic Germans and of the Lutheran Church in the Baltic provinces. Those privileges were to be acknowledged by successive Russian rulers up to Alexander II in 1856. The German-ruled Russian Baltic provinces (to which Courland and Latgale were added after the third partition of Poland) enjoyed a far-reaching autonomy within the tsarist empire. Although Baltic German hegemony was to be undermined by the tsarist government's policy of russification during the nineteenth century and was ended by the emergence of independent Baltic states after the First World War, the German presence was to be finally eliminated only during the Second World War.

The Lithuanians to the south carved out a path which was different from and, for several centuries, more successful than that of their Baltic neighbours. They owed their initial success to the impenetrability of their territories, their military prowess and a remarkable succession of rulers in the thirteenth and fourteenth centuries. Under pressure from the Teutonic Order the Lithuanian tribes achieved political unity in 1248 under the 'modernising autocrat', Grand Duke Mindaugas.[8] For tactical reasons Mindaugas converted to Christianity but his people did not. Nor, for a long time, did his successors. In fact the Lithuanian pagan religion reorganised itself and confronted the social, political and spiritual challenge of the Christian churches with considerable success. The Lithuanians not only held their own against the Teutonic order but also extended their influence far into the interior, over Belorussia and such Russian cities as Kiev and Smolensk, as they fought both the Tatars and the princes of Muscovy. When they ultimately entered western Christendom the last pagans in Europe did so on their own terms. In 1386 their ruler Jogaila (Jagiello) married a Polish queen and ordered the mass baptism of his subjects. He did so because 'he was moved by the prospect of winning the Polish kingdom, not by kindness.'[9] In 1410 Lithuania allied with Poland to inflict a decisive defeat on the Teutonic Knights at Tannenberg. Thereafter Lithuania and Poland rose and fell together. At first loosely joined, the two countries were formally united in 1569. In the eighteenth century the sprawling

8 Christiansen *Norther Crusades* 135.
9 Ibid, p 139.

Polish-Lithuanian commonwealth fell victim to the anarchic politics of its nobility and the rise of powerful, predatory neighbours: Prussia, Austria and Russia. With the third and final partition of Poland in 1795 Lithuania, along with Latgale and the semi-independent duchy of Courland (formerly part of Livonia), was absorbed into the Russian empire.

Although all three Baltic peoples had been subdued by the tsarist state by the end of the eighteenth century, the Lithuanians continued to be divided from the Estonians and the Latvians. The divisions have persisted to the present day. True, the three nations have been brought together by the traumas of the twentieth century but it is all too easy to overlook their differences in emphasising their 'common fate'. Those differences are fundamental and more important than those which exist between Latvia and Estonia, although these too should not be underestimated. The Lithuanians remained faithful to Roman Catholicism; the Estonians and Latvians fell to the advance of Lutheranism. In the tsarist empire Lithuania remained under the influence of a Polonised aristocracy, in contrast to the German ruling class of Estonia, Livonia and Courland. Economic developments also diverged. The Baltic provinces became major centres of Russian industry and trade whereas Lithuania remained an agrarian backwater. Almost every historical generalisation that can be made about the Latvians and Estonians has to be modified to take account of the Lithuanians. The persistence of historic traits, often lost from view amidst the turmoil of recent events, provides vital clues to the differing ways in which today's Baltic republics have responded to the challenges arising from the breakup of the Soviet system.

In the Russian empire the native peasantry of the provinces of Estonia, Livonia and Courland continued to live under a German landed aristocracy until the end of the First World War. The larger towns of the three provinces also remained predominantly German in population and culture. Nevertheless their ethnic diversity became more marked in the second half of the nineteenth century, as industrialisation gained pace and landless peasants flocked to the cities. The population of Riga, totalling just over 100,000 in 1867, was 42.8 per cent German, 25.1 per cent Russian, 23.5 per cent Latvian and 5.1 per cent Jewish.[10] By 1897, when the population had risen to over 280,000 and Riga had become the sixth largest city in the Russian empire, the

---

10 A Henriksson, *The Tsar's Loyal Germans. The Riga German Community: Social Change and the Nationality Question, 1855–1905*, Boulder, Col 1983, p 1.

proportions of Latvian and German speakers had been reversed; there were now 45 per cent Latvian and only 22 per cent German. Other important centres of industry were to be found in Liepaja (Libau), Tallinn, Pärnu (Pernau) and Narva. Tartu (Dorpat), by contrast, became important as a major centre of German culture for all three Baltic provinces. Its famous university, founded by the Swedes in the seventeenth century, was refounded by Alexander I at the beginning of the nineteenth century as a German-speaking institution (it later became a Russian-speaking, and finally an Estonian-speaking university). By contrast, Lithuania saw relatively little urban growth. It had, however, in Vilnius (Wilna/Vilna/Vilno) a city of great ethnic and cultural diversity. For Jews, who made up a large part of its population, it became from the late fifteenth century 'the northern Jerusalem' – one of the leading centres of their culture and scholarship.[11]

Ruling as proxy for the tsar, and often rising to the highest levels of the central government in St Petersburg, the Baltic Germans stamped their mark on the autonomous Baltic provinces. Throughout their lands they ruled in a self-consciously medieval spirit, enforcing their control through the exclusive provincial estates (*Ritterschaften*) and the city guilds and corporations. German was the language of administration, justice and education. Of Tartu (then Dorpat) and its university it has been said that 'its intrinsically German character differed from a Russian institution as much as the gloomy gothic towers of Tallinn or Riga did from the gleaming domes of the Kremlin.'[12] The entrenched power of the Baltic German rulers and the pervasiveness of German culture in the Baltic provinces were such important obstacles to the growth of Latvian and Estonian national identities during the nineteenth century that the erosion of the German position in the last decades of tsarist rule merits particular attention.

The most concerted challenge came in the second half of the century with the tsarist government's policy of russification.[13] By then the regime had become less tolerant of Baltic German autonomy. While the system of regional administration had been valued for its efficiency by Russian bureaucrats of the eighteenth century, those of the nineteenth century had more confidence in the strength of Russian institu-

11 Y Arad, *Ghetto in Flames: The Struggle and Destruction of the Jews in Vilna in the Holocaust,* Jerusalem 1980. For a vivid evocation of life in interwar Vilnius see the memoirs of the Polish Nobel prize winner, C Milosz, *Native Realm,* London 1980, pp 54–107.

12 M Haltzel, *Der Abbau der deutschen ständischen Selbstverwaltung in den Ostseeprovinzen Russlands,* Marburg/Lahn 1977, p 1.

13 E C Thaden (ed), *Russification in the Baltic Provinces and Finland, 1855–1914,* Princeton, NJ 1981.

tions. The tsars, in particular Alexander III, who came to the throne in 1881, felt less need to placate their Baltic German partners in government. The archaic privileges of the Baltic Germans became a natural target for both Russian nationalists and those attempting to modernise and centralise the imperial administration. Panslavists found the anachronistic position of the Baltic German ruling caste a thorn in their side and were determined to bring the provinces into line with the rest of the empire. In his six-volume work, *Borderlands of Russia: The Russian Baltic Coast* (1868–76), the Slavophil publicist Iurii Samarin declared that it was time for the Baltic provinces to stop trying to isolate themselves from Russia and 'to be convinced at last that . . . they are not an advance post of Germany . . . but a western, maritime borderland of Russia.'[14]

It was ominous when Tsar Alexander III failed to reconfirm Baltic German rights on his accession to the throne. This was followed in 1885 by the introduction of Russian as the compulsory language of government and administration. Russian was also introduced into the school system up to and including university level. In 1893 the university of Dorpat (Tartu) became the university of Iurev.

Threatening as russification was to the German position in the Baltic provinces, it is worth emphasising that it took an even more extreme form in Lithuania. Here the aristocracy was closely identified with the abortive Polish uprisings against the tsarist government in 1830 and 1863. The tsarist regime sought to weaken the local nobility by confiscating its estates and dividing them up among the peasants. It also encouraged the Orthodox Church to convert the Roman Catholic peasantry. After 1863, furthermore, russification turned directly against the Lithuanian peasants, who had been even more revolutionary than their Polish counterparts. The study of the Lithuanian language, which had been encouraged by the Catholic clergy, was repressed – even the use of Roman characters was outlawed in favour of Cyrillic – and the Russian educational system was imposed on the schools. Russian peasants were encouraged to settle on estates confiscated from Lithuanian landowners.

The Estonian and Latvian peasants of the Baltic provinces were spared the full rigours of russification which was directed, as we have seen, primarily against the Baltic Germans. Yet russification ultimately posed a less fundamental challenge to Baltic German hegemony than did the emerging national consciousness of the Estonian and Latvian peoples.

14 Cited ibid, p 128.

The nineteenth century saw a series of momentous changes in the status and mentalities of the native Baltic peoples. They had to do in part with economic and social advancement. Even more important, however, was the realisation that education and advancement need not necessarily imply adopting the language and customs of one's traditional rulers. The change sometimes came quite suddenly: 'In an unforeseen and unprecedented development of the late 1850s, educated Latvian speakers at Dorpat and elsewhere began to designate themselves frequently and proudly as "Latvians".'[15] The implications of the emergence of modern Baltic nationalism were profound. By choosing not to be absorbed into the traditional elites of the Baltic provinces, educated Estonians and Latvians were at least implicitly – and to an increasing extent explicitly – rejecting the existing social and political order and bidding to create a new order of which they would be the leaders.[16] This did not necessarily imply a rejection of the position of the Baltic provinces within the Russian empire. It did, however, imply the destruction of Baltic German hegemony.

Ironically, Baltic Germans themselves had helped to provide the economic and cultural foundations for the 'awakening' of Baltic nationalism in the eighteenth and early nineteenth centuries. Under the influence of the Enlightenment individual German landowners had already begun to give peasants rights on their own estates by the late eighteenth century. Self-interest was, of course, also a dominant motive. Reform was seen as essential if the Baltic provinces were not to fall behind the advances being made in western European agriculture. In building up an efficient regional agricultural economy, the Baltic Germans were also underpinning their political control *vis-à-vis* the central Russian government; by emancipating the native Baltic peasantry and giving them a stake in the land the *Ritterschaften* hoped to create a more secure basis for their social and political authority. Full emancipation was decreed for all three provinces – Estonia (1816), Courland (1817) and Livonia (1819) – many decades before it was achieved in the rest of the Russian empire. The agrarian reforms may thus be seen as a sort of pre-emptive strike.[17]

15 A Plakans, Peasants, intellectuals and nationalism in the Russian Baltic provinces, 1820–1890, *Journal of Modern History* **46** (1974): 445–75, p 456.

16 There are obvious parallels with nationalist movements elsewhere in nineteenth-century Europe. For general discussions see E Kedourie, *Nationalism*, London 1960; J Breuilly, *Nationalism and the State*, Manchester 1982, p 31. For the Baltic provinces see also A Loit (ed), *National Movements in the Baltic Countries during the 19th Century*, Uppsala 1985.

17 Pistohlkors, Die historischen Voraussetzungen. In B Meissner (ed) *Die baltischen Nationen*, p 16.

Less cynical considerations were present in the cultural field. In-spired by Lutheranism, the Enlightenment and in particular by Herder (who lived in Riga from 1764 to 1769), Baltic German clerics fostered the study of the Latvian and Estonian languages and contributed to the rediscovery of folk-songs and folklore. A German pastor published the first Latvian grammar in 1761; in 1789 a German–Latvian dictionary was published. German pastors and intellectuals were also prominent in the 'Latvian Literary Society' (founded in 1824) and the 'Estonian Learned Society' (1838). The political importance of folklore should not be underrated for Estonians and Latvians. Unlike the Poles, Hun-garians or even the Lithuanians, they had no historic state to look back to for inspiration. Like the Finns, they substituted a past peopled with mythological heroes.[18] Just as the Finnish poet Elias Lönnrot compiled (and partly wrote) the songs and poems which made up the great national epic *Kalevala*, so F R Kreutzwald produced the *Kalevipoeg* for the Estonians. Since no such fragments could be found in Latvian oral tradition, Andrejs Pumpur published the long poem *Lacplesis* ('The Bear Slayer') in 1888.[19]

Although the Baltic Germans had given unwitting encouragement, national consciousness progressed only slowly among the Estonians and Latvians in the first half of the nineteenth century. The economic position of the peasants gradually improved. They gained economic security as a result of further reforms introduced after 1848, when tenancies were granted against payment of rent. However, peasant landownership was still limited. In Livonia, for example, where the German nobility constituted less than 2 per cent of the population, it owned land estimated at anything between 60 and 74 per cent of the total.[20] Reform did not therefore encourage the peasants to identify more closely with the landowners. In any case, the countryside was not where the decisive struggle for political control in the provinces would be fought out. Under the stimulus of industrialisation there was a massive movement of population into the towns. Here there de-veloped a new Latvian and Estonian bourgeoisie and proletariat which ultimately challenged the political supremacy of the Baltic Germans.

The challenge was an extraordinarily wide-ranging one. By 1900 the Estonians and Latvians were becoming increasingly difficult to govern under the old order. They could no longer be treated as peas-

18 W A Wilson, *Folklore and nationalism in modern Finland*, Bloomington, Indiana and London 1976.

19 Plakans Peasants intellectuals 472–3.

20 C Lundin, The road from Tsar to Kaiser: changing loyalties of the Baltic Ger-mans, 1905–1914, *Journal of Central European Affairs* **10** (1950): 231.

ant masses, to be bought off by timely concessions. The social and economic mix was now much more diverse and volatile. The linguistic reawakening among the Estonians and Latvians heightened national consciousness and made them increasingly unwilling to accept German tutelage, or adopt German culture as a means of social advancement. Economic growth in the Baltic provinces opened further routes to betterment for the majority Baltic peoples. In the process of social and economic differentiation the high degree of literacy among the Estonians and Latvians was of decisive importance. The all-Russian census of 1897 showed literacy levels outside the Baltic provinces of approximately 30 per cent; the corresponding figures for Livonia and Estonia were 92 per cent and 95 per cent respectively.[21]

These high levels reflected the Lutheran preoccupation with literacy. Interestingly, Lutheranism, a religion embracing both the Baltic Germans and their native subjects, helped to frustrate the attempts of the tsarist government to drive a wedge between them. The first manifestation of russification had been the 'conversion campaign' directed towards the Estonian and Latvian peasantry in the 1840s by the Russian Orthodox church and backed by the secular authorities. However, despite the religious affinities between rulers and ruled in the Baltic provinces, the Estonians and Latvians still had to engage in a political campaign on two fronts. The first was against the German monopoly of political, social and economic power. On one level, they were aided by russification, which undermined the power of the *Ritterschaften*. At the same time they did not wish to loosen the German grip only to have it replaced by the iron hand of tsarism. Estonians and Latvians wanted the autonomy of their provinces to continue but under their own control. Like other subject nationalities, such as the Czechs and the Irish, the Baltic nationalists thought in terms of 'home rule' rather than complete independence.

Lithuanian nationalists could not afford to take so sanguine a view of tsarist rule. Their challenge to Russia and to tsarism was direct: there were no German intermediaries to deflect its force or to divert the attention of the tsarist government. In other respects, too, Lithuania's development in the nineteenth century differed radically from that of the Baltic provinces. Agrarian reform was delayed; the emancipation of the serfs did not take place in Lithuania until 1861, at the same time as the rest of the tsarist empire. Despite the legal obligations to which they were still subject after 1861, the Lithuanian peasants had

---

21 Pistohlkors, Die historischen Voraussetzungen. In B Meissner (ed) *Die baltischen Nationen*, p 24.

some advantages over their Estonian and Latvian counterparts. They could purchase land from their impoverished landlords after the failed Polish uprisings of 1830 and 1863 and were later able to profit from the reform programme introduced by Stolypin in 1906. Yet urbanisation and industrial development lagged far behind the Baltic provinces. In contrast to the Latvians and Estonians, landless Lithuanians could not find employment in nearby cities. In the larger towns, such as Kaunas (Kovno) and Vilnius, the population comprised mainly Russians, Poles and Jews, with Lithuanians in a distinct minority. For this reason and because of the policy of russification after 1863, Lithuanians emigrated overseas in massive numbers, mainly to the United States and Canada. As a result of underdevelopment Lithuanian society did not become as diversified as that of the Baltic provinces. It had only a small educated middle class, drawn almost exclusively from peasant stock, on which nationalism could build.

Just as Latvian and Estonian nationalism gained from the high levels of literacy in the provinces, so the relatively poor literacy figures in Lithuania gave Lithuanian nationalism a slow start. Admittedly, the Catholic clergy encouraged the study of the Lithuanian language and the development of education in the first half of the nineteenth century. So little progress had been made, however, that russification when it came was inflicted on a society which was still barely literate. As a result the Russian language was being taught in Lithuanian schools some twenty years before it was imposed on those of the Baltic provinces. In Lithuania as in Poland the Catholic church led the campaign against russification of the schools. Religion and nationalism formed a symbiotic relationship.[22]

By the early twentieth century Baltic nationalism, although not directly threatening the Russian state, was perceived by the tsarist regime as more dangerous than the traditional particularist claims of the German ascendancy. Nationalism was being expressed in increasingly subversive terms as the first generation of leaders gave way to a new and more dynamic cohort of politicians in the 1890s and a variety of political parties came into existence. Many of the younger generation were to go on to play a major role in establishing independent Baltic states. They included, in Estonia, the volatile Jaan Tönisson and the more down-to-earth Konstantin Päts, both men of peasant origin who had made their careers as lawyers and newspaper editors.[23] In Latvia, nationalism was more closely identified with Social Democracy. An

22 Ibid, p 24.
23 G von Rauch, *The Baltic States. Estonia, Latvia, Lithuania: The Years of Independence: 1917–1940*, London 1974, p 10.

expatriate group, founded by Mikelis Valters in Zurich in 1903, not only adopted a Social Democratic platform but even advocated the secession of Latvia from the Russian empire. In forging links with Social Democrats abroad, especially in Germany, the new Baltic leaders were already, as it were, beginning to internationalise the question of their provinces' future.

In Lithuania nationalist activity had to take different forms owing to the greater degree of tsarist repression. Within the country the Catholic clergy continued to take a lead in cultivating the Lithuanian language and coordinating resistance to Russian policy. More overt nationalist activity had to be carried out from beyond the frontiers of the empire. Tilsit, in East Prussia, was a centre from which illicit publications were smuggled across the border. In Lithuania too, future leaders, like Galvanauskas, were active in newly formed political parties. These included a Social Democratic Party founded in 1895 and, after the 1905 revolution, a Lithuanian Peasant League and a Catholic Democratic Party. As in the Baltic provinces, it was difficult to envisage full independence from the Russian empire as a practicable goal. The Social Democrats were committed from the outset to 'an independent democratic republic, consisting of Lithuania, Poland, and other countries, based on a loose federation.'[24] One of the leading founders of the party, Alfonsas Moravskis, believed that the revolutionary potential of the country was simply not strong enough to permit the creation of an independent Lithuanian state.[25] For socialists there was of course the additional consideration that nationalism threatened the international solidarity to which they aspired. Even Lithuanian nationalists, however, had problems in defining their national identity which were in some respects greater than those of their Estonian or Latvian counterparts. The large numbers of Jews and Poles who inhabited Lithuanian territory presented problems for any ethnically based definition of Lithuanian nationality. The old Polish-Lithuanian commonwealth also cast its shadow. Lithuanian nationalists feared exposure to the Polish culture which had made such inroads in the past. 'After having lost their cultural elite once to the Byelorussians (in the fourteenth century) and then to the Poles (after the Union of

---

24 Cited in L Sabaliunas, Social Democracy in Tsarist Lithuania, 1893–1904, *Slavic Review* **31** (1972): 339. At first the 'other countries' were to include Latvia, Belorussia and the Ukraine but not Russia. Russia was included as a possible member from 1897 onwards.

25 Ibid, p 340.

Lublin), the Lithuanians were apprehensive about undertaking a new experiment.'[26]

The revolutionary year of 1905 revealed the full force of discontent among the peoples of the Baltic lands. The Baltic provinces were most deeply affected by the breakdown of tsarist authority which followed 'Bloody Sunday' in St Petersburg at the beginning of 1905. As elsewhere in Russia, rural unrest was endemic. In 1905, however, it expressed itself violently, more so in Livonia, Estonia and Courland than in Lithuania. Here, revolutionary activity was directed less against landowners than against Russian parish clergy and school teachers. In the Baltic provinces, by contrast, the peasants rose with savagery against their German masters; 184 manor houses were burned and 82 Baltic German landowners and clerics were killed. A pathetic anecdote was recorded by a British journalist who met an aged German parson in Jelgava (Mitau):

> His chief delight had been the collection of Lettish songs, riddles, proverbs, and legends. Over this labour he had gone blind, but, with wife and grandchildren around him, he had resolved to write one more book, to be called 'The Happy Life', when suddenly the peasants attacked his parsonage, shot his sexton, threatened his daughter, burnt his library, smashed his china, trampled on his harpsichord, and made a bonfire of his furniture in the garden, kindling it with his manuscripts.[27]

In the cities there were widespread strikes, culminating in the general strike of October 1905. At a stroke it had become all too evident that the Baltic Germans were wholly dependent on the power and military might of the Russian state. Indeed, German landowners cooperated actively in the brutal repression meted out to the peasantry between 1905 and 1908. The impact of the revolution on the Baltic German aristocracy was vividly expressed by Max von Sivers. When he returned to his ancestral home of Römershof he was less shocked by the state of the charred remains of his home, which he had expected, than by the feeling that he was returning 'as a mere stranger, walking amidst the servants, still living untroubled on my estate, who watched me with mocking expressions.' The Baltic German nobility were revealed as an isolated caste, relics of a medieval pattern of colonisation which had made them rulers not of German farmers, but of an alien peasantry. The old patriarchal society of the Baltic provinces had

---

26 M K Dziewanowski, Joseph Pilsudski, the Bolshevik Revolution and Eastern Europe, *Polish Review* **14**, 4 (1969): 23.

27 H W Nevinson, *More Changes, More Chances*, London 1925, pp 154–5.

disappeared, never to return.[28]

For the majority of Baltic peoples the balance sheet of 1905 was a mixed one. On the one hand, the tsarist regime felt compelled to modify its decree making Russian the compulsory language of schooling. The use of Estonian, Latvian and Lithuanian was permitted once more; in Lithuania the Roman script was restored in place of the Cyrillic which had been compulsory for the previous forty years. Thus education became a renewed focus for aspirations to socio-economic and national advancement. When a new wave of repression was unleashed by the tsarist government it was directed not against the Baltic languages but against the political activities of Baltic nationalists. Many prominent leaders faced imprisonment or went into exile. Against this background it was not surprising that the political rights won after 1905 had little practical effect. Baltic delegates elected to the four Russian Dumas after 1906 failed to persuade the tsarist state to concede the Baltic majority peoples control over their own lands. Lithuania's cause made still less progress than that of the Estonians and Latvians. Even Russian liberals were not prepared to concede to Lithuania the kind of restricted autonomy which survived in the Baltic provinces under the remnants of Baltic German authority.

As a result of the revolution of 1905, the tsarist regime reverted to the traditional policy of collaboration with the Baltic German caste. The Germans, however, had been deeply shaken by the events of 1905. They too had to find new solutions. They had answered the call to support the Russian state in its time of crisis but nothing could conceal the growing vulnerability of their position. The Baltic Germans began to develop a distinctly beleaguered mentality. Their options were rapidly closing. One idea, favoured by such liberal Baltic Germans as Eduard von Dellingshausen, was to placate the Estonian and Latvian demands for more political power by giving representation in government at the district level. Yet this offered too little, too late to satisfy nationalist aspirations. The legacy of 1905 soured all such political experiments. A second option for the German nobility was to collaborate with Russian conservatives. In the Third Duma Baltic German representatives affiliated with the conservative Octobrist group. However, Russian conservatives tended to be Russian nationalists and the Germans found themselves the target of frequent attacks by Panslavists.[29]

28 K-H Grundmann, *Deutschtumspolitik zur Zeit der Weimarer Republik: Eine Studie am Beispiel der deutsch-baltischen Minderheit in Estland und Lettland*, Hannover-Döhren, 1977, p 75.

29 R Wittram, *Meinungskämpfe im baltischen Deutschtum währen de Reformepoch de 1 Jahrhundert* Rig 1934 56.

In these circumstances the *Ritterschaften* fell back on emphasising the distinctly German character of the Baltic provinces. Belated attempts were made to recruit a loyal German peasantry from Imperial Germany; a number of nobles were prepared to make land available for this purpose but with relatively little result. More importantly, efforts were made to bridge the gap between the aristocracy and the German urban bourgeoisie. German Associations (*Vereine*) appeared in all three provinces, Estonia, Courland and Livonia. They took as their starting point the reforms of 1905, reviving the German-language schools which had been suspended under russification and exploiting the new right to freedom of association.

The German Associations sought to replace the old stress on tradition and privilege with a new emphasis on nationality and race. Their activities were not, therefore, welcome to many of the conservative Baltic German nobility, who feared further erosion of the old order of closed corporations and estates. The traditionalists felt a continuing loyalty to the tsar, on whose authority what remained of their old position still rested. After 1905, however, other Baltic Germans emigrated to the German empire. Germany had of course long been a place of refuge for those who had fallen foul of the tsarist regime. The activities of Baltic German émigrés were aggressively anti-tsarist. Neither can the work of the Associations in fostering links with pan-German organisations be regarded merely as defensive reactions. On the contrary, they marked a determined attempt to enlist the support of the Reich in maintaining the Baltic provinces as bastions of Germandom.

In reality, Wilhelmine Germany showed little sympathy for the Baltic German cause. Ultra-nationalist circles were naturally an exception. Even German conservatives, however, were distrustful of the archaic privileges of the Baltic *Ritterschaften*, while German liberals and socialists were openly hostile. On this question there was, in fact, an unusual degree of cross-party consensus. More importantly, the Reich adhered for reasons of power politics to the tradition of friendship between Prussia and Russia dating from Napoleonic times. Bismarck was the classic exponent of this policy both before and after 1871. Its cornerstone was collaboration against the Polish cause. Thus Bismarck effectively gave a free hand to Russian policy in Lithuania and the Baltic provinces, despite the vociferous anti-Russian propaganda of Baltic émigrés like the influential historians Theodor Schiemann and Johannes Haller or the publicist Paul Rohrbach.[30]

30 H Rothfels, The Baltic provinces: some historic aspects and perspectives, *Journal of Central European Affairs* **4** (1944): 130–1.

When Russo-German relations did finally deteriorate drastically in the years before 1914, the change had little to do with Baltic issues but was largely a product of growing antagonism between Austria and Russia in the Balkans. There was no German threat to Russia's Baltic provinces before the outbreak of war in 1914. For that reason the loyalties of the Baltic Germans did not have to be put to the ultimate test. Many may have contemplated taking 'the road from tsar to kaiser', particularly after 1905. They had to make up their minds only when the German armies rolled into Lithuania and Courland in 1915. Those who opted for Germany turned their backs not merely on the tsarist government but on any lingering hopes of reconciliation with Baltic nationalism.

War, Revolution and Independence

In 1914 it would have been impossible to predict whether, or at what point, Baltic nationalist demands for autonomy within the tsarist empire would be translated into a call for full independence. The outbreak of hostilities between Germany and Russia removed the possibility of peaceful evolution within the empire. If Russia were to win the war there were likely to be few concessions to the subject nationalities. A German victory would almost certainly bring the Baltic provinces and Lithuania into a closer relationship with the Reich. Few could have guessed in 1914 that neither great power would win. In 1918, after decades of halting progress, the Estonians, Latvians and Lithuanians suddenly saw the chance to become masters in their own house.

That this opportunity should present itself at all was quite remarkable in that 1918 opened with the German armies in the east at the height of their power. War brutally exposed the weakness of Russia's position in the Baltic. Even before 1914 the strategic balance in the region had been tilted to Russia's disadvantage with Japan's destruction of the tsar's Baltic fleet, after its epic voyage to the Far East during the war of 1904. Russia's entente with Great Britain after 1907 had done nothing to restore the balance, since the Royal Navy did not dare to challenge German naval mastery of the Baltic. With the failure of the Russian offensive in East Prussia in 1914–15, there was nothing to stop the German advance into Courland and Lithuania.

Between May and September 1915 the whole of Lithuanian territory and the entire province of Courland came under German control.

By the time the German advance was halted on the Daugava and at the gates of Riga at the end of 1915, three-fifths of the population of Courland, along with much of its industry, had been evacuated. Yet the Germans were unable to break the Russian lines on the Daugava until August 1917. The end of the old order in Russia in the February Revolution had fatally weakened an already faltering war effort. At the end of August the Germans occupied Riga and in September Estonian territory came under German control for the first time, with amphibious operations against the islands of Saaremaa (Ösel), Muhu (Moon) and Hiiumaa (Dagö). Finally, in February 1918, German forces occupied the rest of Estonia and Livonia.

For all practical purposes the German High Command (*Oberste Heeresleitung* – OHL) henceforth effectively decided policy in the *Land Oberost*, as the territories under German control in Courland and Lithuania were known.[1] The military had long nourished a desire to weaken Russia permanently by erecting a ring of 'barrier' states on her western borders, even to the extent of annexing them to the Reich. Additionally, the border territories were seen as vital sources of foodstuffs and raw materials. The Baltic provinces and Lithuania, with their traditions of German settlement and located as they were in a key strategic position, were prime candidates for annexation.[2] Support for annexation was also widespread in civilian circles in Germany after the outbreak of war. As early as August 1914 officials close to the Chancellor, Bethmann Hollweg, were contemplating the annexation of Lithuania and Courland.[3] By September 1915 the German agricultural expert Professor Max Sering had elaborated a scheme for the colonisation by German settlers of all three Baltic provinces – Courland, Livonia and Estonia – as well as Lithuania. These ideas were backed enthusiastically by Baltic German émigrés such as Theodor Schiemann. They also appealed strongly to the leaders of the High Command, Hindenburg and Ludendorff, who were from 1916 onwards the effective dictators of Germany. A colonisation programme was launched in the summer of 1916 and the Baltic region became an integral part of the war aims

1 A Strazhas, The *Land Oberost* and its place in Germany's *Ostpolitik,* 1915–1918. In V S Vardys and R J Misiunas (eds), *The Baltic States in Peace and War 1917–1945,* University Park, Pennsylvania and London 1978, pp 43–62.

2 K-H Janssen, Die baltische Okkupationspolitik des deutschen Reiches. In J von Hehn, H von Rimscha, H Weiss (eds), *Von den baltischen Provinzen zu den baltischen Staaten. Beiträge zur Entstehungsgeschichte der Republiken Estland und Lettland 1917–1918,* Marburg/Lahn 1971, pp 227–30.

3 F Fischer, *Germany's Aims in the First World War,* London 1967, pp 115–17, 273–9.

programme laid down at Bad Kreuznach in April 1917. It stated that Courland and Lithuania were 'to be won for the German Reich as far as the line traced by the OHL', and that the 'acquisition of parts of Livonia and Estonia, including the islands at the mouth of the Gulf of Riga, was also desirable.'[4]

The February 1917 Revolution in Russia had, however, radically altered the terms of the annexationist debate in Germany. Once the idea of national self-determination was placed firmly on the agenda, annexation had to be presented in the guise of autonomy for the subject peoples of the Russian empire. The German authorities had begun to play with the nationality issue as early as the spring of 1916 with their sponsorship of 'the League of Non-Russian Peoples', in which Lithuanian émigrés and Baltic Germans played a prominent role.[5] Before the Kreuznach conference Bethmann Hollweg had already worked out a scheme whereby Poland, Lithuania, Courland, Livonia and Estonia should become autonomous areas, associated economically with Germany and with guarantees for their native German populations. In addition Lithuania and the Baltic provinces would be opened up for colonisation by Germans from the interior of Russia (the 'Volga Germans').[6] The High Command, though initially sceptical, reached agreement with the civilian leadership on the new policy of autonomy at the Bingen conference of July 1917. Genuine independence for the Latvians, Estonians and Lithuanians was impossible, it was argued, because they would not be strong enough to act as buffer states between Germany and Russia or to 'constitute a secure future barrier against Russian expansive ambitions'. They would be of value to Germany only if they were 'brought and permanently kept in a relationship of complete dependence on the Reich, militarily, politically and economically.'[7]

Such a policy meant, however, that Germany had to take at least some account of the wishes of the peoples to whom it was proposing to grant 'autonomy'. In Courland, German policy could rely on the support of the great majority of the local German population, which had become closely identified with the occupation authorities since 1915. The Baltic German estates of Courland still regarded themselves as the natural representatives of their province's interests. In September

---

4 Cited ibid, pp 279, 348.

5 S Zetterberg, *Die Liga der Fremdvölker Russlands 1916–1918: Ein Beitrag zu Deutschlands antirussischem Propagandakrieg unter den Fremdvölkern Russlands im Ersten Weltkrieg*, Helsinki 1978.

6 Fischer, *Germany's Aims*, pp 375–7.

7 Memorandum of 29 November 1917, cited ibid, p 460.

1917 they voted to place the province under the protection of the Reich. Their example was followed by the provincial estates of Livonia and Estonia, suitably bolstered by a small number of complaisant Latvians and Estonians, as the position of the Baltic Germans was threatened first by the Provisional Government in Petrograd and then, after the October Revolution, by the bolsheviks. German appeals for assistance led to the entry of Reich troops into the two provinces in February 1918.[8]

Germany's relationship with the majority peoples of Courland and Lithuania was more problematical. The harsh policies of the occupation authorities had alienated initially well disposed local populations. On the whole the Latvians could be ignored for the moment since the Baltic German ascendancy still existed and so large a part of Courland's population had left the province. The Lithuanians presented greater difficulties. On the one hand Lithuania was central to the OHL's strategic conception as the bridge to Courland, Livonia and Estonia. On the other hand Germany had encouraged Lithuanian nationalists in their defiance of Russia and was therefore obliged to take at least some account of their demands.

In September 1917 a Lithuanian National Committee, the *Taryba*, met under German auspices. It immediately pressed for much wider powers within the prospective puppet state than the occupation authorities were prepared to contemplate and, under pressure from the German Reichstag, some of the more objectionable features of the occupation regime were removed. Nevertheless the Lithuanians were completely at Germany's mercy as the Germans moved, at the end of 1917, towards peace negotiations with the new bolshevik regime at Brest-Litovsk. Ludendorff threatened a partition of Lithuanian territory, with the Vilnius region going to Poland, if the Lithuanians failed to comply with Germany's demands. On 11 December 1917 the *Taryba* therefore proclaimed:

> (i) an independent Lithuanian state with Vilnius as its capital. (ii) an
> alliance between this state and the German Reich, to be realised chiefly
> by a military, transport, customs and currency union.[9]

The Lithuanians still tried to secure a larger measure of sovereignty and in fact made a further declaration of independence on 16 February 1918 which omitted any reference to Lithuania as a German protec-

8 Janssen, Okkupationspolitik, 253.
9 Cited in Fischer, *Germany's Aims*, p 469.

torate.[10] Yet after the signature of the Treaty of Brest-Litovsk on 3 March 1918, and in the absence of any western interest in the question of Lithuania's future, they were forced to acknowledge that independence could be achieved only on Germany's terms. It was therefore on the basis of the December declaration that the kaiser recognised Lithuanian independence on 23 March 1918.

German interest in keeping Russia at bay was heightened by the new ideological threat from bolshevism after October 1917 and the German leadership took full advantage of Russia's plight to inflict a punitive peace on its new leaders. Under the terms of the Treaty of Brest-Litovsk (supplemented in August by the Treaty of Berlin) the bolsheviks were compelled to accept the loss of vast territories, including Courland and Lithuania (but did not renounce their formal sovereignty over Estonia and Livonia until August). The treaties further strengthened the position of the German High Command. In the spring of 1918, with Germany victorious in the east and launching its devastating March offensive on the Western Front, the 'silent dictatorship' of Hindenburg and Ludendorff was at its peak.

There had, however, always been reservations voiced in the Reichstag, particularly by the parties of the left, about the principle of annexation as a war aim, as well as its nature and extent. While the Russian Revolution therefore removed some of the practical obstacles to annexing the Baltic lands to Germany, it greatly intensified the wider debate about the right of smaller nationalities to self-determination. Within the Reich it became more difficult for German annexationists to press their case.[11] In governing circles too, opinion was divided between those who shared the OHL's interest in depriving Russia of its 'border' areas and those who remained concerned about the long-term effect of such a policy on future German–Russian relations.[12] This is why many argued for not going beyond Courland ('the nation's war aim') and depriving Russia of access to the Baltic. Brest-Litovsk was not, therefore, simply a climax to German annexationism but was also the occasion for a protracted struggle to determine the whole future of the Baltic area.[13]

10 S W Page, *The Formation of the Baltic States: A Study of the Effects of Great Power Politics upon the Emergence of Lithuania, Latvia and Estonia*, Cambridge, Mass 1959, pp 52–3.

11 W Ribhegge, *Frieden für Europa: Die Politik der deutschen Reichstagsmehrheit 1917–1918*, Essen 1988, pp 225–74.

12 A Taube, Das Auswärtige Amt und die estnische Frage, *Jahrbücher für Geschichte Osteuropas* **17** (1969): 573.

13 W Baumgart, *Deutsche Ostpolitik 1918. Von Brest-Litovsk bis zum Ende des Ersten Weltkrieges*, Vienna, Munich 1966, pp 69, 74, 82.

Self-determination was an even more explosive issue in the Russian context. In early 1917 it looked as though the Baltic peoples would be content to move through a period of self-government with the ultimate aim of autonomy within the Russian state. With the tsar's fall went the old partnership between his regime and the Baltic German nobility; the Provisional Government in Petrograd professed itself ready to forge a new partnership with Baltic nationalist leaders. Weak as it was, the Provisional Government took some important steps towards the setting up of administrative districts on national lines, which cut across the old provincial boundaries. In April 1917, in response to a campaign led by the Estonian nationalist leader Jaan Tönisson, it divided the Baltic territories still under Russian control into two districts: Estonia, now including the islands off its coast (formerly under a separate administration) and Latvia – the former province of Livonia. In addition the estates and local authorities still controlled by Baltic Germans were deprived of their powers. They were replaced in Estonia in May by an elected provincial assembly, the *Maapäev*, which became the focus for Estonian aspirations to a greater degree of self-determination.[14]

The Latvian cause encountered greater difficulties. Latvian nationalists were trying to unite a people divided among two provinces one of which – Courland – was under German control and one district – Latgale – which was part of the Russian province of Vitebsk. They also faced a challenge from the left in the form of workers' and soldiers' councils which came increasingly under bolshevik influence. The Provisional Government, finally, was not prepared to grant the Latvians the same degree of autonomy as it had allowed the Estonians. The uneasy rapprochement between Baltic nationalism and the government in Petrograd was brought to an end by the bolshevik seizure of power. From that moment Baltic demands for autonomy within the Russian state gave way to the clamour for full independence.

It now found a stronger echo inside Germany, where the so-called majority parties, the Social Democrats, the Centre and the Progressives, were applying greater pressure for far-reaching reform of the Reich. Those same parties, the Socialists in particular, were leading the call for self-determination for the Baltic peoples in accordance with the letter, if not the spirit, of Brest-Litovsk. As long as its military might remained undented, the OHL could resist this pressure and could still manipulate the situation in the Baltic, remote from Berlin.

14 O Arens, The Estonian *Maapäev* during 1917. In Vardys and Misiunas (eds), *Baltic States*, pp 19–30.

Nevertheless annexationism still had to be clothed in the guise of self-determination.

Giving practical effect to this vision dogged German Ostpolitik until the end of the war. It proved impossible to find 'constitutional' solutions to the problem of attaching the Baltic countries to the Reich. Hence the absurd quarrels over which member of which German dynasty should be 'rulers' of the various grand duchies which were to be conjured up from the Baltic territories. The Lithuanians took advantage of such dynastic rivalries to mitigate the full force of German (and more specifically Prussian) annexationism. In July 1918 the *Taryba* proclaimed the Catholic Duke Wilhelm of Urach as King of Lithuania: he was to take the name 'Mindaugas II'. The changing fortunes of war were to relieve the Lithuanians of the need to continue with this ploy. In November 1918 the *Taryba* abandoned the monarchical experiment and reverted to a republican constitution. From the German point of view, however, the episode illustrated the difficulty of accommodating such archaic political entities within the complex federal consitution of the Reich.[15]

In sum, German military success and the Treaty of Brest-Litovsk had created a situation which could not be solved under the conditions then existing in either Germany or Russia. Yet by the very act of separating the Baltic countries from Russia, the Treaties of Brest-Litovsk and Berlin made acute the question of their future. Instead of being a block the treaties became in effect a stepping stone to Baltic independence. Germany's success alerted the western powers, Great Britain, France and the United States to the implications of German domination in the East. This was not merely because the Reich's actions affronted the ideals of self-determination elaborated in President Woodrow Wilson's Fourteen Points of January 1918. They also evoked the spectre of a Germany able to sustain its war effort indefinitely on the basis of Russian resources.

Prospects were ominous in the light of Ludendorff's massive spring offensive on the Western Front and all the Allies could do for the moment was to try desperately to restore at least the semblance of a front in the east. This had implications for the Baltic cause. It must be stressed that the Allied powers treated Baltic problems as a facet of the 'Russian question' as a whole. On the one hand they did not wish to endanger their relations with the Russia of the future (which they did

---

15 H Rolnik, *Die baltischen Staaten Litauen, Lettland und Estland und ihre Verfassungsrecht*, Leipzig 1927, pp 25–6.

not expect to be bolshevik) by acknowledging full independence for the Baltic peoples. At the same time, however, the western powers sought to encourage these peoples in their resistance to German hegemony. Both the Estonians and the Latvians defied the German plan to incorporate their territories into the Reich. The Estonians seized the brief opportunity before the arrival of German troops in Tallinn to declare their country an independent republic on 24 February 1918.[16] They then exploited Allied fears of German ambitions so successfully that Britain, France and Italy were persuaded to give de facto recognition to Estonian independence in May 1918.[17] The deep cleavages in Latvian politics and the fighting that was taking place on Latvian soil delayed a Latvian declaration of independence until November 1918. Although de facto recognition again quickly followed, Allied views on Baltic questions were still far from clear. The inconsistency of Allied attitudes towards the Baltic betrayed their inability to develop a coherent Russian policy. All that was certain was that they did not wish the Baltic area to fall under German dominion.

The collapse of Germany in November 1918 seemed to remove that danger, but a new fear replaced the old. As the weary German troops pulled back from the east the Red Army began to move into the space which they had vacated. It was felt in London and Paris that the German forces in the east provided the best chance of stemming the Soviet advance; hence the Allied insistence under Article 12 of the Armistice of 11 November that Germany maintain its forces in the east for the time being. Ultimately the armistice provided the justification for fresh German volunteers to be drafted into the Baltic early in 1919. In reality the German contribution was largely confined to Latvia, where it certainly helped to keep the bolsheviks at bay. In Estonia and Lithuania it was left to the new governments to organise their own defences as best they could.

The bolshevik advance into Baltic territory, signalled by the proclamation of Soviet republics, had begun immediately after the armistice.[18] In Estonia the Red Army captured Narva but its progress was checked by the arrival of the British fleet at Tallinn in December 1918. A breathing space was provided during which the Estonian government and its new commander in chief, Johan Laidoner, hurriedly

16 K Ast, Estonia's struggle for independence. *Baltic Review* **13** (1958): 52.

17 M-L Hinkkanen-Lievonen, *British Trade and Enterprise in the Baltic States 1919–1925*, Helsinki 1984, p 57.

18 J von Hehn, Der Kampf gegen den Bolschevismus an der baltischen Ostfront im Jahre 1918/1919, *Deutsches Archiv für Landes und Volksforschung* **6** *(1942): 696–702.*

set about organising its own army. Significantly, Baltic German volunteers became part of this force. Most decisive, however, was the arrival of a Finnish volunteer force in Tallinn at the end of December. By February 1919, Soviet forces had been driven from Estonian soil. Lithuania also lost half of its territory, including Vilnius, to the initial bolshevik thrust. As early as January 1919, however, when the Soviet invasion was at its peak, the Lithuanians had managed to organise their own forces and had equipped them with the arms and war materials left by the retreating German occupying forces. Towards late summer the Lithuanians had regained control of their territories. In Latvia the situation was more complex.

First, Latvian territory was the main theatre of Baltic operations for the German forces in 1919. Second, in contrast to Estonia, the Baltic Germans formed their own force, the *Landeswehr*, and worked in conjunction with the Reich German contingents rather than with the Latvian government. Third, the Soviets could draw on a much greater degree of support in Latvia than in the other two countries, partly because the region was more industrialised than its two neighbours and partly because the German occupation had been so protracted. The Latvian Soviet republic was less short-lived than its Estonian and Lithuanian counterparts. The Soviet invasion was spearheaded by Latvian communist troops who initially received warm support from the local population. By early January the communists controlled almost the whole of the former province of Livonia, including the city of Riga. The Latvian government under Karlis Ulmanis was forced to retreat and to organise its defences from Liepaja.

It was in Latvia above all, therefore, that the adventurism and duplicity which came to be the hallmark of the German Baltic campaign of 1919, greatly complicated the tasks of the new Baltic leaders and the western powers. They also hampered the efforts of the new German republic to reorientate its Baltic policy. Under the armistice Germany formally renounced its previous treaties with Russia and the new government in Berlin could proceed to dismantle the wartime administration in the east. In accordance with its proclaimed intention of basing its future policy on collaboration rather than repression, Weimar Germany sought to build friendly relations with the Baltic republics. Regrettably this goal was at once endangered by the situation arising from the German military presence in the Baltic during 1919. Any attempt to lay the blame entirely at the door of the German government for the thoroughly confused events in the Baltic in 1919 would be misguided. In the first place the troops were there at the behest of the Allies, whose Russian policy was still unfathomable. Second, the uncertainty provided a perfect recipe for the resumption of conflicts over Ostpolitik between the German civilian and military leaders. The latter, as ever, controlled events at the front while the political leadership was overwhelmed by the problems of postwar readjustment and the conduct of the peace talks at Versailles.

German military high-handedness in the Baltic area was encouraged by the fact that the armistice arrangements were in effect associating Germany with the hesitant beginnings of an Allied intervention against the Soviets. The German military anticipated better peace terms if they made common cause with the Allies and White Russians in an antibolshevik crusade. For the moment at least, there was broad agreement between the Allies, the Germans and the native Baltic peoples on the need to reverse the bolshevik advance in the Baltic. In that respect General Rüdiger von der Goltz, who had arrived in Latvia on 2 February 1919 to command the German forces in the field, could claim to be carrying out the provisions of the armistice to the letter in immediately launching a counter-offensive. The German Freikorps were supported by the Baltic German *Landeswehr*. However, this combination led, after von der Goltz's rapid advance, to a coup launched by the *Landeswehr* against the Latvian government of Karlis Ulmanis in Liepaja on 16 April 1919. The formidable Ulmanis was replaced by the malleable Andrievs Niedra.

The putsch therefore threatened to create a new German power base in the eastern Baltic. Indeed, von der Goltz was among those German leaders who still favoured securing this strategically important 'land bridge' to a restored 'White' Russia. What alarmed the German government as a whole, although some were more sympathetic to von der Goltz than others, was the damage the events would do to Germany's proclaimed intention of building up friendly relations with the Baltic countries. Berlin signalled its intention to pull its troops back from the Baltic on 9 May but the Allies insisted two days later that Germany continue to fulfil its obligations under Article 12 of the armistice. Under these circumstances it is not surprising that it proved exceptionally difficult for Berlin to slow the momentum of the German advance, which resulted in the recapture of Riga from the bolsheviks on 22 May 1919. Georg von Rauch has neatly underlined the importance of this victory by terming it the 'miracle on the Daugava', preceding by a year the better known 'miracle on the Vistula', when the Poles pushed back the Red Army from the gates of Warsaw.[19]

19 G von Rauch, *The Baltic States. Estonia, Latvia, Lithuania: The Years of Independence 1917–1940*, London 1974, p 62.

Flushed with success, von der Goltz tried to press the advance beyond Riga but clashed with a joint Estonian–Latvian force supporting the deposed Ulmanis government. The Allies were finally obliged to take a stand on the continued presence of German troops in the Baltic. On 13 June the Supreme Council decreed that all Reich German soldiers must leave the region in the shortest possible time. Shortly afterwards, on 3 July, von der Goltz was ordered to evacuate Riga and the city was placed under the temporary governorship of a British official, Stephen Tallents.[20] Even this could not guarantee a rapid end to the German Baltic campaign since the troops still had to be brought back in good order, under leaders who remained unwilling to return to the Reich. A further opportunity to sidestep Allied controls presented itself in the shape of the White Russian forces under Bermondt–Awalof, who claimed to be part of the Allied intervention.[21] In reality his own ambitions provided an umbrella for dissident German Freikorps members to pursue their objectives even when von der Goltz was finally recalled in October 1919. The German Cabinet acknowledged the general's services but stressed that the evacuation of the Baltic area had become a 'matter of prestige' for the Allied powers.

Hitherto the only substantial Allied presence had been the Royal Navy whose squadrons, under the command of the irascible Admiral Sir Walter Cowan, virtually 'ran the Baltic' after the downfall of the German High Seas Fleet.[22] British warships at Tallinn had been of decisive importance against the bolsheviks in December 1918 and again in the autumn of 1919 against Bermondt-Awalof at Riga. The first serious Allied disquiet about the role of the German Baltic troops was aroused by the Liepaja coup in April. They insisted on the reinstatement of the Latvian government. Limited material support began to arrive for the native Baltic forces and on May 23 an Allied military mission was set up under General Sir Hubert Gough. It proved to be the prelude to a succession of agents and further missions sent to give advice and aid to the Baltic governments and to find out exactly what was going on.

The first lesson they learned was how difficult it would be to dislodge von der Goltz. This impressed itself immediately on one British official, Herbert Grant-Watson:

20 Sir Stephen Tallents, *Man and Boy*, London 1943, pp 332–41.

21 H-E Volkmann, *Die Russische Emigration in Deutschland 1919–1929*, Würzburg 1966, pp 61–74.

22 E Anderson, British policy towards the Baltic States 1918–1920, *Journal of Central European Affairs* **19** (1959): 288; G Bennett, *Cowan's War: The Story of British Naval Operations in the Baltic, 1918–1920*, London 1964.

He [von der Goltz] knew of the arrival of the Cruiser Squadron (at Libau) and of the fact that Bosanquet and I had come ashore but we could not foretell whether he would allow us to enter the city. According to the terms of the armistice, all German troops, beyond the German frontiers, were to return to Germany when the Allies so demanded but General von der Goltz had openly defied the orders of the Allies and of his government and was in a position of a rebel . . . He regarded the bolsheviks as a threat . . . and was convinced the Allies would hold similar views. As he commanded the best-trained and best-equipped army in Eastern Europe, he anticipated that they would make overtures to him and commission him to drive back the slav hordes.'[23]

Yet the very presence of men like Grant-Watson was to demonstrate to von der Goltz that his plans were not realistic. Intervention was no longer the first priority of the British government, even though Winston Churchill at the War Office continued to press for a crusade against Bolshevism. Lord Curzon, the foreign secretary, told Gough before his departure that although it was important not to endanger Britain's relations with Russia's future government, he was to try 'to establish our influence in the countries between Germany and Russia.'[24]

It followed that reliance on the German forces in the Baltic had to be ended as quickly as possible. The only viable alternative was that provided by the Baltic peoples themselves, whose governments capitalised on this reality. The flurry of activity on the part of the Allied powers increased the opportunities for Baltic leaders to lobby the peace-makers at Versailles. At last the Baltic peoples could more actively and effectively counter the belief that the existence of independent Baltic countries was somehow less important than the continuation of the West's struggle against bolshevism. They could correct the tendency noted by the Estonian socialist, Martna, to regard 'the defensive struggle of our country as some sort of intervention.' As he bitterly reminded the West, 'the Russians attacked us and we did not want to be subjected.'[25] This very obvious point is a significant one. After the April coup in Liepaja, the Allied powers, whatever their long-term ideas about 'Russia', necessarily gave encouragement to the cause of Baltic independence.

23 H A Grant-Watson, *An Account of a Mission to the Baltic States in 1919*, London 1957, p 13.

24 H de la Poer Gough, *Soldiering On*, London 1954, p 191.

25 Cited in Baron W Wrangell, Ausschnitte aus der estnischen Politik, 1918–1920, *Baltische Monatsschrift* (1930): 521–42.

As channels of communication were opened between the Allied and Baltic peoples following the Liepaja coup, so the Baltic question was internationalised. In the final months of 1919, the slow, if still painful process of evacuating the Reich German troops was set in motion. Meanwhile, the more reliable members of the Baltic German *Landeswehr* were put under the command of Colonel Alexander (the future British Field Marshal). The native Baltic forces were reorganised and re-equipped with the aid of the Allies. The implications for Germany were graphically described by General von Seeckt of the Army Command at Kolberg in an intelligence report for July 1919: 'In the Baltic itself an increase in English influence is undeniable . . . England wants in this way to make the Baltic provinces into an English colony and to destroy at any price the bridge between Germany and Russia.'[26] Seeckt's pessimism was vindicated by reports from German commercial representatives, who noted mounting Allied economic interest in the Baltic in the second half of 1919.[27] Significantly, the Allied missions which had been sent out to the Baltic to supervise the final evacuation of the German forces, were exploring commercial deals, by which money and military equipment would be supplied against future payments in the form of Baltic raw materials – notably flax and timber.[28]

From the Baltic point of view the changing emphasis of Allied policy was evidence of the flagging of the interventionist cause. That cause was further discredited by the cynical but incompetent machinations of Bermondt-Awalof and other White Russian leaders. Even the German Army Command observed in July 1919 that Bermondt was 'scarcely in touch with reality with his plans' while Henkel, the German chargé d'affaires in Estonia, was even more dismissive: 'Such demoralisation and lack of preparation was revealed on the side of the Russian intelligence and Russian officer corps, that one must doubt whether these circles will ever be capable of conducting any sort of fruitful recon-

26 Bundesarchiv Koblenz (BAK), Nachlass von Schleicher, Akten betreffend Umdrucke des Grossen Generalstabes, Abteilung Fremde Heere und Fremde Heere Ost.

27 Report of German trade representative Lorenz-Myer, 12 June 1919, Auswärtiges Amt, Akten betreffend Wiederaufnahme des Warenaustausches, Frieden II Wirtschaftliches, Baltenland Nr 4 Bd 2, Bundesarchiv Koblenz (BAK).

28 W Duranty, *I Write as I Please*, London 1935, p 37; *Documents on British Foreign Policy* (DBFP); Series 1, Vol III, pp 60–5; Grant-Watson, *An Account*, pp 45–8; Lt-Col du Parquet, *Der Drang nach Osten: L'aventure allemande en Lettonie,* Paris 1926, pp 129–31, 248.

struction.'[29] In sum, the bolsheviks, who wished to end Baltic independence, were too weak to do so; the White Russians, with similar ambitions, were too disorganised; the Allied powers, whose actions had encouraged the idea of independence, preferred not to think too deeply about it.

It was therefore imperative for the Baltic peoples themselves to seize the initiative. This they did with remarkable courage in the last stages of their 'War of Liberation' in the latter part of 1919. In a fitting climax to a year of bewildering complexity the Latvian and Estonian forces who had defeated the bolsheviks now joined forces to drive out the White Russians. Other units of Bermondt's army which clashed with the Lithuanians were pushed out in December. In the same month the last remnants of the German Freikorps left for the Reich, although German involvement in Bermondt's attack on Riga caused Latvia to declare a state of war with Germany in late November 1919. Meanwhile, the failure of the White Russian offensive against Petrograd had resulted in a counter-offensive by the Red Army which brought it to the Estonian frontier. Here it was halted when Lenin overruled Trotsky and prevented his pursuit of the White Russians into Estonian territory. Finally, the Latvians went over to the offensive, in alliance with Poland, in order to liberate the ethnically Latvian province of Latgale from bolshevik rule. By February 1920 the territory had been conquered and an armistic signed with Soviet Russia.

The above events overlapped with and complicated the task of all of the Baltic states in trying to reach final peace terms with the Soviets. This was all the more urgent in the light of the Allies' tacit acceptance, in embracing the concept of a *cordon sanitaire* in East Europe at the end of 1919, that the bolsheviks were there to stay. In December the Allied Supreme Council formally withdrew support from the White Russians and from January 1920 it lifted the blockade of Soviet ports. It was consistent with this development that the Allied powers, in a reversal of their attitude in the summer, chose not to advise the Baltic republics against responding to Soviet overtures for peace.

The earliest Soviet peace offers to Estonia had been made in spring 1919 in order to prevent the White Russian forces from using Estonian territory as a base for operations against Petrograd. Estonia made

29 Politisches Archiv des Auswärtigen Amtes, Bonn (PAB), Gesandtschaftsakten betreffend des Beauftragten Mitau, 25 Geheim, Paket Nr 198; For Henkel see FO Microfilm, Auswärtiges Amt, Akten betreffend politische Beziehungen Estlands zu Russland 3, Vol 1, K249/K076313–4.

abortive attempts to arrange coordinated talks with its Baltic neighbours late in 1919, but faced with the victorious Red Army on its
frontier it felt compelled to negotiate alone with the Soviets. In December peace talks officially opened in Tartu and a peace treaty between Estonia and the Soviets was concluded on 2 February 1920.
Soviet peace talks with Latvia and Lithuania did not take place until
April–May 1920. The process was complicated by the onset of war
between the Soviets and the new Polish state. Lithuania's reward for
making peace with the bolsheviks at such a time (in Moscow on 12
July) was recognition of its sovereignty over the Vilnius district: the
bolsheviks were more than ready to concede Lithuanian rights to a
territory which Poland claimed for its own. Latvia was the last Baltic
republic to make peace with the bolsheviks. When it did so on 1
August 1920, ethnic Latvians, long separated by the vicissitudes of history, were at last brought together in one state.[30]

Lenin portrayed the peace treaties as an 'incomparable victory over
western imperialism', but there is little doubt that good relations with
the new Baltic leaders were essential after the Red Army's defeat at
the battle of Warsaw in August 1920. The treaty with Estonia deprived the anti-bolshevik forces of a jumping-off point for the White
Russians and also provided an opening for trade.[31] By signing separate
peace treaties with the Baltic states the Soviets had also warded off the
danger of a united front between Finland, Poland and the Baltic states,
of the kind that was under discussion at the Conference of Balduri
(near Riga) in August 1920.[32] The conference had thrown up the
menacing outline of a regional alliance system which could have been
directed against the Soviets in what were to be the last stages of western intervention. The end of that intervention can be dated formally
from the conclusion of peace between Poland and the Soviets in the
Treaty of Riga of March 1921.

Although the treaty increased Polish territory at the expense of
Russia, the bolshevik regime had survived and had defeated its internal
enemies. The peace process coincided with the introduction of Lenin's
New Economic Policy and energies were now absorbed by the battle
for economic reconstruction and the establishment of a Soviet state.
The goal of world revolution had not been abandoned and was indeed
actively promoted by the Communist International (Comintern). From

30 For details of peace treaties, A N Tarulis, *Soviet Policy towards the Baltic States
1918–1940*, Notre Dame 1959, pp 53–68.

31 G Sepols, *Za kulisami inostrannoy interventsii v Latvii*, Moscow 1959, pp 182–5.

32 Latvian Legation, *Minutes of the Baltic Conference held at Balduri in Latvia in 1920*,
Washington, DC 1960.

1921, however, Comintern had to contend with the policy of peaceful coexistence promoted by the Commissariat for Foreign Affairs (Narkomindel) under Chicherin. There was therefore a contradiction in Soviet policy towards the states which had emerged from the former Russian empire. Some members of the regime undoubtedly believed that there was still revolutionary potential in the Baltic republics. Comintern was certainly active clandestinely in all the border states. The Soviet leadership as a whole had every reason for anxiety about the role the Baltic republics might play in any future western crusade against bolshevism. However, tactical considerations and the doctrine of self-determination required an acknowledgement of Baltic independence.

Was this acknowledgement anything more than tactical? There is a danger in reading back from the 1939–40 period and assuming a consistent intention to reabsorb the Baltic republics into the Soviet state. The available evidence is at the very least inconclusive. It is helpful to compare the Soviet attitude with that of the White Russians and indeed the West. The White Russians refused to contemplate any diminution of Russian rule over the former subject nationalities of the empire. The bolsheviks at least propagated the idea of self-determination. Lenin's pragmatism on the nationality question did after all make it possible for the Soviets to recognise Baltic independence, even though it 'was not considered a positive development either by Russian nationalists or bolsheviks.'[33] Diplomatic recognition may have been merely a 'tactical retreat', yet tactical retreats have a habit of creating new realities over time. Simply by existing the Baltic states acquired legitimacy. It is significant that the Soviet peace treaties, the first to accord full recognition to Baltic statehood, have become a central plank in today's drive to independence by the Baltic peoples.

Soviet recognition in 1920 has to be seen in the context of the West's own dilatory treatment of Baltic claims to de jure recognition. Although sympathetic to the plight of the Baltic republics, the Allies tended to believe that sooner or later they would have to revert to a closer relationship with the Russian state, if with a greater degree of autonomy. If the Soviets expected the Baltic states to revert to Russian rule, therefore, they were hardly alone in doing so.

---

33 R Misiunas, The role of the Baltic states in Soviet relations with the West during the interwar period. In J W Hiden and A Loit (eds), *The Baltic in International Relations between the Two World Wars*, Stockholm 1988, p 171.

PART TWO

States of Europe 1918–40

CHAPTER THREE
Building New States

Today's Baltic leaders, facing the problems of separation from the Soviet Union, can take comfort in the knowledge that their forebears faced no less daunting tasks in establishing the independent republics of Estonia, Latvia and Lithuania. They would also recognise with exasperation the note of reserve struck even among their sympathisers in the West. A good example is provided by an analysis made by the head of the Northern Department of the British Foreign Office, J D Gregory, in April 1920.[1] First, Gregory admitted that the Allied attempt to find a compromise between Baltic nationalism and the 'dogma of indivisible Russia' had failed with the end of intervention: 'In Russia, the Social revolution, in the ex-Russian states the Nationalist revolution have . . . come to stay.' Yet the conclusions which he drew from the 'radically changed' circumstances betrayed an imprisonment in older modes of thought. The Baltic states, he said, must realise that their 'chances of independent political existence are entirely bound up with the economic liberty of Russia':

> This vast country from the western boundaries of Poland to the Urals forms a single economic area, and its future prosperity depends on the recognition of this fact. Eventually, therefore, the component parts of the old Russian Empire are bound to come together again, but this time in a strictly limited economic federalism, and decentralised politically to the fullest extent. Economic union, but cultural independence, finding expression in the separate political existence of Sovereign States, affords the best hope for the future, and in so far as we can help forward that solution, we shall have made a serious contribution to a comprehensive Eastern peace.

1 Memorandum of 9 April 1920, *Documents on British Foreign Policy* (DBFP), Series 1, Vol XI, pp 352–5.

The clear implication of such views, even when Allied de jure recognition had been given to the three republics in 1921–2, was that the Baltic peoples would have to do all the essential work of state-building themselves. Like the other states which had emerged at the end of the First World War, Estonia, Latvia and Lithuania had to construct new political systems, reconstruct their economies and settle their frontiers among themselves and with their neighbours.

Latvia and Estonia had difficulty over only one frontier area, surrounding the small railway town of Valga (Walk), and turned to Great Britain for mediation. As a result of Colonel Tallents' decision in 1920 the town was divided between the two countries – a judgement which both came to regard as equitable, although the story that the frontier ran down the middle of the main street was an exaggeration.[2] Lithuania's frontier problems were far more serious. Its border with Latvia was agreed through the arbitration of Professor Simpson, the British expert, in 1921. In 1920, however, Polish forces occupied the Vilnius district, depriving Lithuania of its historic capital and largest city and creating a permanent source of contention between the two countries, as well as removing Lithuania's common frontier with the Soviet Union. The Lithuanian government, now ruling from Kaunas, gained partial compensation by wresting the predominantly German-populated city of Klaipeda (Memel) from League of Nations' control in 1923.

Even after the truncation of Lithuanian territory the combined area of the three Baltic republics was sufficient to make contemporaries question the habitual description of them as 'small states'. Writers seeking to introduce the Baltic states to western audiences in the 1920s tried to make helpful comparisons. The area of Latvia alone, they pointed out, with its 65,791 square kilometres, surpassed that of Switzerland, Holland, Denmark or Belgium. Together, Estonia and Latvia formed 'a region roughly resembling in shape a Holland magnified to more than thrice its size but with only some two-thirds of its population.'[3] With Lithuania their total territory was not far short of that of the United Kingdom shorn of Wales. Such analogies may still be of value today in fixing an image of the Baltic republics in western minds. It is significant that in 1990 the three republics felt it necessary to establish an information bureau to counter damaging misconceptions, among these the assumption that the 'tiny' Baltic countries are unable to survive on their own. They rightly insist on being regarded

2 Sir Stephen Tallents, *Man and Boy*, London 1943, pp 371–9.
3 J Buchan (ed), *Baltic and Caucasian States*, London n.d. (c. 1923), p 121.

simply as states and their achievements during their period of independence more than justify that claim.

Contemporary writers also tried to convey something of the 'feel' of the Baltic countries in terms of geography and landscape. This presented problems as there were few prominent natural features. 'Geographically the country is uninteresting', wrote Bernard Newman of Estonia, 'its low ridges relieved only by occasional lakes and many forests.'[4]

The description of Estonia and Latvia to which readers of the relevant volume of John Buchan's series *The Nations of Today* were treated was still less inviting:

> There are no mountains, but wide tablelands and low hills; no great rivers save the Dvina, but many lesser streams; much sand, bog and forest, but also much fairly fertile soil. The climate is hardly kind. 'Kurland weather' has an evil renown even in the gloomy province of East Prussia. A winter which seals every port except Libau for four months, the curt northern spring, summers so torrid that the night-time is the best for harvest, a dismal, rainy autumn — such is the customary sequence of the year.[5]

Lithuania, by contrast, was presented in almost rapturous terms:

> Between the Vistula and the Dvina lies a great plain. In the winter the snow lies deep upon it and in summer the fields are a riot of wild-flowers. Waves of green wheat and strips of blue-flowering flax sweep up to the dark barrier of fir-forest beyond. Swift, shallow rivers water it, and a multitude of lakes, fringed with reeds and haunted by wild duck, lie dotted about it.[6]

Perhaps the best descriptions, however, come from those who knew the countryside intimately, like Tania Alexander's recollections of summers spent at her family home of Kallijärv in Estonia between the wars,[7] or those of Sir Stephen Tallents:

> The countryside derives, like other plains, an air of tranquil spaciousness from the unbroken width of its luminous skies, and there rests upon it in summer a mellow and tranquil light. The colouring is subdued, a little like that of Northumberland. I recall its dun stubbles, pale grasses and grey willows; its grey-green corn touched delicately by the passing wind as by the shadow of flying smoke; the airy lightness of its birch trees, standing among dark pines like children in an old house. But here and there the

---

4 B Newman, *Baltic Background*, London 1948, p 132 (the description is based on a visit paid to the country between the wars).

5 Buchan, *Baltic and Caucasian States*, pp 77–8.

6 Ibid, p 137.

7 T Alexander, *An Estonian Childhood*, London 1987.

countryside breaks into vivid colour. The green of the young rye, sheets of gay primulas in the spring meadows, the shining miles of harvest and the brief flaming gold of the birch trees in autumn win a special brilliance from their sober setting.[8]

The year 1920 was the first in which the Baltic countries enjoyed anything like full control over their own affairs. The problems they faced in the political, social and economic fields were formidable. 'The Baltic peoples, who had hitherto been the least considered members of society, were now masters in their own house, chaotic though that house might be.'[9] In seeking to satisfy the aspirations of the Latvian, Estonian and Lithuanian majorities, the leaders of the new states wisely chose the course of accommodation with the numerous minorities within their borders. In numerical terms, unlike today, they were under no compulsion to do so. Ethnic Estonians constituted over 88 per cent of Estonia's 1.1 million inhabitants in 1934; the figures for Latvia were 75.5 per cent of a population of just under 2 million and for Lithuania, with a population of just over 2 million in 1923, 84 per cent. If not large in absolute terms, the minorities in the three states were varied. Russians formed the largest minority in both Latvia (12 per cent) and Estonia (8.5 per cent). In Estonia Germans constituted the second largest community (1.7 per cent) and in Latvia the third largest (3.2 per cent). The pattern in Lithuania was very different. Here Jews formed the largest minority (7.6 per cent, compared with Latvia's 4.8 per cent and Estonia's 0.4 per cent). The Poles formed the second largest minority in Lithuania (3.2 per cent) followed by the Russians (2.7 per cent) and Germans (1.4 per cent). Other minorities included Latvians in Lithuania (0.7 per cent), Poles in Latvia (2.5 per cent) and Swedes in Estonia (0.7 per cent). Such ethnic complexity reinforced the argument that the Baltic countries faced either 'tribalism and ruin, or alternatively, racial tolerance and prosperity.'[10]

The whole question of minority rights preoccupied the constitution makers of the Baltic republics. It found expression in systems of proportional representation for parliamentary elections. More specifically, enlightened attempts were made to enshrine the rights of minorities in the Baltic constitutions. The constitution of Estonia specifically guar-

8 Tallents, *Man and Boy*, p 275.

9 Royal Institute of International Affairs (RIIA), *The Baltic States: A Survey of the Political and Economic Structure and the Foreign Relations of Estonia, Latvia and Lithuania*, London 1938, p 29.

10 Cited in J W Hiden, *The Baltic States and Weimar Ostpolitik*, Cambridge 1987, p 51.

anteed instruction in the mother tongue to racial minorities and promised them control over their own schooling and cultural life. These promises were put into effect in the Estonian Law on Cultural Autonomy of 1925. Any minority of over 3,000 persons had the right to become a corporation at public law and to administer its own educational, cultural and charitable affairs – even to the extent of being able to raise 'culture taxes'. These were supplemented by funds from the central and local authorities. The Estonian minority legislation has been rightly regarded as a model of its kind.[11] In Latvia's case, the minorities had to be content with developing the opportunities available under the school autonomy law of 1919. Plans for detailing rights in the second part of the constitution were shelved after internal disputes which led some to describe it as a 'rump constitution'.[12]

On this basis the Germans in particular went on to develop a highly successful school policy, although the Latvians did not follow Estonia and introduce a formal structure of cultural autonomy. Eventually the Germans were able to set up an autonomous school board, which could influence policy through its representation in the Latvian Ministry of Education. The Baltic German communities in Latvia and Estonia were fortunate in being able to attract financial support from the Reich. As *Auslandsdeutsche* they could not be seen to receive overt political support, for this would damage relations with their new masters. But under Baltic legislation, they could receive modest German subsidies for cultural and welfare activities. Despite the destruction of the old landed order, the Baltic German communities adapted to the new constraints with some success, certainly in the cultural field and indeed in the economic. The flourishing German theatre at Riga, the Herder Institute and a whole range of cultural exchanges with the Reich testified both to the continuing vigour of Baltic German life and to the tolerance of Latvians and Estonians, so recently subjected to German military occupation. This positive picture has to be set against the long-term demographic decline of the Baltic German communities after independence.[13]

On paper, the minorities in Lithuania had virtually the same rights as those in Estonia. In reality, Poles and Jews in particular were subject to discrimination from an early date. The early collapse of democracy

11 For details see E Maddison, *Die nationalen Minderheiten Estlands und ihre Rechte*, Tallinn 1930

12 A Silde, Die Entwicklung der Republik Lettland. In B Meissner (ed), *Die baltischen Nationen: Estland, Lettland, Litauen*, Cologne 1990, p 65.

13 For a discussion of the German minority and its ties with the Reich see Hiden, *Weimar Ostpolitik,* pp 36–61, 190–7.

in Lithuania (1926) ensured that there was little time for tolerance of minorities to take root. With greater or lesser success, however, each of the Baltic republics had attempted to go beyond the minimum guarantees of minority rights stipulated by the League of Nations as a condition of their membership.[14]

The parliamentary representatives of the minorities helped to swell the considerable number of political parties represented in the rather small legislatures (between 100 and 120 members) of the Baltic republics. All three states adopted constitutional systems similar to that of the Weimar Republic, with single chamber parliaments, elected on the principle of proportional representation. A common feature of the Baltic constitutions was their great stress on parliamentary supremacy at the expense of the executive. The Estonian constitution in force from 21 December 1920 allowed the head of government, who was also head of state (*Riigivanem* – State Elder), no right of veto over parliamentary decisions. The three-year parliaments (*Riigikõgu*) could be dissolved only by referendum, the basic right to do this residing with the people. The ultra-democratic nature of the Estonian constitution could be seen from the powers which the population had (as in Switzerland) to initiate laws through referendums. In Latvia, too, the constitution of 7 November 1922 gave extensive powers to parliament (*Saiema*). The president, however, had powers to initiate legislation and to appoint the prime minister, while the government of the day could temporarily resort to rule by decree when parliament was not in session. The authority of the executive was similar under the Lithuanian constitution of 1 August 1922. Although the president could dissolve parliament (*Seimas*) his own political fate then depended on the outcome of new elections.

The operation of parliamentary politics in the Baltic countries was itself profoundly affected by the social transformation which accompanied the birth of the new republics. Land reform provides the most dramatic example of this change. In each of the three republics a deliberate attempt was made to counter any threat of communism by creating a new landed peasantry. The step was essential to securing the social stability and economic progress which were preconditions of national survival. In postwar conditions it was vital for the Baltic governments to control and plan all available economic resources, including land. Inevitably, reform was carried out at the expense of the former

14 Cf R Pearson, *National Minorities in Eastern Europe 1848–1945*, London 1983; C A Macartney, *National States and National Minorities*, London 1934.

landowners; Baltic German in Estonia and Latvia; Polish and Russian in Lithuania. In Estonia alone, 96.6 per cent of all estates were taken over. The German element in Estonia was left with only a small residual holding and received very little compensation under the legislation of 1926. In the case of Latvia no compensation was paid by the state but rather more land was left with the original owners. Lithuania's former landed aristocracy shared much the same fate. As a result of the reforms the Baltic governments acquired huge land funds for redistribution in the 1920s and the old landowning elites lost at a stroke most of their inherited wealth.[15]

Reforms of this magnitude could hardly fail to mould the day-to-day political struggle in the parliaments of the three republics. Most obviously, the parties representing the new landowning peasantry emerged as a major political force in all three countries, usually on the moderate right of the political spectrum. These included in Estonia the Homesteaders and Farmers Parties, which merged to form the Agrarian Union in 1931–2. In Latvia there were the Peasant Union, the New Farmers and the Latgalian Christian Farmers. The division between farming and non-farming interests was less clear cut in Lithuania in so far as they were largely encompassed by the Christian Democratic Party: here the Catholic bond blurred the classic rural–urban and class divisions.

The other main grouping in Baltic parliaments comprised the socialist parties, drawing their support from the landless peasants and urban working class. The Estonian moderate left was represented by the Labour and Social Democratic Parties; further to the left stood the Independent Socialist Party and the Communists, the latter proscribed after their abortive coup of December 1924. As in Estonia, communism received little electoral support in Latvia and its influence was mainly confined to the trade union movement. Latvian socialist politics were dominated, as they had been before the war, by the Social Democratic Party. Lithuania had a People's Socialist Party as well as a Social Democratic Party.

Around the two main political groupings of farming and labour interests revolved a wide range of smaller parties, some representing the interests of the urban bourgeoisie, others reflecting the ethnic diversity of the Baltic republics. Most nationalities had more than one 'party' ostensibly representing their interests. In Latvia, for example, the Russians were divided between five different parties and the Jews

---

15 E Fromme, *Die Republik Estland und das Privateigentum*, Berlin 1922; A Heyking, *The Main Issues Confronting the Minorities in Latvia and Estonia*, London 1922.

had three. Although the Germans in Latvia had several parties, they increasingly functioned as one interest group under the umbrella of the so-called committee of German Balt Parties. Instead of reporting back to their separate parties, the German delegates in the *Saiema* reported to the committee under the chairmanship of the highly influential Paul Schiemann, nephew of Theodor Schiemann. His initial six-month term of office was extended by popular consent to ten years in 1920. 'So arose the paradox that Schiemann was leader of a 'party' which consisted chiefly of members of other parties.'[16] The Baltic Germans in Estonia were equally well organised.[17] Such discipline paid dividends in the bewildering patterns of coalition politics during the parliamentary epoch in the Baltic republics. It enabled the German element to exert a parliamentary influence disproportionate to its numerical size, some of its members even rising to ministerial rank.

Democratic politics in Estonia, Latvia and Lithuania were all too easy to caricature. In Latvia, the most extreme case, thirty-nine separate parties were represented in parliament between 1922 and 1934. Putting together coalitions was exceptionally difficult in all three countries and governments rarely lasted more than a few months. At first sight the propensity for Baltic parties to proliferate seems to be reasserting itself in the 1990s, leading some observers in the West to make dismissive references to the politics of the interwar period.[18] It is, however, vital for today's Baltic politicians to distil that experience and to look for the good as well as the bad points. A deeply frustrating mixture of hope and disillusion was after all characteristic of many parliamentary systems in the 1920s and 1930s, as the example of Weimar Germany shows. Even in Britain, two-party politics was the exception rather than the rule between the wars. In the Baltic states, as in the French Third Republic, key parties and political figures gave some continuity of administration through frequent changes of government. The Farmers' Party was represented in all eighteen governments of independent Latvia and Karlis Ulmanis headed five administrations in the period of parliamentary rule up to 1934. Päts provides a similar example in Estonia; in Lithuania, too, a relatively small group of names constantly recurs in government lists. Frequent changes of government were no bar to legislation. In Latvia alone 3,267 laws were drafted in the sixteen years of parliamentary rule.[19]

---

16 W Wachtsmuth, *Von deutscher Arbeit in Lettland 1918–1934. Ein Tätigkeitsbericht. Materialen zur Geschichte des baltischen Deutschtums,* 3 vols, Cologne 1951–3, Vol 3, p 41.

17 In general, M Garleff, *Deutschbaltische Politik zwischen den Weltkriegen,* Bad Godesberg 1976.

18 Cf T Tammerk, It's party time, *Homeland,* 27 December 1989.

19 Silde, Die Entwicklung. In Meissner (ed) *Die baltischen Nationen,* p 68.

Inevitably, the Baltic peoples were no more able than Poles, Germans, Hungarians, Italians and all too many others to give credit to the positive features of their new democratic systems. Too often they saw only the weaknesses. Ultimately, all three republics were to abandon democracy in favour of authoritarian dictatorship. Lithuania was the first to take flight in 1926, when Antanas Smetona and Augustinas Voldemaras were brought to power by a military coup. In the same year the first of a series of calls for strengthening the executive was made in Estonia, on this occasion from Konstantin Päts and the Farmers' Party. Pressure for change in Estonia grew with the onset of the great depression after 1929. One response on the part of the democratic parties was to merge into larger groupings. More ominously the cause of constitutional reform was captured by the extra-parliamentary extreme right in the form of the League of Freedom Fighters (VAK).

Originally a non-political organisation representing veterans of the war of independence, the VAK had grown rapidly. Led by the youthful Artur Sirk and General Andres Larka, it became a para-military movement on fascist lines. Its draft proposals were accepted by a public traumatised by economic crisis and disillusioned with parliamentary government.[20] Under the terms of the new constitution of 1933 the powers of the executive were greatly enhanced. The state president was to be elected for five years by the people and he now had the right to appoint a Cabinet and to pass emergency decrees. Estonia passed from a system of extreme parliamentarianism to one of presidential dictatorship.The beneficiary, however, was not the Freedom Fighters but Konstantin Päts. Rather than risk losing the elections required by the constitution which became law in January 1934, Päts engineered a pre-emptive strike on 12 March, more than a month before the poll was due to take place, by declaring a state of emergency and banning the dangerously popular VAK.

Latvia followed the path to authoritarian rule very shortly afterwards. Again there were calls for constitutional reform and again the government was faced with an extreme right-wing challenge, in this case from the Thunder Cross movement. More consciously moulded in the image of German National Socialism, Thunder Cross was yet anti-German as well as anti-Semitic. In response to the mounting threat and undoubtedly influenced by the success of Päts in Estonia, Karlis Ulmanis used the occasion of his appointment at the head of a new government on 16 March 1934 to declare a state of emergency.

20 T Parming, *The Collapse of Liberal Democracy and the Rise of Authoritarianism in Estonia*, London and Beverly Hills, California 1975.

The Thunder Cross movement was proscribed with little or no resistance. In May Ulmanis completed his assumption of dictatorial powers, eventually becoming president as well as prime minister in 1936.

Like the Estonians, therefore, the Latvians 'came to be governed by an authoritarian regime, which insisted that it had assumed absolute power in the defence of democracy.'[21] In this respect, they differed from Hitler, who explicitly used democratic procedures to destroy the Weimar system and dismissed with contempt the 'men of 1918' who had built the German republic. There was much justification in the claims of the Estonian and Latvian leaders. Both men had, after all, played a key role in the struggle for independence and in the construction of their states. The same was true of Smetona in Lithuania. Nevertheless, the claims of Päts and Ulmanis have to be viewed with some scepticism. The former merits particularly close scrutiny precisely because he has had a good press in the light of his constitution of 1938 which restored a measure of democracy to Estonia, and which is still regarded as being in force by those who desire the restoration of Estonian independence.[22]

Päts dealt harshly with his political opponents, real or imagined. His victims included Jaan Tönisson, himself hardly an undistinguished fighter for Estonian independence, and the prominent diplomat Kaarel Pusta. The role of Päts' notably efficient secret service also deserves scrutiny. It may have had a hand in the death of the VAK leader Sirk, whose body was found in mysterious circumstances beneath his Luxemburg hotel window in August 1937. More importantly, the affinity of his regime and the ideas behind it with those of more overtly fascist systems must not be overlooked.[23] In 1935 Päts followed better-known dictators in proscribing all political organisations, including the democratic parties. They were immediately replaced by his own creation, the Fatherland League (*Isamaaliit*). This was structured on the lines of the banned VAK, many of whose ideas Päts had taken over. The Estonian version of a *Volksgemeinschaft* was rounded out by a re-structuring of the economy which had a strong affinity with Italian corporatism.

Yet it remains difficult to fit Päts neatly into the pattern of interwar dictatorships. Hitler and Mussolini never contemplated dismantling their regimes but that is precisely what Päts seemed to be doing in the

21 G von Rauch, *The Baltic States. Estonia, Latvia, Lithuania: The Years of Independence 1917–40*, London 1974, p 154.

22 Parming, *The Collapse*, p 61.

23 A Isberg, *Med demokratin som insats: Politiskt-konstitutionellt maktspel i 1930-talets Estland*, Uppsala 1988.

late 1930s. In this respect the resemblance is rather with the 'Liberal Empire' of Napoleon III than with the fascist dictators. The new constitution which took effect in Estonia in January 1938 was ostensibly an attempt to strike a balance between the executive and legislature; one avoiding the parliamentary extremes of the 1920s and the presidential excesses of the period after 1934. In practice Päts continued to reserve many powers to himself and did not end the ban on parties or lift press censorship. Given Päts' declaration as late as 24 February 1940 that he did not favour the re-establishment of political parties, it is difficult to see the 1938 constitution as an ideal model for democratic development in present-day Estonia. There was a choice of candidates but only for the eighty-seat state assembly. Members of the other chamber of parliament, the Council of State, were either appointed by the president or delegated by professional and eccesiastical corporations.[24] These conditions bear a remarkable resemblance to some of the post-perestroika electoral arrangements in the Soviet Union.

It therefore remains difficult to endorse wholeheartedly what seems to be a rehabilitation of Päts amongst Estonian historians.[25] In comparison with Päts, Karlis Ulmanis seems to have been a less intolerant figure. He did not feel the urge to set up a one-party system and prominent party politicians continued to serve under him. Nor did he introduce a new constitution: the democratic constitution of 1922 theoretically remained in force, as it does to this day. Ulmanis does not appear to have been impressed in any way by either Hitler or Mussolini and had a distaste for totalitarian methods of government. Ulmanis did, however, share Päts' liking for corporatist institutions. Indeed, reorganisation on these lines went further in Latvia than in either Estonia or Lithuania. In creating some fifteen corporative bodies, including a Chamber of Culture, Ulmanis was at the very least undermining the egalitarian values of Latvian political life. Yet there was little outright opposition to his regime and the state of emergency was lifted in 1938. To the end, however, Ulmanis was never prepared to put his popularity to the test in a referendum.

As ever Lithuanian politics differed in important respects from those of Estonia and Latvia. By the time Päts and Ulmanis were establishing authoritarian rule in their countries, the Lithuanians could look back

---

24   Rauch, *Baltic States,* p 158; Rein Taagepera, A note on the March 1989 elections in Estonia, *Soviet Studies* **42** (1990): 330.

25   H-J Uibopuu, Die Entwicklung des Freistaates Estland. In Meissner (ed) *Die baltischen Nationen,* pp 52–61.

on almost eight years of dictatorship. Augustinas Voldemaras, the prime minister, and Antanas Smetona, the president of Lithuania, had also fought to establish their state's independence. Their small Nationalist Party had, however, been unable to achieve control of the government through the ballot box, gaining not a single seat in the first three parliaments and only three in the last free elections in 1926. Their opportunity came in December 1926 when, perhaps prompted by the example of Pilsudski in Poland, they carried out a coup with army backing. They were able to exploit nationalist resentment against the Soviet–Lithuanian pact concluded by Lithuania's left-wing government in September. The 'Voldemaras dictatorship' of 1926–9 promulgated a new constitution in 1928 which greatly enhanced the president's powers. It also imprisoned large numbers of its political opponents. While the democratic parties fell by the wayside, Voldemaras moved to the extreme right, eventually becoming leader of the Iron Wolf, a secret, para-military organisation. Although Smetona was an honorary member of the Iron Wolf, his ambitious prime minister hoped to use the movement as a power base to unseat the president. Smetona proved the more skilful politician; in 1929 he dismissed Voldemaras and replaced him with his brother-in-law, Tubelis. The former prime minister made several attempts to regain power by force, the last in June 1934. With Voldemaras in prison during the years 1934 to 1938, Smetona consolidated his dictatorship.

The Smetona regime had close affinities with those of Päts and Ulmanis. Smetona also merged the nationalist groupings into one patriotic front and reorganised his own Nationalist Party along Nazi lines in 1933. The other political parties remained in limbo. Smetona remained deaf to the pleas for a return to parliamentary democracy, except in May 1935, when he permitted elections in response to peasant unrest. Even then a new law was passed on the eve of elections reserving the government the right to nominate all electoral candidates. Not surprisingly, few people turned out to vote. The ensuing parliament was composed of forty-nine members, forty-six of whom were members of the Nationalist Party (the other three being German). When a new constitution finally came into effect in 1938 it made gestures towards democracy but in reality consolidated Smetona's authoritarian rule. As head of state and leader of the only permitted political party, he retained wide powers for his seven-year term of office. Smetona's regime perhaps went further than those of Ulmanis or Päts in seeking to establish a unifying nationalist ideology. It claimed to draw inspiration not from National Socialism or Fascism but from Lithuanian culture – the factor which Lithuania's great medieval rulers had neglected to develop.[26] As Smetona put it, 'the Italians have their marble, the Germans their iron, and we have our clay, wood and stone.'[27] In practice the regime developed distinctly totalitarian overtones, with the Nationalist union acting as the means by which the leader's ideas were transmitted to the public at large, and a heavy emphasis on the indoctrination of youth in the schools and the Young Lithuanian movement.

Yet Smetona, like his fellow Baltic dictators, presents problems of classification. All three dictators have to be given some credit for their determination to defend the states they had helped to found. As dictatorships go, moreover, 'their rule was the mildest in Europe'.[28] There seems little point in trying to distinguish between them as types. Some have argued that Päts and Ulmanis represented 'authoritarian democracy' while Smetona's was a 'presidential regime'. This distinction has rightly been criticised: all were equally 'presidential'.[29] Comparisons with other 'presidential' systems, such as the classic one under Hindenburg in Germany between 1930 and 1933, are complicated by the fact that the three Baltic dictators themselves headed fascist-type movements. Yet whereas Hindenburg gave way to a fascist solution in the form of Hitler, the Baltic leaders headed off full-scale fascism by adopting some of its features. This is not to deny that they had a genuine affinity with Baltic variants of fascist ideology. Nor did they find the role of 'Führer' wholly uncongenial. More fruitful comparisons might be made with the regimes of Salazar in Portugal or the 'clerico-fascism' of interwar Austria. What the Baltic regimes did not resemble, however, were the kind of military/royalist dictatorships prevalent in parts of south-eastern Europe, such as Romania and Bulgaria.

There is nothing in this analysis which suggests that Päts, Ulmanis and Smetona were little Hitlers. The question of the impact of their policies on non-Baltic nationalities must, however, be confronted. The most obvious point to make is that their constitutional changes, in particular the abandonment of proportional representation, drastically limited the political representation of the minorities. Cultural auton-

---

26 L Sabaliunas, *Lithuania in Crisis: Nationalism to Communism, 1939–1940*, Bloomington, Ind 1972, p 28.

27 Cited ibid, p 28.

28 V S Vardys, The rise of authoritarian rule in the Baltic states. In V S Vardys and R J Misiunas (eds), *The Baltic States in Peace and War 1917–1945*, University Park, Pennsylvania and London 1978, p 77.

29 Ibid, p 78.

omy might continue, alongside the many self-help organisations which had developed in the 1920s to cater for the welfare and schooling of the various minorities. Such networks, however, always depend on access to political influence if they are to function effectively. More seriously, as the rising tide of Baltic nationalism infected the political process, minority interests came under direct attack.

The process is seen most clearly in the realm of schooling, the very interface of national coexistence in the Baltic republics. After the coup of 1926 in Lithuania, some forty-eight Polish schools were closed while in the Klaipeda district the government applied pressure for German children to attend Lithuanian schools. The situation had become so bad by 1936 that Poles and Germans joined forces to protest against Smetona's education policy. Polish schools were also closed in Latvia but the main thrust of the policy of Latvianisation introduced by the education minister, Kenins, in 1931, was directed against the Baltic German community. The rather successful Baltic German school system which had been built up in the 1920s was subverted by Kenins' policies. Curriculum changes were introduced and grants to Baltic German schools were reduced. In 1934 a new education act downgraded the head of the autonomous German school board; he could now only give advice to the Latvian minister of education and exerted no influence on policy. Similar legislation was introduced in Estonia, where the education authority responsible for the German schools was disbanded and its powers transferred to the Ministry of Education.

All of these measures undermined the hitherto enviable framework of cultural autonomy. Closely linked to them but even more far-reaching were the expressions of linguistic nationalism in the new laws of 1934–5 in Estonia and Latvia. The use of Estonian and Latvian was required for place-names and in the transaction of government business. Latvian and Estonian spelling was insisted on for personal names: for example the Estonian politician Einbund became Eenpalu. This was a trivial but depressing manifestation of growing intolerance of national diversity. 'Latvianisation' and 'Estonianisation' unintentionally echoed the 'russification' of decades past and sadly anticipated the Russian-language signs and street names which were inflicted upon the Baltic republics after the Second World War.

Nationalism was not confined to symbols but penetrated to the very heart of Baltic economic life. All three dictators were successful in developing the Baltic economies and pushing them further along the path of modernisation. Inevitably, however, this was often at the expense of the minorities: particularly the German element in Latvia and Estonia. By 1938 the situation was so dire in Latvia that many felt 'there were barely any prospects for the long-term survival of the *Volksgruppe.*'[30] This was not, of course, entirely caused by Baltic nationalism. It had much to do with the rising influence of the Third Reich in the Baltic German community.

Subsidies for Baltic German activities from the Reich increased under Hitler but they were accompanied by growing political control from Berlin. Estonians and Latvians had been well aware of financial aid from the Reich throughout the 1920s but became anxious about it only after Hitler's seizure of power. Nor were some of the leaders of the Baltic German communities unconscious of the dangers. Doubts about becoming over-dependent on the Reich were expressed as early as 1930 by Rüdiger, the head of the Baltic German political organisation in Latvia.[31] Yet after 1933 relations between the Baltic Germans and the Reich intensified, not just financially but through exchanges and contacts at every level. Even so it was with some difficulty that those Baltic Germans who were genuinely National Socialist extended their control over the existing Baltic German organisations. The leader of the Estonian National Socialists, Viktor von zur Mühlen, even had to resort to an alliance with the Estonian Freedom Fighters in his attempt to seize control of the Baltic German party leadership. Nor was Erhard Kroeger, the leader of the German National Socialists in Latvia, any more successful in his bid to secure the political leadership of the German community.

Tragically, however, as the nationalist policies of Päts and Ulmanis began to bite, the mood in the German communities as a whole grew more pessimistic. Competing nationalisms began to feed on one another, although the situation was marginally less severe in Estonia where there had never been such antagonism between the German and Estonian communities as existed in Latvia. These developments are a sad commentary on the breakdown of the vision of multi-national Baltic states enshrined in the legislation of the 1920s. A prime minister of Latvia could actually say in 1927: 'We Latvians feel as one with the Germans . . . as a nation pursuing common goals and tasks.'[32] Under the conditions of the 1930s, little remained of the 'common Baltic home'. Nevertheless, it is wrong to assert that the tenets of National Socialism 'were taken over quite indiscrimately by the Baltic Germans.'[33] The quarrels within the Baltic German camp

---

30 J von Hehn, *Die Umsiedlung der baltischen Deutschen – das letzte Kapitel baltischdeutscher Geschichte*, Marburg 1982, p 59.
31 Wachtsmuth, *Von deutscher Arbeit*, Vol 1, p 421.
32 Cited by Silde, Die Entwicklung. In Meissner (ed) *Die baltischen Nationen*, p 66.
33 Rauch, *Baltic States*, p 167.

refute this notion.

In the end it was Hitler's policy which sealed the fate of the Baltic Germans, who were evacuated from Estonia and Latvia in the autumn of 1939 in the aftermath of the Nazi–Soviet pact. In compelling the Baltic Germans to leave the lands to which they, like the native Baltic peoples, had tenaciously clung, Hitler removed a bastion of western civilisation as well as of German influence. More immediately, their departure made it easier for Hitler to use the Baltic territories as a battlefield, and for Stalin to reap the rewards.

CHAPTER FOUR

The Diplomacy of Survival

By 1920 the Baltic republics had driven foreign invaders from their soil and were in the process of negotiating peace treaties with the Soviets in which the bolsheviks recognised the full independence of the three small states. They had also secured de facto recognition from the western powers, although Lithuania had had to wait until September 1919 – much longer than Estonia or Latvia – partly because it had become independent under German auspices and partly owing to the complications of its frontier dispute with Poland. However, the West had still not given the Baltic republics full diplomatic recognition. It was of course to their advantage that the victor powers had embraced the doctrine of self-determination and had enshrined it in the peace settlement. To this extent the three republics were in the same position as the other new states of central and eastern Europe. Yet they had a harder task than the other states in convincing the Allied powers to give them de jure as well as de facto recognition. Baltic representatives had to continue lobbying the foreign ministries of the western powers and the peace-makers in Paris until Estonia and Latvia were finally accorded de jure recognition in 1921, and Lithuania in 1922. While, therefore, the bolsheviks could not prevent Baltic independence, the West had to be persuaded to accept it.

There were several reasons for western hesitation. There was, first, a large measure of ignorance in the Allied capitals about some of the basic facts of Baltic geography, politics and history. 'At that time,' wrote J D Gregory, the head of the Northern Department of the Foreign Office, (inaccurately) of the Estonians, 'we knew little about their country (which generically with a piece of Latvia had been called Courland and was mostly known abroad as the home of Baltic barons) and still less about their properly native inhabitants and leading men.'[1] As for the Lithuanians, they had in Gregory's view made the mistake of cultivating the Germans rather than the West during the war: as a result the Foreign Office heard 'very little of Lithuania and the Lithuanians until they had become involved in active controversy with Poland.'[2]

More importantly, the Allies still tended to subsume Baltic problems in the 'Russian problem'. Admittedly their perception of that problem had changed significantly by 1920. They had not abandoned their opposition to bolshevism, or indeed the hope that it would disappear, but they could no longer be wholly confident of the time scale. Military intervention had failed. The threat of bolshevism had to be met by other means. One option was to contain the Soviets by a ring of independent border states linked by defensive treaties to the western powers. In December 1919 Clemenceau spoke of a *cordon sanitaire* in eastern Europe; in the same month the British foreign secretary Balfour referred to the need for a 'barbed-wire fence'.[3] A second approach was to tame the bolsheviks by economic means. The advantage of this was that the Soviets could be implicated in the reconstruction of postwar Europe. Lloyd George, the British prime minister, believed such a step to be imperative. Britain's own accommodation with the Soviets was already under way by the beginning of 1920, when the O'Grady trade mission was sent to Moscow.

Whatever conflicts might arise between the two strategies, both containment and reconciliation created a more favourable climate for Baltic independence. Although the West remained sceptical about the viability of the new Baltic countries, the collapse of intervention against the bolsheviks eliminated the need to respect White Russian objections to the breakup of the former Russian empire. Once the bolsheviks themselves had recognised Baltic independence there seemed no reason for further hesitation on the part of the Allies. Indeed Gregory at the Foreign Office thought in April 1920 that any further delay in recognising Estonia and Latvia might endanger the prospects for British trade.[4] However, the outbreak of the Polish–Soviet war in the spring of 1920, which brought the Red Army to the gates of Warsaw by August, strengthened the case for caution. If Po-

---

1 J D Gregory, *On the Edge of Diplomacy: Rambles and Reflections, 1902–1928*, London 1928, p 186.

2 Ibid, p 178.

3 *Documents on British Foreign Policy* (DBFP), Series 1, Vol II, pp 738–48.

4 M-L Hinkkanen-Lievonen, *British Trade and Enterprise in the Baltic States 1919-1925*, Helsinki 1984, p 88.

land fell, the Baltic states might soon follow and Britain did not want to go to war with Russia on their behalf. In the end it was France which, in January 1921, took the lead in recognising Estonian and Latvian independence, in order to assist the efforts being made by its Polish ally to create a Baltic alliance. Lloyd George followed the French lead against the advice of the Foreign Office. Here there was greater anxiety about Soviet intentions and, as we have seen (Chapter 3), the idea of a Russian federation was still strong. The Foreign Office did wish to maintain the British naval presence in the Baltic, partly out of consideration for Britain's 'growing commercial interests' in the region.[5] The Baltic squadron was, however, withdrawn at the Admiralty's insistence in 1921 and in July the British government told the Baltic states that it could no longer promise material support against a Soviet attack.

If recognition for Estonia and Latvia came late and was heavily qualified in practice, Lithuania had to wait still longer. The British Foreign Office tended to place more blame on the Lithuanians than on the Poles for the intractability of the Vilnius issue, and came round in the course of 1920 to the view that the best solution was a Polish–Lithuanian federation. The French, for obvious reasons, backed Poland's claims still more strongly. Only after the irretrievable breakdown of the federation plan, and more than a year after Lithuania's recognition by Germany and several other countries, not to mention its entry into the League of Nations, did the Allies finally grant de jure recognition in December 1922.

Both the internal consolidation of the three Baltic states and the beginnings of détente between the Soviets and the West made the prospects for Baltic independence far more promising than the tortuous deliberations of the Allied governments on the question of recognition seemed to imply. The Baltic states had every hope of participating in the expected resumption of economic relations between East and West. On this point they were in unexpected agreement with the Soviets. Lenin described the Soviet–Estonian peace treaty of February 1920 as 'an actual break through the blockade', and as a 'fact of tremendous universal historical significance' because it 'opened a window on Europe'.[6] Estonia was the first of the republics to benefit from what the Soviet commissar for foreign affairs, Chicherin, described as 'the first experiment in peaceful co-existence with the

5 Cited ibid, p 91.

6 A N Tarulis, *Soviet Policy towards the Baltic States 1918–1940*, Notre Dame, 1959, p 56.

bourgeois states.'[7]

There were of course still risks in acting as an intermediary between East and West. Ulterior motives were present in the bolshevik camp as much as in the West. Just as Lloyd George hoped to tame bolshevism by economic means, so the Soviets could, as the German representative in Tallinn observed, spread propaganda through their trade with western Europe.[8] Baltic leaders faced conflicting pressures. They were attracted by the prospect of a resurgence of trade across their territories. At the same time, their distrust of the bolsheviks made them receptive to schemes for creating a barrier against Soviet communism or a German–Russian combination.

The Allied concept of a 'barrier' complicated the discussions which the Baltic republics were beginning to hold among themselves and with their neighbours in Scandinavia and eastern Europe, for a regional alliance system. The leaders of the three Baltic states had to take into account not merely the interests of Great Britain, Germany and the Soviet Union but also those of their prospective alliance partners in the Baltic region. Of these, Poland was the most important. It had aspirations to play a great power role in the Baltic in its own right; it was also on bad terms with both Germany and Russia, at whose territorial expense it had been reconstituted. Polish policy was compelled to defend not only its disputed Versailles frontiers with Germany, but also the territories wrested from Russia in the Polish–Soviet war of 1920. Finally, Polish relations with the Baltic states were poisoned by Poland's seizure of Vilnius, the ancient capital of Lithuania, in October 1920.

To the north stood Finland, which ostensibly had much in common with the three Baltic republics. Closely related ethnically to the Estonians, the Finns had been under tsarist rule since 1809. They, too, had been forced to fight their way free of the bolsheviks in 1918. Yet Finland had enjoyed much greater autonomy within the old Russian empire than had the Baltic provinces. Its right to independent statehood was more readily accepted by the Allied powers. Culturally, and to an increasing extent politically, Finland looked to Scandinavia rather than towards the Baltic states. The Scandinavian countries were more distant prospects as alliance partners for the Baltic republics. Norway took almost no interest in Baltic affairs; Denmark played an important economic role in the immediate postwar period but was not active

7 J W Hiden, *The Baltic States and Weimar Ostpolitik*, Cambridge 1987, p 75.
8 Ibid, p 75.

politically. Sweden was a different matter. Sweden had long since lost the Baltic empire which it had won by conquest in the seventeenth century. Since the Napoleonic wars it had followed a policy of neutrality and non-involvement in European affairs. In the early 1920s, however, Sweden was tempted by the prospect of a more active role in Baltic diplomacy.

In considering their respective foreign policy options the Baltic states and their neighbours did not, therefore, see themselves merely as agents of western interests. On the contrary, they wished to improve security in the region with the ultimate aim of avoiding being drawn into great power confrontations. The problem was that most conceivable combinations seemed to entail many of the risks they were hoping to avoid. Between 1917 and 1934 almost every permutation of northern and eastern European states was contemplated at one time or other.[9] The options were gradually whittled down. Ultimately, in 1934, only the so-called Baltic Entente between Latvia, Lithuania and Estonia came into being. This achievement may appear meagre in the light of the ambitious early schemes for a huge regional bloc stretching from Scandinavia in the north to Romania in the south. Indeed, the few studies that exist on Baltic diplomacy tend merely to recite a gloomy story of mutual mistrust and frustrated hopes. Many argue that 'whatever these countries did or failed to do was ultimately immaterial.'[10] To focus only on the failures of Baltic diplomacy between the wars is, however, to overlook the potential benefits of Baltic cooperation not merely for the states concerned but for European stability as a whole. The current Baltic reawakening, together with the end of the Cold War division of Europe, has suddenly made such schemes appear less visionary and more worthy of serious attention. Present-day Baltic leaders are learning from the mistakes and achievements of this era of intra-Baltic diplomacy.

Jaan Tönisson talked in 1917 of a possible Scandinavian–Baltic bloc which would 'have, as a union of thirty million people, a certain amount of influence during the negotiations at the Peace Conference.'[11] In 1989 his words were echoed by Vytautas Landsbergis, addressing the First Congress of People's Deputies in Moscow:

9 Cf B J Kaslas, *The Baltic Nations – The Quest for Regional Integration and Political Liberty*, Pittston, Pa 1976.

10 A Dallin, The Baltic states between Nazi Germany and Soviet Russia. In V S Vardys and R J Misiunas (eds), *The Baltic States in Peace and War 1917–1945*, University Park and London 1978, p 107.

11 Cited in O Arens, The Estonian *Maapäev* during 1917, In Vardys and Misiunas (eds), *Baltic States*, pp 24–5.

We need new conceptions that take the best from Lenin's legacy and nothing from Stalin's. . . . Once again there will arise self-governing people's states. And then they can decide for themselves, what mutual agreements and unions they will sign and enter into as nations and states. Such a conception could embrace and unite entire regions of Eastern or Northern Europe and offer a much more feasible future for our trumpeted 'Common European Home'.[12]

It is worth recalling that the sort of blocs envisaged by Tönisson and others could have been a military factor of some significance. Even the minimum combination of the three Baltic states could muster more than 500,000 soldiers (at a time when Weimar Germany was restricted to an army of 100,000). In addition they disposed of one hundred tanks, four hundred front-line aircraft, four modern submarines and an extensive range of other weaponry.[13] Combined with Poland on the one hand – a formidable military power in its own right – or with Finland and Sweden – both well-armed by Scandinavian standards – the military potential of a 'Baltic bloc' was considerable. Indeed, some of the potential for collaboration was realised. The Estonians and Latvians concluded a military convention in 1923, which Lithuania was to join in 1934. Yet military collaboration between the three Baltic states remained a dead letter. The Estonian and Latvian armed forces held joint manoeuvres in 1931 but the experiment was not repeated. General Laidoner of Estonia was reported to have said that relations between Estonia and Lithuania were so bad that if they were attacked by a common enemy it would be 'extremely hard to induce Estonian and Lithuanian soldiers to fight side by side.'[14] Close links were, however, forged between the Finnish and Swedish general staffs,[15] while the Finnish and Estonian military authorities collaborated in the early 1930s in reconstructing the tsarist naval batteries on either side of the Gulf of Finland. The American military attaché in Riga wrote in August 1939 that the coastal artillery on the Finnish and Estonian sides of the Gulf would 'be a serious menace to the operations of the Soviet

12 O Glebov and J Crowfoot (eds), *The Soviet Empire; its Nations Speak out. The First Congress of People's Deputies, Moscow, 25 May to 10 June 1989*, Chur 1989, pp 22–3.

13 E. Anderson, The Baltic Entente 1914–1940: its strength and weakness. In J W Hiden and A Loit (eds), *The Baltic in International Relations, between the Two World Wars*, Stockholm 1988, pp 81–2.

14 Cited in H I Rodgers, *Search for Security: a Study in Baltic Diplomacy 1920–1934*, Hamden, Conn 1975, p 75.

15 M Turtola, Tornionjoelta rajajoelle, Poorvoo 1982 (English summary pp 246–55); idem, aspects of Finnish–Estonian military relations in the '20s and '30s. In Hiden and Loit (eds), *Baltic in International Relations*, pp 103–4.

vessels.'[16] The twelve-inch cannons which the Finns installed in 1931–3 represented 'the strongest, longest-range gun and the best armoured gun turret in the whole world.'[17]

The concern of the Baltic states remained, of course, to avoid using their military firepower. For this reason they were anxious to build links with Finland and, through Finland, with Sweden, the most influential of the Scandinavian states. Yet although as we have indicated the Swedes were attracted by 'a foreign policy other than the old neutrality', the weight of tradition and their habitual caution held them back.[18] The Finns for their part came increasingly to see security in an orientation towards Scandinavia rather than in closer links with their Baltic neighbours to the south. The Finnish parliament thus failed to ratify the Warsaw Accord signed on 17 March 1922 by Finland, Poland, Estonia and Latvia – the high point of large-scale Baltic collaboration. Finnish and Swedish hesitation was understandable but regrettable. Paradoxically, in distancing themselves from the Baltic alliance projects they may have lessened the chances of keeping the Baltic free from conflict. Their present-day successors seem to have learnt the lesson: Sweden and Denmark, at least, have been more ready than the western powers to acknowledge the right to independent nationhood of the Soviet Baltic republics.[19]

The absence of a Scandinavian element made all the more problematic the question of collaboration with Poland, the other major prospective partner for the Baltic states. Any scheme involving Poland was likely to increase the risk of conflict with either Germany or Russia. Moreover, Poland had its own aspirations to Baltic hegemony. Underlying Poland's regional alliance projects was a sustained attempt, under Pilsudski's guidance, to achieve a division of the Baltic area into spheres of influence with Finland. The latter country would count Estonia within its orbit while Poland expected a free hand over Latvia and Lithuania.[20] There remained, furthermore, the bitter dispute over Vilnius which clouded all discussions for a Baltic bloc. Nevertheless it was difficult to leave Poland out, if any regional security arrangement

16 Ibid, p 106.

17 Ibid, p 106.

18 T Norman, 'A foreign policy other than the old neutrality.' Aspects of Swedish foreign policy after the First World War. In Hiden and Loit (eds), *Baltic in International Relations*, pp 235–50. See also K Kangeris, Die Schwedische Baltikumpolitik 1918–1925. Ein Ueberblick. Ibid, pp 187–207.

19 Sweden was the first country to open a foreign consular office in the Baltic republics (in Tallinn in December 1989). *Homeland*, 15 November 1989.

20 K Hovi, *Interessensphären im Baltikum: Finland im Rahmen der Ostpolitik Polens 1919–1922*, Helsinki 1984.

was to be credible. Thus in spite of the Vilnius issue the Baltic republics as a group continued to keep open the Polish option, at least until the Locarno conference of 1925 transformed the framework of European security. Latvia and Estonia, the two states which *were* able to negotiate with Poland, were not prepared to do so at the expense of Lithuania. In signing the Warsaw Accord, as the Latvian foreign minister, Meierovics, made clear, they wished to retain the option of including Lithuania in due course.[21] By the time that Lithuania felt able to join Estonia and Latvia in 1934, the prospects for a larger bloc had, however, long since vanished.

Poland, of course, was never an independent actor since it was also the key to France's eastern alliance system (through the Franco-Polish alliance of 1921). Regional arrangements were therefore intercut by the security concerns of France and the other major European powers. Wipert von Blücher, a key official at the Russian desk in the German foreign ministry, the Auswärtiges Amt, rightly stressed that 'the problem of the Baltic, because of the present allocation of its shores and the way in which this came about, is closely linked with the Versailles question and the Eastern question as a whole.'[22] The problem for the European powers was to move beyond the punitive Versailles 'diktat' and the crude notions of containing the bolshevik infection towards a more equitable and more stable European settlement. For the Baltic republics, then as now, it was imperative to be seen as part of any new *European* order. The trouble with the order which emerged in the 1920s was that it had an anti-Soviet slant. Until Locarno it had an anti-German slant as well. The dilemma for Baltic leaders was that while their political loyalties lay firmly with the Allies, they could not afford to antagonise either Germany or Russia. These two powers had been weakened by war and revolution but for the Baltic republics they remained 'great powers' and had to be treated with circumspection.

The best hope for the Baltic states was for a reconciliation between Germany and the West and ultimately between the West and the Soviet Union. This would square the political circle and would also be economically advantageous. The vision appeared to be on the point of realisation during the run-up to the world economic conference at Genoa in April 1922. For the first time Germany, the Soviet Union and the Allied powers convened to attempt the reconstruction of Europe.

21 Berndorf report 22 March 1922, Foreign Office Microfilm, Auswärtiges Amt, Akten betreffend Aufzeichnungen über die auswärtige Lage, Vol 1, 3177H/D686179.
22 Hiden, *Weimar Ostpolitik*, p 142.

Lloyd George set the tone with his remarks on the tasks facing the conference:

> He did not want to see Russia attacking other countries, nor did he want to see other countries attacking Russia. No good could come of it; it kept Europe in a sort of tumult and excited nationalist feeling on both sides; Russia would not calm down and the others would not be able to come to any European understanding with a view to the reconstruction of that battered and shattered old continent.[23]

In this climate the Baltic republics hoped to profit from being the interface between western capitalism and the Soviet Union under Lenin's New Economic Policy (NEP).[24]

What they got instead was the Rapallo treaty. Concluded by the German and Soviet delegations to the Genoa conference on 16 April, Rapallo shattered Lloyd George's plans. The agreement provided for the mutual liquidation of German–Soviet war debts and Germany's diplomatic recognition of the Soviet state. It also committed the two powers to economic cooperation and in doing so cut the ground from under the planned international consortium to trade with the Soviets. What appeared at the time to be a Russo-German combination against the West also had implications for the Baltic republics. The collapse of the Genoa conference, together with the disappearance of the prospect of a greater role for the Baltic countries in East–West trade, came as a shock to Baltic leaders. Politically unwelcome as the German–Russian agreement undoubtedly was, they could hardly ignore its professed intention to intensify German–Russian economic relations. Rapallo engendered a new realism. Baltic delegates at Genoa told their German counterparts that, as a result of the agreement, it seemed 'more than ever necessary to form a quite open and reliable bridge between Germany and Russia.'[25]

For the time being therefore the Baltic republics prepared themselves to live with the enforced separation of their ultimate political goal of East–West reconciliation, and their immediate economic interests. The latter dictated Baltic participation in the development of German–Soviet trade. For this reason alone it would be a mistake to see Rapallo, as many have done, merely as a threat to Baltic inter-

---

23 Genoa Conference Proceedings, Vol 2: Minutes of the First (political) Commission, 3rd Meeting, 16 May 1922, in PRO FO 371/7435.

24 E Anderson, The USSR trades with Latvia: the treaty of 1927, *American Slavic and East European Review* **21** (1962): 296–321.

25 Cited in Hiden, *Weimar Ostpolitik*, p 122.

ests.[26] Yet Rapallo had anti–western implications which continued to trouble the Baltic states. Not until Locarno, in 1925, did the desired German–western reconciliation come about. Even then, the Locarno treaties guaranteed only the borders between Germany and France and between Germany and Belgium; they left open the question of Germany's eastern frontiers as a matter for future arbitration. In refusing to accept the frontier with Poland, the German government continued to nourish Polish feelings of insecurity. Furthermore, the activation of the Franco–Polish alliance of 1921 was now made dependent on prior agreement between the Locarno signatories instead of being automatically invoked in the event of an attack on either party by Germany.

Nor did Locarno placate the Soviet Union. On the contrary, together with Germany's entry into the League of Nations it aggravated Soviet fears of a hostile West. These were not allayed by the German–Soviet Treaty of Berlin in 1926, in spite of Stresemann's success in persuading the League of Nations to exempt Germany from any League action directed against Russia. Moscow mistrusted Stresemann's determined cultivation of economic links with western Europe and the United States and the inclusion of Germany in a coalition of western powers. The Soviets entertained exaggerated fears about Germany being used by Great Britain in an anti–bolshevik crusade. Soviet anxieties were expressed in warnings to the Baltic republics not to allow themselves to become military outposts of Great Britain.

Moscow remained sensitive to threats, real or imagined, on its Baltic flank. Further evidence comes from the Soviet refusal to sign collective agreements with the Baltic republics and its preference for bilateral non-aggression treaties.[27] The Soviet Union also remained indifferent to the idea floated briefly in 1925 by the German representative in Riga, Adolf Köster, of a Soviet–German guarantee of the Baltic states – an idea to be revived by Litvinov in much changed circumstances in 1934.[28]

For the Baltic states, therefore, Locarno was a frustrating mixture. On the one hand, as we have just seen, it made Poland and Russia more nervous. On the other hand it had many positive aspects. Locarno made war less likely and thus contributed to the 'appeasement of Europe'. In conjunction with the financial arrangements made for German reparations under the Dawes Plan (1924), it represented a sig-

26 Ibid, pp 119–21; K Hildebrand, *Das deutsche Reich und die Sowjetunion im internationalen System 1918–32: Legitimät oder Revolution*, Frankfurt 1977.

27 R Ahmann, *Nichtangriffspakte: Entwicklung und operative Nutzung in Europa 1922–1939*, Baden-Baden 1988.

28 Hiden, *Weimar Ostpolitik*, pp 152–5.

nificant step towards the 'recasting of bourgeois Europe'.[29] Locarno was a necessary precondition for integrating the Baltic economies into the western European trading system. After 1925, the notion of a Baltic league directed against either Germany or the Soviet Union was redundant. It was not by chance that the series of regular meetings of Baltic foreign ministers was terminated in 1925, a year which also saw the accidental death of one of the major architects of the Baltic bloc idea, the Latvian foreign minister, Zigfrids Meierovics.

The Baltic states got as much from Locarno as any such treaty could have been expected to provide. It was up to the European great powers to make the Locarno system work. Meierovics' successor, Albats, was unduly pessimistic in asserting that 'without the pacification of Eastern Europe a Western peace pact remains but an insignificant scrap of paper.'[30] Although an 'Eastern Locarno' never materialised, largely due to German and Soviet resistance, many of the conditions which it was expected to bring about were in fact being realised by the late 1920s. Any direct threat from Germany to Baltic independence had long since disappeared and Berlin had put the military adventurism of 1919 firmly behind it. The German foreign minister, Curtius, could say with some justice to his Estonian counterpart in 1931 that Germany had tried 'to encourage the independence of the Baltic states, since we were hardly keen to see them becoming dependent on Russia or joining a Polish-led bloc.'[31]

It was in Germany's interest to use political persuasion and economic aid to maintain a gap between the Baltic republics and Poland. Admittedly, Germany kept up the revisionist pressure on Poland but even here, beneath the public rhetoric and away from the glare of domestic politics, the officials of the two states worked slowly to hammer out a modus vivendi.[32] With the three Baltic states, and with Latvia in particular, Germany developed a much more positive relationship. In part this was because Latvia represented a bridge to an improved relationship with the Soviet Union. This aim survived both the death of Meirovics and the failure of Köster's scheme for a joint German–Soviet guarantee of the Baltic states in 1925. Both Albats and

29 C S Maier, *Recasting Bourgeois Europe: Stabilisation in France, Germany and Italy in the Decade after World War One*, Princeton, N J 1975.

30 Cited in Rodgers, *Search for Security*, p 48.

31 Cited in W Hubatsch, Die aussenpolitischen Beziehungen des Deutschen Reiches zu Lettland und Estland, *Deutsche Studien* **13** (1975): 308–9.

32 H Lippelt, 'Politische Sanierung'. Zur deutschen Politik gegenüber Polen 1925/1926, *Vierteljahrshefte für Zeitgeschichte* **19** (1971): 323–73.

Cielens, who succeeded him as Latvian foreign minister in 1926, made it clear that they wished to continue the policy of consolidating relations with Russia and Germany.[33] Although large-scale diplomatic initiatives failed to materialise, positive links were established when the signature of a trade agreement between Germany and Latvia in 1926 was followed by a Soviet–Latvian economic agreement in 1927.[34]

If Latvia was the key to German policy in the Baltic area, Lithuania was the key to the Soviet Union's. Russia played on Lithuania's preoccupation with Vilnius to divide it from the other two Baltic states. In exchange for Soviet recognition of its claim to Vilnius, Lithuania signed a non-aggression treaty with the Soviet Union in September 1926. Here too, however, there was the possibility of a stabilisation of German–Soviet–Baltic relations. A German–Lithuanian trade agreement concluded in May 1926 was of more than merely commercial interest. For Stresemann trade talks were a means of conducting a political dialogue with Lithuania at a time when the Memel issue precluded a more overtly political approach. At the same time he encouraged the Lithuanians in their negotiations with Moscow while taking care to keep the Soviets informed of Germany's exchanges with Lithuania.[35] The Baltic states therefore formed channels of communication between Germany and Russia but were also independent actors in the diplomatic process. The more their relations with their two powerful neighbours were fixed in the form of trade agreements, non-aggression treaties or arbitration treaties, the more all parties to those agreements were embedded in the emerging European security system. The longer the status quo continued, the more likely it was to resist change. Far from threatening the Baltic states, the effect of Weimar 'revisionism', as pursued by Stresemann, was therefore to consolidate their international position.

Nor does there appear to have been any significant threat from the Soviet Union. The retreat to 'socialism in one country' which was associated with Stalin's rise to supreme power was underway. Faced with the gigantic if self-imposed task of rapidly industrialising the Soviet Union, Stalin signally failed to take any opportunity for aggression against the Baltic states. On the available evidence at least, Stalin was not actively seeking to undermine the independence of the Baltic countries. There was no repetition of the abortive communist coup in Estonia of December 1924, alarming as it appeared at the time.[36] The

---

33 Rodgers, *Search for Security*, pp 58–9.
34 Hiden, *Weimar Ostpolitik*, pp 163–4.
35 Ibid, pp 164–6.
36 T U Raun, *Estonia and the Estonians*, Stanford, Calif 1987, p 115.

subversive activities of Comintern were increasingly overshadowed by the more pragmatic policies of Narkomindel, the Soviet Commissariat of Foreign Affairs, under Chicherin and, in the 1930s, under Litvinov. Soviet policy was exemplified by the non-aggression treaties of the period 1926–33. These treaties, while still aiming to keep the border states divided, none the less underpinned the peace treaties of 1920, in which the Soviet Union had acknowledged Baltic independence.

Under such conditions it is not surprising that German–Soviet collaboration against the border states simply failed to materialise during the life of the Weimar Republic. The idea that there was no automatic threat coming from Germany's friendship with Russia was for a long time difficult to accept in the West because of misleading parallels drawn between Rapallo and the Nazi–Soviet pact. The terrible legacy of the Molotov–Ribbentrop agreement ensured that from 1939 onwards little could be said in favour of Germany's eastern policies. With the onset of the Cold War, furthermore, it was all too easy to telescope the period and to characterise Germany's relations with the Soviet Union between 1922 and 1941 as an 'unholy alliance'. The claims of historians in the eastern bloc that Rapallo was an early model of 'peaceful coexistence' were not taken seriously. Now that the Cold War is over it is possible to dwell not so much on the 'continuities' between 1922 and 1939, as on those between 1922 and 1992. The parallels which are really worth exploring are those between Weimar Germany's Ostpolitik and that of the Federal Republic.[37]

From today's perspective it has also become more apparent that German economic dominance of East Europe and the Baltic did not necessarily have sinister implications. Weimar governments certainly used trade for political ends and those ends were indeed revisionist.[38] *Any* improvement in Germany's international position implied revision of the Treaty of Versailles because that treaty touched on virtually every aspect of Germany's existence. The point is that such revision was not, of itself, a threat to European peace in general or to the interests of the Baltic states. Further support for this proposition is

37 P Krüger, *Die Aussenpolitik der Republik von Weimar*, Darmstadt 1985, p 555.

38 J W Hiden, The 'Baltic problem' in Weimar Ostpolitik. In V R Berghahn and M Kitchen (eds), *Germany in the Age of Total War*, London 1981, pp 147–69; H-J Schröder, Zur politischen Bedeutung der deutschen Handelspolitik nach dem Ersten Weltkrieg. In G Feldman *et al* (eds), *Die deutsche Inflation. Eine Zwischenbilanz*, Berlin and New York 1982; P Salmon, Anglo-German commercial rivalry in the depression era; the political and economic impact on Scandinavia 1931–1939. In M-L Recker (ed), *Von der Konkurrenz zur Rivalität: Das britisch–deutsche Verhältnis in den Ländern der europäischen Peripherie, 1919–1939*, Stuttgart 1986, pp 101–42.

provided by the reactions to Weimar Baltic policy of the one great power which was indisputably regarded as the protector of the smaller Baltic countries and of paramount importance to their 'diplomacy of survival': the United Kingdom.

At the end of the First World War Britain's attitude towards the German presence in the Baltic was naturally one of deep hostility. Shortly before Brest-Litovsk, early in 1918, Lloyd George warned the Cabinet that: 'Under one name or another, and the name hardly matters, these Russian provinces will henceforth in reality be part of the dominion of Prussia. They will be ruled by the Prussian sword in the interests of the Prussian aristocracy.'[39] In the course of the 1920s, however, the British moved towards a less jaundiced view of Germany's Baltic presence. The fear of a hostile German–Soviet combination receded after Locarno; it became apparent that the Baltic Germans who remained in Estonia and Latvia were no longer a disruptive force, and that they were concentrating their energies on making the most of their reduced socio-economic position. Above all, however, the Anglo-German economic rivalry in the Baltic, which was so acute in 1919–20, had all but disappeared by the late 1920s. More accurately, it had been transmuted into a triangular trading relationship between Britain, the Baltic states and Germany, which in the pre-depression era operated to the advantage of all parties.

The trading pattern whereby Britain bought Baltic agricultural produce, thus providing the revenue which the Baltic states devoted overwhelmingly to the purchase of German manufactured goods, will be examined in detail in the next chapter. It was yet one more aspect of the European stabilisation effected in the Locarno era. Yet there were still no concrete guarantees for the security of the Baltic states. They therefore continued to look not merely towards the League but above all to their mentor, Great Britain. Admittedly, Britain made no formal commitments to European security beyond those entailed in the League covenant and the Locarno treaties. Moreover as late as 1926 a British Foreign Office memorandum still professed indifference to the ultimate fate of the Baltic states: 'Apart from obligations which may arise under the Covenant of the League, we should not feel called upon to object to any change such as the federation of the Baltic States, or their reabsorption by Russia.'[40] This prognosis, however, did

---

39 Public Record Office, London (PRO), Cabinet Office, WC314/Appendix 4 January 1918.

40 DBFP, Series 1A, Vol I, p 866.

less than justice to the evolving relationship between Britain and the Baltic states.

Central to that relationship remained the fact that British naval power and military aid had contributed decisively to the independence of Estonia and Latvia. British officials continued to concern themselves with Soviet threats to the integrity of the Baltic states, as shown by their sharp reaction to the attempted communist coup in Tallinn in 1924. The British armed forces and intelligence services made use of Tallinn and Riga (as well as Helsinki) as listening posts for the Soviet Union. This role became particularly important after the breaking off of diplomatic relations with the Soviet Union in 1927.[41] The British also resolutely opposed proposals for the neutralisation of the Baltic Sea, many of them emanating from the Soviet Union, a device clearly aimed at keeping the Royal Navy out of Baltic waters.[42]

Of course Britain could not commit itself to the kind of unqualified support in time of crisis which Baltic leaders seemed to expect. Gregory, who was fully aware of the ambiguity of Britain's role in the achievement of Baltic independence, expressed the characteristic British attitude of embarrassed benevolence when faced with Estonian and Latvian gratitude. 'We found ourselves [he said] with two grateful little friends who, on account of our initiative, will always look for a moral support to us, though not, I trust, for military protection in grave emergency.'[43] Despite Britain's formal statements to the contrary, Baltic leaders continued well into the 1930s to believe that the Royal Navy would be on hand once again when the moment of crisis came. The inexperienced diplomats of the Baltic countries were prone to misread the signals coming from Whitehall. They suffered from the understandable optical illusion that a relationship which was of paramount importance to them was equally important to Great Britain.[44]

Nevertheless, Foreign Office officials, including Gregory himself, took a paternalistic interest in the welfare of the new Baltic states. From 1920 onwards the Foreign Office worked actively to reconcile Poland and Lithuania over Vilnius in the interests of general stability in the Baltic region. Gregory himself played a major part in this process. The familiar assertion that Britain was inactive in eastern Europe finds no echo in the response of the foreign secretary, Lord Curzon, to the

41 P Salmon, Perceptions and misperceptions: Great Britain and the Soviet Union in Scandinavia and the Baltic Region 1918–1939 (forthcoming).

42 P Salmon, British security interests in Scandinavia and the Baltic 1918–1939. In Hiden and Loit (eds), *Baltic in International Relations*, p 124.

43 Gregory, *On the Edge of Diplomacy*, p 188.

44 Hinkkanen-Lievonen, *British Trade and Enterprise*, pp 107–9.

Vilnius crisis: 'It seems quite certain that no satisfactory settlement will ever be reached between the Poles and the Lithuanians themselves: a settlement must be imposed upon them.'[45] Or, as Gregory less bluntly phrased it, 'Great Britain alone has the requisite moral authority in those regions to attempt advice and guidance.'[46] In 1925, following visits to Poland and the Baltic states, R W Leeper of the Northern Department advocated a more active British role in the region. The thrust of his argument was that the Baltic states did not want political or military guarantees 'but the quiet assurance that England at any rate considers that these countries are sufficiently stable for her own economic expansion in them.'[47]

Such expressions of British interest in the Baltic also sent messages to the other great powers active in the region. In 1924, for instance, the German legation in Riga reported a conversation in which the Labour Foreign Office minister Ponsonby had told Meirovics that the 'prevention of Russian expansion in the Baltic was a vital issue' for London.[48] Britain's continuing vigilance towards Soviet activities in the border states indicated to Berlin that it should not go too far in its collaboration with Russia over Polish and Baltic issues.

The passage of time and Britain's growing trade with the Baltic states led to a growing acceptance of their economic and political viability in Whitehall. By 1932 a member of the Foreign Office felt able to assure an audience at the College of Imperial Defence that 'it was not necessarily to be assumed' that either Estonia or Latvia would 'ultimately be re-incorporated with Russia, though that this fate was in store for them both was regarded as axiomatic a few years ago.'[49] Beneath Britain's guarded approach to eastern Europe, and indeed continental Europe as a whole in the late 1920s, the ground had been laid for the more active Baltic role which it would be compelled to adopt after the onset of the depression. In general, however, the Baltic states could gain more during the 1920s from the hard-headed self-interest of Weimar Germany than from the benevolent detachment of Great Britain.

45 Curzon minute on dispatch from Warsaw of 7 October 1920, PRO, FO 371/5374.

46 Gregory memorandum, 'Poland and Lithuania', 25 February 1925, FO 371/10978.

47 DBFP, Series 1, Vol XXV, pp 850–8.

48 Hiden, *Weimar Ostpolitik*, pp 145–6.

49 Draft lecture by J Perowne, August 1932 FO 371/16292, N5579/5579/63.

By the end of the 1920s the Baltic republics had convinced the European powers of their right to exist. They had found a place in the international economic order and a niche in the European security system established at Versailles and Locarno. Both of these pillars were to be fractured by the slump of 1929. The Baltic republics had survived as states. They would now have to struggle for their continued existence under radically changed conditions.

CHAPTER FIVE

The Economics of Survival

When the Baltic provinces became the Baltic states they lost the foundations of their economic prosperity. As integral parts of the Russian empire they had enjoyed the benefits of guaranteed markets, a plentiful supply of raw materials and a highly favoured position in the flow of trade between Russia and western Europe. The major Baltic ports of Riga, Liepaja (Libau) and Jelgava (Mitau), Ventspils (Windau) in Latvia, and Tallinn and Narva in Estonia, were favoured by location and climate as major access and exit points to and from the Russian interior. Between 1908 and 1911 one-third of all the exports and imports of European Russia was conveyed through the ports of Riga, Libau and Windau. They handled a flourishing export trade in flax, timber, hides, rye, butter and eggs and imported products such as rubber, steel and coal. These imports were converted by Baltic industries into finished products for the Russian empire.

Riga was particularly favoured by foreign shippers, whose vessels could always return with a full load of timber after unloading their inward-bound cargoes. In the process Riga became the biggest timber exporting harbour in Europe, its shipping trade doubling between 1900 and 1913.[1] Western interest in Baltic transit trade was supported by the presence of French, Dutch, Belgian, British and above all German capital. Such funds helped to make possible the concentration of industry and commerce in the major Baltic cities. This, together with the practice of setting up branches of west European industry in the Baltic to circumvent Russia's high tariff wall, ensured a vigorous industrial development. Estonia could boast in Tallinn the Dvigately

1 H F Crohn-Wolfgang, Die Republik Lettland und ihre wirtschaftliche Zukunft, *Jahrbücher für Nationalökonomie und Statistik* 1: 118 (1922): 44.

Railroad Car Factory and one of Russia's most important shipbuilding centres, the Baltic Shipyards. Narva housed the world's biggest cotton works, the famous Krainholm mills.[2] Latvia, the 'Belgium of the East', supported, like Estonia, a range of metal, chemical and wood industries. In Riga alone were the world's largest metal file manufacturer, the Salamandra plant, the huge Provodnik Rubber Factory, the Felser Shipboiler Works and the Phoenix Railroad Car Factory. Two-thirds of the inhabitants of Riga were dependent on industry for their livelihood.

As in other respects economic developments in Lithuania had followed a different course. Less favoured by geography, Lithuania had not experienced such intensive industrialisation as either Latvia or Estonia. Agriculture and forestry retained their traditional dominance. The few industries that did develop were based mainly on the processing of agricultural products and timber. When Lithuania gained control of Klaipeda (Memel) in 1923 it secured for the first time a major port and significant industrial centre. The absence of a common frontier with the Soviet Union, due to Poland's seizure of Vilnius in 1920, was to prevent it from playing a major role as a transit route between east and west and as a result its industrial development remained stunted in comparison with that of the other two Baltic states.

All three Baltic economies, however, were devastated by the impact of the First World War and the prolonged military campaigns on Baltic territory until the end of 1919, when the last German troops were evacuated and the bolsheviks driven out. By then the great industrial centres in Latvia and Estonia had virtually collapsed. Industries were ruined, with buildings often empty, their machinery and assets stripped by the retreating Russian authorities from 1915 onwards. The impressive banking and financial network serving Baltic trade and industry, which had been greatly dependent on parent companies in Russia, had also vanished. The centre of banking in Estonia and Latvia had been St Petersburg and the numerous commercial banks in the provinces had had their head offices in the Russian capital.[3] To wartime destruction were added the strains of Baltic involvement in the Allied intervention in Russia, the further disruption of trade caused by the Allied blockade throughout 1919 and the absence of any worthwhile Baltic currency. Independence was proclaimed by the Baltic countries with ruined industries, empty coffers and plundered rural economies.[4]

2 E Anderson, The USSR trades with Latvia: the treaty of 1927, *American Slavic and East European Review* **21** (1962): 296–321.

3 J W Hiden, *The Baltic States and Weimar Ostpolitik*, Cambridge 1987, p 100.

4 A Blodnieks,*The Undefeated Nation*, New York 1960, p 183.

The magnitude of the task of reconstruction facing the Baltic peoples in 1919 should be kept in mind when today's Soviet spokesmen insist that the Baltic republics cannot survive on their own. The achievements of the first decade of Baltic independence bear eloquent witness to the absurdity of this claim.

In common with other Europeans, the Baltic peoples expected to return to economic normalcy by reconstructing the bases of their pre-war prosperity. The fact that there were now three independent states each trying to build its own economic structures was not seen as an obstacle to the resumption of their historic roles in the flow of East-West commerce. The world's major trading powers, notably Great Britain, Germany, France and the United States, also saw the future of the Baltic republics in these terms. The political upheaval in Russia was not expected to alter such ingrained trading patterns. As the German economic expert Crohn-Wolfgang argued in 1922, the advantages of Riga

> were a product of nature which could not be changed by political events and will never be changed by these . . . However the political relations in the east develop, one thing is certain, namely that the geographical area constituting European Russia . . . will continue to use Riga as its main economic outlet; and here all human reason suggests that Riga's future as a harbour is determined, as is that of Latvia, as a transit region.
> Specifically, the country will continue to be the coastal transit zone for Russia and the bridge between western Europe and Russia.[5]

If anything, the bolshevik revolution had heightened the importance of Latvia and Estonia as intermediaries in East-West trade. As independent capitalist states on the edge of Russia the Baltic countries appeared to western enterprise as ideal 'springboards' from which to open up the postwar Russian markets. Businessmen and officials in both Germany and Britain, the two powers which came to dominate Baltic trade between the wars, were alert to the potential from the outset. The title of Crohn-Wolfgang's book, on 'Latvia's significance for the Eastern question', speaks for itself. In it he argued that history had shown that to open up new areas economically a beginning had to be made in the frontier regions, which for Russia after 1919 meant the Baltic countries. These, he affirmed, would 'be the bridge across which we can reach Russia, whereas the leap from Berlin to Moscow is bound to be a blunder.'[6] The sentiment was echoed in London in

5 Crohn-Wolfgang, Republik Lettland, p 427.
6 H F Crohn-Wolfgang, *Lettlands Bedeutung für die östliche Frage*, Berlin and Leipzig 1923, p 10.

the words of Owen O'Malley, an official in the Northern Department of the Foreign Office. In assessing an early British banking venture in the Baltic states he wrote that the scheme 'would give this country a paramount position in the economic and political life of the Baltic provinces and . . . that they would afford a very good jumping off ground for British trade with Russia whenever this becomes possible.'[7]

The assumption that Russia's needs would be virtually limitless fostered a widespread illusion that it was an 'Eldorado' for western trade. This explains why so many adventurers, alongside the more solidly based concerns, flocked to the Baltic area in 1919–21, there to prepare for the coming bonanza in the east. In reality this failed to materialise. Even under the New Economic Policy of Lenin from 1921 the opportunties for western participation in the Soviet economy were limited. As the Soviet Union slowly turned in on itself and moved towards 'socialism in one country' the overall levels of trade and transit through the Baltic states remained deeply disappointing. Whereas in 1922 25 per cent of Estonia's trade was with the Soviet Union, by 1935 the figure had dropped to 3 per cent. Although Latvian exports to the Soviet Union rose from 2 per cent to 15 per cent following the conclusion of a trade agreement between the two countries in 1927, they had fallen back to 1 per cent in 1933 and had still reached only 3 per cent by 1938.[8]

The parallels with today's situation are worth considering, as western enterprise attempts to size up the economic consequences of the Gorbachev revolution. In fact the prospects for the Baltic republics of profiting from any resurgence of East–West trade are arguably now much better. There seems virtually no prospect of a reversion to Stalinist economics and Gorbachev is manifestly desperate for intensive economic relations with the West.

For the newly independent Baltic states, however, the 1920s were a period when they were forced to come to terms with the fact that the most obvious route to economic prosperity was no longer open to them. Instead, they were compelled by the middle of the decade to restructure and reorientate their economies on an entirely new basis. They were thrown back on their own resources – largely agricultural and with potentially valuable reserves of flax, timber and (in Estonia) shale oil. In developing these assets the Baltic states created profitable trading relations with the industrial powers in the West. In the process

---

7 O'Malley minute of 20 October 1920, PRO, FO 371/5376.

8 G von Rauch, *The Baltic States. Estonia, Latvia, Lithuania: The Years of Independence 1917–1940*, London 1974, p 126.

new types of industry were created. They were never, therefore, merely 'peasant republics'.

Forging relations with the West presented difficulties in the early stages of Baltic reconstruction. In all three countries fervent nationalism and the presence of strong and influential socialist parties combined to produce radical approaches to postwar problems which often alarmed foreign capitalists. The most drastic example was the dispossession of the once dominant Baltic German landowning caste in Estonia and Latvia. What struck many in the West as close to bolshevism in fact provided an effective barrier to the spread of communism through the creation of a landowning peasantry. At first agrarian reforms added to the postwar disruption of agricultural production; ultimately, however, the restructuring of the rural economy helped to provide the mainstay of Baltic foreign trade.[9]

That trade was at first burdened by emergency legislation giving the state monopoly control over the most important raw materials, notably flax and timber. Such controls formed the basis of a complex system of export and import licensing which remained in place until 1921. In Latvia, for example, priority was given, in the interests of the survival of the new state, to the conservation of scarce currency reserves and the securing of food supplies. Non-essential goods were effectively banned: licences were given only for vital imports, such as agricultural machinery. Other legislation which upset foreign investors related to the enforced exchange rates introduced by the currency laws in Estonia and Latvia, which were highly arbitrary and affected above all German enterprise.[10] Similar doubts were expressed in Britain. In an article entitled 'Fiscal gymnastics', the *Manchester Guardian Commercial* declared of Estonia: 'The country has gone theory mad.'[11]

By 1921–2 in any case the emergency controls had outlived their usefulness and were being dismantled. This enabled an attack to be made on the problems of inflation, shortages and unemployment characteristic of the first phase of economic development in the Baltic countries. A particularly interesting illustration of the switch away from state controls and towards a freer economy is provided by the work of the Latvian finance minister, Ringold Kalnins. He was ap-

9 I Romas, *Die wirtschaftliche Struktur der baltischen Staaten und die Idee einer Zollunion*, Rytas 1934, p 31.

10 Report of German representative in Riga, Wever, 9 November 1920, Foreign Office Microfilm, K2330/K663648–51, AA, Akten betreffend politische Beziehungen Deutschlands zu Lettland, Bd 1.

11 Cited in M-L Hinkkanen-Lievonen, *British Trade and Enterprise in the Baltic States 1919–1925*, Helsinki 1984, p 191.

pointed in 1921, the year in which Latvia's confidence was given an important boost by the Allied recognition of its de jure independence. The absence of that recognition had, of course, been another major deterrent to foreign enterprise in all three Baltic states.

Kalnins, a private businessman and wealthy in his own right, was determined to break away from the rigid state controls of his predecessors. He published a robust declaration of intent in the journal of his ministry, *Ekonomist.*

> The monopoly of economic life by the state is to be ended. In this way, together with other drastic measures, the budget will be balanced as far as possible. At the same time to facilitate currency reform steps must be taken at the earliest moment to set up a [state] bank. Yet reform of the currency can only go hand in hand with a reorganization of foreign trade.

The message from Kalnins was 'thrift in the whole economic life of the state.'.[12]

The intimate connection between the restoration of a Baltic banking system and the development of foreign trade had been widely insisted upon by the businessmen seeking access to the new markets in the East. Until the Baltic states had viable currencies of their own they remained dependent on foreign credits to finance a flow of goods. This was repeatedly pointed out by agents and commercial representatives of both British and German firms.[13] In spite of the immense political good will towards Britain and a dislike of Germans in the immediate postwar atmosphere, the latter enjoyed significant advantages in early banking operations in the Baltic countries. This was partly because the Weimar Republic could take advantage of the fact that large amounts of German occupation currency, the so-called *Ostmark*, were still circulating in all three countries. Indeed Lithuania retained the *Ostmark* as its currency until 1922, which partly explains the very early and overwhelming dominance of German enterprise in that state.[14] Germany had a 72 per cent share of Lithuanian imports in 1920. The British vice-consul in Kaunas (Kovno) reported on the handicap to British trade represented by the fact that: 'Every bank of importance in Lithuania is at the present time largely or partly German

---

12 B Siew, *Lettlands Volks- und Staatswirtschaft*, Riga 1925, p 45.

13 See for example letters from the Frankfurt am Main Chamber of Commerce, 29 August 1919 and 11 September 1919, BAK, Auswärtiges Amt, Akten betreffend Finanz, Bank- und Wirtschaftsfragen, Baltenland Nr 1, Bd 1.

14 H F Crohn-Wofgang, Die baltische Randstaaten und ihre handelspolitische Bedeutung, *Schmollers Jahrbuch* **45** (1921): 214.

capitalised or German controlled.'[15] Even in Latvia and Estonia, however, where Britain was more active, the *Ostmark* provided a useful foothold for German traders in the sense that it was still prized more highly as a unit of exchange than the worthless Estonian and Latvian currencies.[16]

By 1922 it was clear that Germany's early lead in penetrating the Baltic banking system had been consolidated. The modus operandi of German banking is revealed by briefly examining the examples of the Riga Commercial Bank and the Libau Bank. The Riga Bank, founded in 1871, largely on the basis of German capital, was Latvia's oldest and one of its largest commercial banks. When it was reconstructed after the war its management remained chiefly in German hands although it received substantial financial backing from American sources. Through its branches in Estonia and Lithuania, and even in Poland, the Riga Commercial Bank was in a position to support German business throughout the Baltic countries.[17] The establishment of the Libau Bank in 1922 is even more instructive in showing how Germany overcame the obstacles created by Baltic chauvinism. Ultimately, the various Baltic and German financial institutions participating in the Libau Bank were all financed by the powerful Darmstädter Bank in Berlin. However, as Wallroth, the German minister in Riga noted with quiet but evident satisfaction, 'The extent of the orginal German participation is masked through the mutual collaboration of the Lithuanian, Estonian and Latvian banks.'[18]

Germany's prominent position in the Baltic banking system was soon reflected in its dominance of Baltic markets. This was a very different situation from that existing during the period 1919–20. In 1920 Britain had provided nearly 21 per cent of Latvia's imports, against Germany's 18.6 per cent. The figures for Estonia were respectively 26 per cent and 30 per cent. By 1922 Germany was providing over 40 per cent of Estonian imports and 48 per cent of Latvian. The position was much more advantageous to Germany in key areas like industrial and agricultural machinery. By the time Latvia held its first international trade fair in 1921, Germany's domination of the Latvian market was inescapably clear to contemporary observers.[19] Germany took 45 per

15 Blennerhassett to Department of Overseas Trade, 4 April 1921, PRO, FO371/6725, N4836/359/59.

16 Hiden,*Weimar Ostpolitik,* pp 72–3.

17 Wallroth report of 21 April 1922 Deutsches Zentralarchiv, Potsdam (DZA), AA, Akten betreffend Bank-und Sparkassenswesen in Lettland, Bd 1, 64562.

18 Ibid, Wallroth report of 8 February 1922.

19 O Lehnich,*Währung und Wirtschaft in Polen, Litauen, Lettland und Estland*, Berlin 1923, p 251.

cent of the exhibition space while France and Britain could manage only 4 per cent and 2 per cent respectively.[20]

Germany's dramatic revival – in the face of anti–German sentiments and British resistance – can hardly be explained by reference to banking systems alone. Germany had important advantages over Britain in its foreign trade owing to a tradition of state involvement in the economy and 'the close interlocking of finance, trade and industry.'[21] Of course, Germany also enjoyed the benefits of geographical proximity to the Baltic republics and long experience of local conditions. The Estonian Cooperative Wholesale Society commented in 1933 on the care with which German firms cultivated Baltic markets:

> Germany has been most active in this respect. Thus, every more important branch of trade and every bigger firm appoints local agents to deal with the customs, attend to the regular advertising of goods, and to obtain and supply any information.[22]

Another advantage possessed by German goods was that they were almost invariably cheaper than those of British origin. Among the most important reasons for this were the favourable exchange rates resulting from Germany's postwar inflation, which gave it an edge until the end of 1923, and the overvaluation of the pound following Britain's return to the gold standard in 1925. The representative of a leading British engineering firm reported wryly: 'Anti-German feeling will no more prevent the purchase of German machinery than British patriotism prevented buyers in England purchasing thousands of American cars at lower prices in the autumn of 1920, when several British motor car manufacturers went into liquidation.'[23]

Much as they valued the high quality of British goods, the Baltic countries simply found them too expensive. In any case, British businessmen seemed reluctant to adapt to local markets. Whereas 'other competing countries readily comply with their customers' wishes, even on very small orders', some English firms were simply 'not sufficiently interested in offering their wares to Estonia'.[24] Not only were the German exporters far more enterprising than their British counterparts, but also they received much more positive support from their govern-

20 Hiden,*Weimar Ostpolitik*, p 104.

21 Minute by Owen O'Malley 23 Feb 1925, *Documents on British Foreign Policy* (DBFP), Series 1, Vol XXV, p 857.

22 The Estonian Cooperative Wholesale Society,*Anglo-Estonian Trade Relations*, Tallinn 1933, p 30.

23 Report of J A Goodwyn of Ransomes, Sims & Jeffries Ltd of Ipswich on a visit to Latvia in February 1921, PRO, FO 371/6731, N3363/3363/59.

24 Estonian Cooperative Wholesale Society, *Anglo-Estonian Trade*, pp 28–9.

ment. German governments realised only too well the value of economic influence in offsetting Germany's political weakness after Versailles. Finally, German business was simply more determined to get whatever share it could, even of relatively small markets.[25]

British officals recognised the absence of such determination on the part of UK manufacturers. Wilton, who was sent to Lithuania at the end of 1920 precisely to promote Britain's commercial presence more effectively than his predecessor Colonel Ward had done, rightly observed: 'The Lithuanian direct trade can never be of any considerable magnitude, but it is worth having and there is no reason why we should not try to get what we can of it'.[26] This presupposed an active attempt to make British business aware of the situation in the Baltic. Here the carelessness of even the serious press in Britain could dismay Baltic officials. When the Estonian Consulate in London objected to the *Manchester Guardian*'s practice of lumping the trade of the 'successor states' under that for 'Russia', it stressed that Baltic trade with the UK

> is annually gaining in importance and deserves to be clearly brought
> before the notice of the British public instead of including it in the totals
> for a 'Russia' which no longer exists, since the successor states form
> independent political and economic units and the rest of the former
> Russian Empire is now known as the Union of Soviet Socialist
> Republics.[27]

It is important to pause at this stage to recall that the Baltic republics had hoped to fund the restructuring of their economies from the profits of a resurgent transit trade across their territories; revenue from customs duties and from storage facilities at the ports was deemed vital. The lower than expected returns from the transit trade made it even more important for the three states to increase their own exports.[28] These were largely agricultural. The initial damage to production caused by war and land reform was slowly repaired. The modernisation of agriculture and the development of cooperative movements, as well as specialisation in high quality dairy and meat products, provided the Baltic countries with openings in world markets, above all in Bri-

25 On the contrast between German and British business expertise see Bank of England memorandum 'Baltic business methods', appended to report by Sir James Cooper on Lithuania's economic position, 13.11.1933, Bank of England Archive, OV 119/1.

26 Wilton (Kaunas) to FO, 5 April 1921, PRO, FO371/6725, N4424/359/59.

27 Riiklik Keskarchiv (Tallinn). Eesti Saatkond Londonis, F1583 N1 A813, letter of 24 October 1924.

28 Royal Institute of International Affairs (RIIA), *The Baltic States*, London 1938, pp 126–7.

tain and Germany.[29] They were remarkably successful in cornering a share of these markets in the face of competition from established suppliers, such as Denmark, Canada and New Zealand.

Agriculture alone was not, however, a safe or reliable basis for long-term economic development in the interwar period. World over-production and depressed prices made it essential for the Baltic countries to diversify their economies. Beyond this consideration was the inbuilt imperative of the new postwar states to move in the direction of greater economic self-sufficiency. That entailed building up manufacturing industry.[30] However, this could no longer be carried out on the prewar basis of processing expensive imports of raw materials for the Russian market. The giant factories which had once serviced Russian requirements were doomed to remain empty. Instead, industrial development had to be based on local resources and geared to supplying local needs. To a limited extent it could also hope to fill gaps in the demand of the Scandinavian and western powers. Notable examples were the new plywood and furniture factories of Estonia and the woodworking industries of Latvia, as well as the opening up of oil-shale workings in Estonia for the export of oil, petroleum and asphalt.[31] A more deliberate drive to industrialise the Baltic countries was launched by the three dictators in the 1930s. Although their efforts met with some success in Latvia and Estonia, Lithuanian industry remained underdeveloped and inefficient, producing high-cost, low-quality goods behind a high tariff wall.[32]

In relating this diversification of the Baltic economies to the earlier discussion of Anglo-German rivalry, two important phases can be identified. During the first phase, lasting until 1922 at the latest, the Baltic republics derived some profit from the influx of speculative capital at the height of the race for the Russian Eldorado. Once it was proved beyond reasonable doubt that this was an illusion many of the early and insecure foreign ventures collapsed. Nevertheless, some of these important early ventures survived and paved the way for more solidly based enterprises. It was fortunate for the Baltic countries that in the second phase, which lasted until 1929–30, the Anglo-German

29 Cf B Gernet, Lettlands auswärtige Handelsbeziehungen. In J Bokalders (ed) *Lettlands Oekonomist*, Riga 1929, pp 27–31.

30 Romas, *Wirtschaftliche Struktur*, p 132.

31 For an insight into the way western speculators sought to exploit the oil shale industry see Tallinn, Eesti Saatkond Londinis, F1583 N1 A864, Memorandum (nd) 1926 concerning the Anglo-Estonian Oil Development Syndicate.

32 L Sabaliunas, *Lithuania in Crisis: Nationalism to Communism, 1939–1940*, Bloomington, Ind 1972, p 100.

economic presence continued to provide benefits. Instead of having to play one rival off against another, more substantial advantages could be derived from exploiting the very different roles undertaken by Britain and Germany in their foreign trade. By the mid-1920s these roles had become clearly defined. Britain was buying much more from the Baltic countries than it sold; Germany was selling more than it bought. In becoming the most important market for Baltic agricultural produce, Britain provided the three republics with the sterling reserves which they used to buy German products. Among these were the capital goods with which they hoped to diversify their economies. This was hardly what the British or Germans had foreseen in 1919. In the second half of the 1920s, however, the Anglo-Baltic-German triangular trade relationship worked to the advantage of all concerned. It was in a sense fortunate that the British proved better at buying than selling. All this was to be changed by the world depression.

The triangle of trade did represent for the Baltic republics a kind of dependence. It avoided, however, many of the dangers associated with great power – small power relationships. It did not degenerate in the 1920s to the situation where the Baltic republics were in danger of becoming parts of an 'informal empire' of either Britain or Germany. In this respect, and particularly against the background of the Locarno and Dawes settlements, it would be more accurate to talk of interdependence. In other words, the Baltic republics were drawn into a network of European-wide most-favoured-nation trade treaties. The fact that the Baltic republics were seen as part of this European system was underlined by the way in which a loan raised through the League of Nations helped to stabilise Estonia's currency in 1926–7. Within this broader European context it mattered less that the much discussed systems of regional economic cooperation, kept nominally alive by the so-called 'Baltic clause' which was inserted into Baltic trade treaties, never really took off. Largely because the Baltic countries produced similar goods, trade between the three republics remained very low indeed.

Reviewing the situation after ten years of independence the Baltic countries could derive considerable satisfaction from their achievement. They had above all demonstrated that they could survive economically without being part of Russia and in that sense had passed the acid test of independence. Even earlier the Estonian chargé in London had felt it necessary to react sharply to an ill-conceived article by Stephen Graham called 'In Estonia' in *The Times* in November 1924.

> We do not exist on international charity, and will not become a burden
> on anyone, thanks to the conscientiousness and hard work of our people,

who by their racial characteristics . . . . are able to tackle their difficulties in an efficient manner, and who are not prone to indulge in lamentations and throw themselves on foreign mercy if any calamity befalls them. It would require a very nervous and imaginative person indeed to fancy himself 'sitting on a volcano' in Estonia.[33]

Today's embattled Baltic leaders can draw not merely inspiration but also practical lessons from the economic reconstruction of Estonia, Latvia and Lithuania in the 1920s. As the Estonian Consul already cited admitted, there were difficulties 'but we are hard at work to become a self-supporting unit in the family of European nations'.[34] This was true of all three states and the 1920s provide more than enough ammunition to refute the charge that when today's Baltic republics are cut adrift from the Soviet empire they will not be able to stay afloat. On the contrary, if the Baltic republics do not succeed in severing their ties they may well go down with the Soviet ship.

---

33 Letter of 6 November 1924, Tallinn, Saatkond Londonis F1583 N1 A813
34 Ibid.

CHAPTER SIX
Lives of the Hunted

In September 1934 the British minister to the Baltic states, Hughe Knatchbull-Hugessen, sent a long dispatch from Riga summing up the momentous changes in their international position which had taken place since he first arrived there four and a half years earlier.[1] 'It would be idle to pretend,' he wrote, 'that the Baltic States are a factor of first importance in European affairs; nevertheless, placed as they are between Russia, Poland and Germany, their reaction to the political changes around them must be of interest.' He went on:

> There is a 'lives of the hunted' element in the attitude of these small
> States to their great neighbours; and it would be difficult to decide which
> in the last resort they fear most – the protective solicitude of the Soviet
> Union, the clumsy directness of Germany, or the devouring overtures of
> Poland. Obviously the intentions of none of the three are strictly
> honourable, and the question, 'how will it all end?' must frequently arise
> in the minds of Baltic statesmen.

By 1934 the international framework established at Versailles and Locarno, on which the existence of the Baltic republics depended, had been fatally undermined – first by the world economic crisis after 1929; second by the rise of powers determined to overturn the postwar international order: Japan in the Far East; Nazi Germany and Fascist Italy in Europe. As Knatchbull-Hugessen indicated, the reactions of Poland and the Soviet Union to the German challenge in eastern Europe could not fail to have direct repercussions on the Baltic states. Their position would be influenced, too, by the responses of the two western powers, France and Great Britain. Economic crisis also desta-

1 (DBFP), Series 2, Vol VII, pp 736–40.

bilised the internal politics of the Baltic countries: in 1934 Estonia and Latvia followed the example of Lithuania in setting up authoritarian dictatorships (see Chapter 3).

With the onset of the great depression both Britain and Germany, the two leading trading partners of the Baltic states, made it clear that they were no longer prepared to continue in its existing form the triangular trading relationship that had evolved in the 1920s. The two industrial powers both sought to overcome the depression by limiting imports and increasing exports, with all too obvious repercussions on Estonia, Latvia and Lithuania. In particular they sought to appease do-mestic farming interests by limiting the imports of agricultural produce which were of vital importance to all three Baltic republics. The econ-omic crisis brought home to them the fact that economic interdepend-ence with western Europe carried risks as well as benefits.

The risks were not only economic but also political. They were vastly increased when Germany turned towards National Socialism. This had two immediate effects. First, it made it even less likely that the Anglo-German-Baltic trade triangle would be restored. Second, Hitler's coming to power disrupted German–Soviet relations and, by intensifying Soviet fears, increased the risk of the Baltic states being squeezed between the two giants. For most of the period after 1933 the danger appeared to lie in a German–Soviet war. In August 1939 it became apparent that the real threat lay in German–Soviet collabora-tion – not of the kind negotiated at Rapallo but the new variety hammered out by Molotov and Ribbentrop in Moscow.

For the Baltic states the crucial year proved to be not 1933 but 1934. In that year a quite remarkable conjunction of events came about which determined Baltic developments for at least the next four years. Briefly, these were, on the economic front, the conclusion of the Anglo-Baltic trade treaties and the inception of Hjalmar Schacht's 'New Plan' in Germany. Politically, 1934 witnessed a diplomatic rev-olution in eastern Europe encompassing the German–Polish non-ag-gression treaty, the conclusion of a Baltic Entente, an abortive proposal for a Soviet–German guarantee of Baltic integrity and the plan of the French foreign minister, Barthou, for an Eastern Locarno.

Nothing signalled more clearly the breakup of the tacit Anglo-German partnership in Baltic trade than the commercial agreements concluded between the United Kingdom and the Baltic states in 1934. The back-ground to these treaties was the revolution in British economic policy marked by the abandonment of the gold standard in 1931 together with the adoption of tariff protection and the establishment of imperial preference at the Ottawa conference in 1932. In 1933 Britain embarked on a programme of bilateral trade agreements with foreign countries designed to increase British exports. First came the arrangements with Scandinavia and Argentina; the three Baltic states were next in line.[2] What all these countries had in common was that they sold much more to Britain than they bought in return; it was therefore easy to put pressure on them. As a leading British financier put it: 'Today hard facts and economic pressure have brought home to the government and people of Lithuania that if they sell to us, they must buy from us.'[3] In addition the British were able to profit from the catastrophic fall in German trade with the Baltic countries resulting from the German shift towards agrarian protectionism after 1929.

Instead of tolerating the expenditure of sterling on German goods, the British now expected the Baltic republics to use the profits of their trade with Britain to finance purchases of UK products. The key innovation in these treaties was that the most-favoured-nation clause, the traditional bar to discrimination in international trade, was circumvented by quota agreements which obliged the Baltic countries to buy minimum quantities of certain specified goods. The concessions in the so-called (and ostensibly private) purchase agreements covered a long and varied list. It included: iron and steel products, jute wrappers, salt, saltpetre, motor vehicles, chemicals and pharmaceutical products, agricultural, dairy and road-making machinery, wool, supplies for woodworking industries and cotton thread. Quite apart from these there were of course tariff reductions on an enormous range of goods, including: herrings, whisky and gin, photographic plates, mustard, metal polishes, boot blacking, bicycles and fountain pens. If nothing else the Baltic leaders were reminded that Britain was still a nation of shopkeepers.[4] Coal was, however, the principal British preoccupation. The British coal industry had been forced to witness the capture of its traditional Baltic markets by Poland after the general strike of 1926. It now used government pressure to win them back. Each Baltic government was obliged to give an undertaking that a certain percentage of its country's annual coal import would come from Britain: for Estonia

2 For details see M-L Hinkkanen-Lievonen, *Britain as Germany's commercial rival in the Baltic States 1919–1939*. In M-L Recker (ed), *Von der Konkurrenz zur Rivalität: Das britisch-deutsche Verhältnis in den Ländern der europäischen Peripherie 1919–1939*, Stuttgart 1986, pp 15–49; P Salmon, Anglo-German commercial rivalry in the Depression era: the political and economic impact on Scandinavia 1931–1939. Ibid, pp 101–41.

3 Report by Sir James Cooper on Lithuania, 27 October 1933, Bank of England Archive, OV 119/1 Lithuania.

4 Details of all three Anglo-Baltic treaties are to be found in PRO, CAB 24/249.

the figure was 85 per cent, for Latvia 70 per cent and for Lithuania 80 per cent.

The combined effect of German economic weakness, the devaluation of the pound sterling and the trade agreements of 1934 brought about a significant increase in British exports to all three Baltic republics in the course of the 1930s. The British share of Estonian imports rose from 10 per cent in 1929 to 19 per cent in 1935. In Latvia the share rose from 8.4 per cent to 20.4 per cent over the same period. The turn-around in Lithuania's case was the most dramatic of all. A Bank of England official observed in 1936 that Lithuania had made a 'tremendous effort' to increase its purchases from Great Britain. These had risen from £830,000 in 1930 to £1,650,000 in 1935, representing an increase from 8.5 per cent to 37.3 per cent of Lithuania's total imports.[5] Lithuania was the only one of the three Baltic states where Britain managed to replace Germany as the leading supplier. Britain's gains were at the expense not only of competitors such as Germany and Poland, but also of the industries of the Baltic countries themselves. The protectionist barriers behind which those industries had been built up in the 1920s were penetrated so that in Estonia, for example, the old-established textile industry was obliged to accept a five-fold increase in the import quota for British cotton piece goods.[6]

However, although the value of British exports to the Baltic states increased up to 1938, Britain's share of Baltic markets was under renewed threat from Germany by the end of the decade. By 1938 the German share of the Estonian market, which had fallen to 21 per cent in 1934, had risen to 31 per cent – slightly above the figure for 1929. In the case of Latvia, too, the German share rose from 24.5 per cent in 1934 to 39 per cent in 1938 – just two percentage points lower than the 1929 figure. Only in Lithuania did Germany fail to recover its commanding pre-depression position. Here its 49 per cent share of the market in 1929 had fallen to 24.5 per cent in 1938. It should be noted, however, that this represented a distinct improvement on the meagre 9.2 per cent scored by Germany in 1936 and points up another weakness of the British position. Britain's success in Lithuania was due much less to the competitiveness of its products, or even the negotiating skill of the British government, than to the collapse of

5 Note by Loynes of 8 May 1936, Bank of England Archive, OV 119/2 Lithuania.
6 Hinkkanen-Lievonen, *Britain as Germany's commercial rival*, p 37.

German–Lithuanian trade which resulted from a heated dispute over Klaipeda (Memel) in the mid-1930s.[7]

Behind the apparent British obsession with the minutiae of tariff negotiations lay a profound shift in Britain's world view. Just as it was attempting at Ottawa to turn the Empire into a closed economic bloc, so in northern Europe and the Baltic Britain was seeking to establish a sphere of economic and financial influence whose implications were ultimately political. The Treasury placed its hopes in the sterling area created when a number of currencies, including those of the Scandinavian and Baltic countries, followed sterling off gold in 1931. Britain's leadership of a sterling bloc offered 'the best opportunities for mutual trade' among its members and a restored prestige for sterling itself.[8] In the Foreign Office officials like Laurence Collier, the head of the Northern Department; and Frank Ashton Gwatkin, head of the newly created Economic Relations Section, saw 'an opportunity not likely to recur' for 'establishing our influence over those countries which are now being injured and antagonized by the policy of our principal competitor' and which, 'as uncertainty increases in Germany and central Europe', were 'looking towards London rather than towards Berlin or Moscow.'[9] By 1935 Ashton Gwatkin felt justified in claiming that the Scandinavian and Baltic agreements had 'developed into something like an imprecise and pacific alliance over the whole political, financial, commercial and cultural field. The United Kingdom has called the Baltic into existence to rectify the lack of equilibrium elsewhere.'

This declaration of Britain's interest in the Baltic is all the more remarkable in view of its enormous range of foreign policy and defence preoccupations in Europe and the world at large. Britain, alas, was not alone in attempting to consolidate its position in the Baltic. Germany too had its vision of a *Grossraumwirtschaft* encompassing north-eastern Europe. The desire for this started to crystallise in the final stages of the Weimar Republic, when Germany's foreign trade declined catastrophically and a rising crescendo of voices clamoured for agricultural protection. Successive governments from Brüning to Schleicher gave way steadily to the pressure to dismantle the Weimar system of most-

---

7 Ibid, p 38; D E Kaiser, *Economic Diplomacy and the Origins of the Second World War: Germany, Britain, France, and Eastern Europe, 1930–1939*, Princeton, NJ 1980, p 137.

8 Cited in I M Drummond, *The Floating Pound and the Sterling Area 1931–1939*, Cambridge 1981, pp 15–16.

9 Sir John Simon to Runciman, 7 March 1933 (drafted by Ashton Gwatkin), PRO, FO 371/17212, N1141/1/63.

favoured-nation trade treaties. A further important ingredient in the emergent *Grossraumwirtschaft* was the introduction of clearing agreements. Clearings, originally intended as a short-term response to the banking crisis of 1931 by substituting barter for the use of scarce foreign exchange, were to become the chief instrument of National Socialist foreign trade policy. Thereafter the ad hoc measures of Weimar policy converged with National Socialist ideology and economic theory. Schacht brought them together in his 'New Plan' of 1934.

The immediate objective of the plan was to conserve Germany's foreign currency reserves. Extending the system of clearing agreements offered Germany a means of intensifying its economic relations with the predominantly agrarian states of northern, eastern and south-eastern Europe – from Scandinavia, through the Baltic states to the Balkans. Instead of money having to change hands, these countries exchanged their raw materials and foodstuffs for imports of German manufactured goods, including armaments. Payment took place only through blocked accounts at the Reichsbank and the respective national banks. Such arrangements were not necessarily harmful to the smaller powers of Europe. Indeed many profited, for a time at least, from the high prices Germany was prepared to 'pay' for their goods.[10] Yet although profits were high, they could be used only to purchase German products: which meant, to an increasing extent, only the goods Germany was prepared to sell. At a stroke the Germans achieved the automatic linkage between exports and imports which the British had tried to realise in the bilateral agreements of 1934. However, the Germans never dominated the trade of Scandinavia and the Baltic as effectively as they did that of the Balkans. Britain's grip on Baltic trade, consolidated by the 1934 agreements, was never entirely loosened.

Both British and German policy therefore threatened to absorb the Baltic countries into a closed economic bloc. Only one, however, threatened their existence. Germany aimed in the short term for war-readiness and in the long term for the economic and political reorganisation of continental Europe under German dominance.[11] The Baltic countries were to be an integral part of the German new order, serving the economic requirements of Hitler's war machine. Apart from

---

10 A S Milward, The Reichsmark bloc and the international economy. In G Hirschfeld and L Kettenacker (eds), *Der 'Führerstaat': Mythos und Realität*, Stuttgart 1981, pp 377–413.

11 On this subject see J Freymond, *Le IIIe Reich et la réorganisation économique de l'Europe 1940–1942*, Leiden 1974; A Barkai, *Das Wirtschaftssystem des Nationalsozialismus: Der historische und ideologische Hintergrund 1933–1936*, Cologne 1977.

concluding trade and clearing agreements, Germany took steps to assure itself of supplies of essential raw materials from the Baltic states. After 1935 the German navy purchased large quantities of Estonian shale oil on long-term contracts, while the German chemical combine IG Farben concluded an agreement with the Estonian phosphates industry.[12] However, the attraction of the Baltic countries to the National Socialist leadership went far beyond economic considerations. In his 'Second Book' of 1928 Hitler had written: 'What the Mediterranean Sea is to Italy, the eastern coast of the Baltic sea is to Germany.'[13] In January 1934 Hitler's ill-fated henchman, Ernst Röhm, enthused about the song of Walther von der Vogelweide, the medieval bard, which told of a Reich uniting the German people 'from the Baltic lands to the Alps'.[14] Less poetically, what the National Socialists were contemplating was in the exploitative tradition of Ludendorff and the *Land Oberost*. It was no coincidence that so many high-ranking Nazis were Freikorps veterans hardened in the Baltic campaigns of 1914–19, or that one of their leading ideologists, Alfred Rosenberg, was a Baltic German born in Tallinn and educated in Riga.

In turning their back firmly on the Weimar Republic's rapprochement with the Baltic countries, the National Socialists also gave new encouragement to the unrepentant elements in the Baltic German communities of Latvia and Estonia. While the majority of the Baltic Germans who remained in the new states were participating in the rebuilding of their homelands, National Socialism did penetrate their ranks. It appealed especially to the young but a number of leading figures in the German communities also felt that in 1933 the moment had come to call once more for attaching the border states to Germany. A memorandum of April 1933 assured the new German chancellor of their support in 'the struggle for the final victory of German freedom and the greatness of the Reich.' Other Baltic Germans argued that the precondition for an effective German thrust in the east was a position of primacy in the Baltic.[15]

The diplomatic revolution of 1934 can be understood only if these grandiose power policy visions are kept in mind. European diplomacy

---

12 S Mylliniemi, *Die baltische Krise 1938–1941*, Stuttgart 1979, p 20.

13 G L Weinberg (ed), *Hitlers Zweites Buch: Ein Dokument aus dem Jahre 1928*, Stuttgart 1961, p 206.

14 Cited in H-E Volkmann, Oekonomie und Machtpolitik. Lettland und Estland im politisch-ökonomischen Kalkül des Dritten Reiches, 1933–40, *Geschichte und Gesellschaft* 2 (1976): 473.

15 Ibid, p 473.

entered a new phase when Hitler turned his back on the Weimar tradition of coexistence with the Soviet Union. The termination of the working relationship between Germany and the Soviet Union after January 1933 removed a vital element of stability in the Baltic region. Baltic fears of a deal being done behind their backs were rekindled. Indeed the Soviet Union's principal response to the new situation was to propose in December 1933 a joint Soviet–Polish guarantee of the integrity of the Baltic states, a step which would have had the advantage of forestalling a Polish–German rapprochement. The full import of Hitler's ideological reversal of German policy became apparent in January 1934, when he concluded a non-aggression pact with Poland.

Even then the Soviets did not abandon their attempt at dialogue with Germany. Over the Baltic states they thought that there must still be common ground. In March 1934 the Soviet commissar for foreign affairs, Litvinov, proposed to the German ambassador in Moscow, Rudolf Nadolny, a German–Soviet guarantee for the Baltic states, which were 'previously a part of the former Russian empire.'[16] Nadolny, a longstanding advocate of Russo-German friendship, resigned after Hitler vetoed the proposed deal. Any such obligation would have unacceptably limited Germany's freedom of manoeuvre in eastern Europe. Thwarted by Hitler, the Soviets turned to the plan for an Eastern Locarno proposed by the French foreign minister, Barthou, in June 1934. This plan aroused the distrust of the three Baltic states since, in providing for 'mutual assistance', it would have allowed Soviet troops to enter their territory.

Their response was a timely reminder that the Baltic countries were not entirely passive in the face of great power concern for their welfare. For the first time since independence all three Baltic states concluded a collective foreign policy agreement. The process began when the Latvian–Estonian defence pact of 1923 was renewed and extended on 17 February 1934, deliberately leaving the door open for other states to join them if they wished. They had Lithuania in mind. Kaunas had clearly grasped that the end of German–Soviet friendship and the conclusion of the German–Polish agreement left them with no defence against Polish ambitions. In April 1934 Lithuania proposed a triple alliance with its fellow Baltic states which was finally signed on 12 September 1934. The Baltic Entente had at last materialised. Admittedly it had no formal military clauses and provided only for regular conferences of the foreign ministers of the three states – resuming the practice of the first half of the 1920s.

16 Nadolny to AA, 28 March 1934, *Documents on German Foreign Policy* (DGFP) Series C, Vol 2, p 684.

It is facile, however, to conclude that 'The Baltic Entente of 1934 had no significance as a security measure.'[17] Only by the narrowest definition of security can this claim be sustained. The Baltic Entente could not actually stop any of the great powers militarily. In 1934, however, National Socialist Germany was still inadequately prepared to confront even Poland, let alone repel the attack from France which Hitler feared. In the same year Kirov's murder set the Soviet Union on the path which was to lead, through the purges, to the decimation of the Red Army's High Command. Seen in this wider context, the Baltic states, with their manpower reserves and armaments, and their economic and political links with Scandinavia and Great Britain, could not be dismissed lightly: they presented enough imponderables to give both Hitler and Stalin serious food for thought. This is why both governments devoted so much attention to Baltic diplomacy and why their military advisers pondered at such length on the strategic challenges in the region.

The Soviet Union devoted considerable efforts in 1935 to trying to persuade the members of the Baltic Entente to participate in the proposed Eastern Locarno.[18] As the German menace grew with the signature of the Anglo-German Naval Agreement in 1935 and the reoccupation of the Rhineland in 1936, the Soviets sought to win the Baltic countries over to their view of the strategic situation. All three chiefs of staff were invited by Marshal Voroshilov to attend the 1936 May Day celebrations in Moscow. During their visit an Estonian officer was taken aside by the Soviet intelligence chief, Uritski, who warned him of Germany's aggressive intentions and indicated that Estonia's only hope lay in a military alliance with the Soviet Union.[19] More ominously, the Leningrad Party boss Zhdanov warned the border states in a speech to the eighth Soviet congress in Moscow in November 1936, against acting as agents of the fascist powers: they should beware lest the Soviet Union opened its 'window on Europe' and sent out the Red Army to see what was happening on the other side of the frontier.[20] The members of the Baltic Entente continued, however, to emphasise their neutrality and their desire to remain clear of any great-power bloc. The Soviet Union for its part remained conciliatory in its diplomatic relations with the Baltic states in 1937–8.

17 H I Rodgers, *Search for Security: a Study in Baltic Diplomacy 1920–1934,* Hamden, Conn 1975, p 102.

18 Mylliniemi, *Baltische Krise*, pp 18–19.

19 Ibid, pp 19–20.

20 G von Rauch, *The Baltic States. Estonia, Latvia, Lithuania: The Years of Independence 1917–40,* London 1974, pp 191–2.

However, there were numerous indications of the build-up of Soviet defences on the borders of Finland, Estonia and Latvia, as well as a number of frontier incidents and infringements of airspace by Soviet military aircraft.

If 1934 marked the first radical change in the international position of the Baltic states, 1938 was a year which shaped their destinies still more decisively. Hitler's diplomatic triumphs – over Austria in March and Czechoslovakia in September – had profound implications for the balance of power not only in central Europe but also in the Baltic. Lithuania was the first to be made aware of the fragility of its position when, on 17 March 1938, the Polish government delivered an ultimatum demanding the resumption of diplomatic relations which Lithuania had broken off over the Vilnius question eighteen years earlier. As a directive from Hitler to the Wehrmacht of 18 March made clear, the Poles would have been backed by a German invasion of southern Lithuania if the Kaunas government had refused to comply. Without support from either their Baltic neighbours or any of the great powers, the Lithuanians gave in to the ultimatum and effectively recognised Polish sovereignty over Vilnius. It was a damaging blow to the internal authority of the Smetona regime and a portent of worse things to come.

In April 1938 Hitler gave the German ambassador in Rome, von Mackensen, a hint of his future intentions: the Sudeten Germans would come first, he said, followed by the 'Baltikum': 'We are not seeking to rule over non-Germans, but if we have to (!) then let it be over the border states.'[21]

From Munich onwards the Baltic region became central to European diplomacy. Hitler's ambitions were now focused on the few remaining pieces of unfinished business from the postwar settlement: Danzig and the Polish 'corridor', and the Lithuanian occupation of Klaipeda (Memel). Until the spring of 1939 he was uncertain whether he could solve the Danzig question through agreement with Poland or whether he would have to use force. Klaipeda posed fewer problems. After Munich it was marked out for a Sudeten-type solution, with the leader of the local National Socialists, Dr Neumann, playing the role of Henlein. Klaipeda was not merely to be returned to the Reich, but Germany was to establish 'a dominating influence in Lithuania, which will ensure the closest possible political, military and economic associ-

---

21 Cited in G von Rauch, *Geschichte der baltischen Staaten*, 2nd edn, Munich 1977, p 193.

ation with Germany'.[22] The Lithuanian government did nothing to halt the nazification of Klaipeda and indicated that it would not use force to resist the return of the district to Germany. After the German occupation of Prague in March 1939, Ribbentrop summoned the Lithuanian foreign minister, Urbsys, and demanded on 20 March that Klaipeda be handed over to the Reich. Two days later Kaunas bowed to the inevitable, losing at a stroke 30 per cent of the country's industrial capacity and its only major port.[23] The Lithuanians had, however, feared even worse: after Prague they thought that Germany might have occupied the whole country. In answer to widespread charges of defeatism a member of the Foreign Ministry retorted: 'Do you think suicide would have been better?'[24]

The dismemberment of Czechoslovakia had far wider consequences. It began the chain of events which led, on 29 March 1939, to the British and French guarantee of Polish integrity.[25] Hitler's response was an order of 2 April to prepare for the invasion of Poland ('Case White'). His decision ensured that the question of peace or war in Europe would now be decided in the Baltic. Though hurried, the Anglo-French decision to halt their policy of appeasement over the Danzig issue was not wholly arbitrary. True, Poland's record of collaboration with Germany over Lithuania and Czechoslovakia was hardly admirable. Nor was Poland, despite its pretensions to great-power status, any more capable than Czechoslovakia of mounting a credible defence against German aggression. Yet resistance to German expansion in the Baltic was a logical consequence of the policies pursued by Britain in the region since 1933.

On the eve of the Second World War the Baltic was for Great Britain anything but a far away country of which it knew nothing. British interests in northern Europe were too important to be sacrificed to the appeasement of Germany. The United Kingdom mounted a vigorous counter-offensive to the growth of German economic and political influence in the Baltic and Scandinavia. It stood stubbornly in the way of the German drive to achieve its *Grossraum* ambitions in the region even though the Reich whittled away the commanding position in

22 Memorandum by Grundherr (Auswärtiges Amt) of 11 November 1938, cited ibid, p 28.

23 Sabaliunas, *Lithuania in Crisis: Nationalism to Communism, 1939–1940*, Bloominton, Ind 1972, pp 116–18 (Table 19).

24 Cited in Mylliniemi, *Baltische Krise*, p 31.

25 A Prazmowska, *Britain, Poland and the Eastern Front, 1939*, Cambridge 1987; D C Watt, *How War Came: The Immediate Origins of the Second World War 1938–1939*, London 1989, pp 162–87.

Baltic trade which Britain had won in the early 1930s. Britain's Baltic presence must be set in the balance when judging what has been seen as Britain's failure to oppose Hitler before March 1939, when it guaranteed Poland. In other words, Britain's reluctance to incur formal military commitments should never be equated with indifference to the break-up of the postwar settlement in north-east Europe, of which Britain had been one of the leading architects. Even if Neville Chamberlain did not share those sentiments, others in Britain had retained something of that earlier vision.

Admittedly the Anglo-German Naval Agreement of June 1935 showed that the Admiralty had effectively abandoned the idea of intervention in the Baltic by the British fleet. By then German naval and air supremacy in the area had been clearly established. Yet this made it all the more important that Britain did resist the growth of Germany's influence by other means. British politicians started to visit the area: Anthony Eden in 1934; Lord Plymouth, a junior Foreign Office minister, in 1937 and Robert Hudson, the minister for overseas trade, in March and April 1939. When the Foreign Office drew up a priority list of twenty countries for British arms exports in 1937, Finland was placed eleventh, immediately followed by Estonia, Latvia and Lithuania. Priority is the key word here. Given the range of Britain's global commitments – likened by Michael Howard to being forced to play an entire score by Mahler on a penny whistle – this rating was respectable.

Above all the Foreign Office sought to counteract the deteriorating position of British trade with the Scandinavian and Baltic countries. It attempted to restrain the Ministry of Agriculture's enthusiasm for tariff and quota controls on imports of foreign agricultural produce, arguing that 'exaggerated protectionism in the United Kingdom should not be allowed seriously to weaken our commercial influence' over these countries, since British trade played a vital part 'in maintaining the influence of the United Kingdom against rival influences, mainly that of Germany, potentially perhaps, that of the U.S.S.R.'[26] Collier in particular also tried to persuade the Treasury and the Board of Trade of the need to counter the ratchet effects of the clearing agreements on German–Baltic trade, which bore 'some resemblance to the commercial penetration which Germany has so successfully pursued in South-Eastern Europe.'[27] In the case of Estonia, for example, a visiting

---

26 Ashton Gwatkin memorandum, 'Scandinavian and Baltic Trade Agreements', 4 January 1937, PRO, FO 371/21078, N59/59/63.

27 Cited in Salmon, Anglo-German commercial rivalry, p 126.

delegation from the London Chamber of Commerce reported in 1936 their impression that 'Estonia is sincerely doing its utmost to encourage trade with the United Kingdom, and that only the compulsion brought by clearing agreements, especially with Germany, prevents the trade from growing larger.'[28] However, the economic orthodoxy of the other ministries proved impervious to Collier's arguments up to the eve of war in 1939. 'There are so many vested interests in the City of London living on the past proceeds of free multilateral trade that we are not allowed to adapt our policy to the new situation', Collier complained in 1938.[29]

After Munich, Foreign Office officials made even more determined efforts to ensure that Germany should not achieve the 'informal empire' in north-eastern Europe which it had by then won in the Danubian and Balkan states.[30] In December 1938, following big gains for the National Socialists in the Klaipeda district elections, Neville Chamberlain, at Collier's prompting, initiated an Anglo-French diplomatic attempt to persuade Germany to respect the status quo established by the Klaipeda Convention of 1924.[31] Germany naturally refused to do so, and when it ultimately absorbed Klaipeda Britain contented itself with a modest protest. More generally, Collier demanded 'a public statement by a prominent member of His Majesty's Government – if possible, the Prime Minister himself – denying explicitly any intention of abdicating our commercial or cultural position in that part of the world.'[32] This time Chamberlain made no response. His rhetoric, on the contrary, sent the wrong signals to both Hitler and Stalin. It contributed to their serious misreading of the lessons of Munich for British policy. Any illusions entertained in Berlin or Moscow about British indifference to the fate of the Baltic were dispelled when London and Paris gave their joint guarantee to Poland at the end of March 1939.

If it were to deter Hitler, the Anglo-French guarantee of Poland would have to depend on Soviet support. Equally, in order to localise his war against Poland, Hitler needed to ensure that Stalin would not intervene. After being left on the sidelines at Munich the Soviet

28 PRO, FO 371/20332, N4173/40/63.

29 Cited in Salmon, Anglo-German commercial rivalry, p 117.

30 H-J Schröder, Südosteuropa als 'Informal Empire' Deutschlands 1933–1939. Das Beispiel Jugoslawien, *Jahrbücher für Geschichte Osteuropas* **23** (1975): 70–96; J W Hiden and J F Farquharson, *Explaining Hitler's Germany*, London 1983, pp 138–40.

31 D M Crowe, Jr, Great Britain and the Baltic States, 1938–1939. In V S Vardys and R J Misiunas (eds), *The Baltic States in Peace and War 1917–1945,* University Park and London 1978, pp 110–19.

32 Minute of 14 November 1938, PRO, FO 371/22265, N5489/64/56.

Union now assumed a decisive role. In courting the Soviet Union, both Germany and the West would have to take account of Soviet views on the Baltic states. Ever since Hitler's arrival in power the Soviet leadership had been less hostile towards the idea of a Baltic bloc. The Baltic states, with their valuable naval facilities, were crucial to the defence of Leningrad, Russia's second city. Keeping the Baltic states neutral would at the very least narrow the front on which Hitler could launch his armies in any possible attack on Soviet territory. For this reason Moscow had renewed its non-aggression treaties with the Baltic states in 1934 and welcomed the Baltic Entente. A Soviet Marshal, Yegorov, visited the three Baltic capitals in 1937.

Such expressions of interest alarmed rather than reassured Baltic leaders. The Soviets for their part found it difficult to convince themselves that the border states would not be drawn into hostile coalitions against them. The Soviet leadership were obsessed by the danger of what they referred to during their negotiations with Britain and France in 1939 as 'indirect aggression'. They feared not merely a physical assault on the territorial integrity of the Baltic states, which would obviously threaten the Soviet Union; but they were also concerned about a further radical rightward shift in Baltic domestic politics of the kind which they had witnessed in Estonia and Latvia in 1934. Such outbursts as Zhdanov's November 1936 speech were not mere paranoia, but the expression of a deep-seated Soviet determination that the Red Army should not have to meet a foreign invader on Russian soil.[33]

Viewed from the Baltic capitals, the attention being directed by the world towards their corner of Europe could only be a source of deep anxiety. This applied even to what were intended to be benevolent initiatives, such as Roosevelt's famous address of 15 April 1939. The inclusion of the Baltic states in a huge list of countries whose integrity Roosevelt asked Hitler to respect, simply aroused the Führer's derision. More seriously, it gave German foreign minister Ribbentrop the opportunity to pressurise Latvia and Estonia into declarations that they felt no threat from Germany. The effects of this on the Soviet Union may be imagined. Well-intentioned but ill-informed gestures from outsiders did nothing to lower the temperature.[34] Anxiety in the Baltic states would have been greater still had they known of the tentative beginnings of German–Soviet contact in the spring of 1939. As it was,

33 See the remarks made by a Soviet diplomat cited in Mylliniemi, *Baltische Krise*, p 18.

34 Cf D C Watt's scathing judgement on Roosevelt's initiative in *How War Came*, pp 260–4.

their attention was captured by the public diplomacy of Britain, France and the Soviet Union between May and August 1939, as the good and the great laboured to find the basis for a partnership to deter Hitler from further aggression.

The British and French were made aware from the outset that any arrangement acceptable to the Soviet Union must include a guarantee of the 'Baltic states', among which the Soviets significantly included Finland but not Lithuania, which did not border directly on their territory. For the Baltic states the only worthwhile 'guarantee' was one leaving them entirely alone. The guarantees on offer in 1939 could only draw them into conflict.[35] The constant reality of their existence was their position at the interface of East and West. In stable times they could derive benefit from their intermediary role; in times of crisis they were on the front line. Any power which offered them a guarantee would in the process implicate them in its own security system. For the Baltic states the only security systems on offer in 1939 were German or Soviet. All that Britain and France could do was to deliver the Baltic states into the Soviet network in their attempt to construct a barrier against Germany in eastern Europe. By this stage the western powers had to accept that they could no longer play a direct military role in the Baltic. On the other hand, their prolonged discussions with the Soviets in the summer of 1939 showed that they recognised only too clearly the vital strategic significance of the region.

The Baltic peoples were given many indications that Germany, too, was increasingly preoccupied with the strategic importance of the Baltic area. As early as 1936 Hitler had described the Baltic states in terms which he previously reserved for Poland: 'a glacis of the European anti-bolshevist powers against Russia.' The German navy, furthermore, regarded control of the Baltic coastline as essential in case of war with the Soviet Union.[36] At that time, of course, it is unlikely that Hitler was seriously contemplating anything other than a Nazi–Soviet clash. He did not think about a deal with Stalin until he had started to plan his campaign against Poland in 1939. Even then, he did not know until very late in the day, perhaps not before August, whether he would be able to secure a satisfactory arrangement with the Soviets. In

35 Note the anxious remarks of Nikolai Kaasik, Head of the Political Department of the Estonian Foreign Ministry about the western–Soviet talks, cited by H Arumäe, *At the Crossroads: The Foreign Policy of the Republic of Estonia in 1933–1939*, Tallinn 1983, p 118.

36 R Ahmann, The German treaties with Estonia and Latvia of 7 June 1939 – Bargaining ploy or an alternative for German – Soviet understanding?, *Journal of Baltic Studies* **20** (1989): 344–5.

these circumstances it was vital to ensure that Soviet forces should not be able to make use of the territory of the Baltic states in the coming conflict between Germany and Poland. On 12 May Wipert von Blücher, German minister in Helsinki and a longstanding expert on Baltic affairs, reported information that 'in case of a German–Polish war the Russian army would occupy Estonia and Latvia and would operate from there against Germany.'[37]

One way of preventing the Russians from interfering in Germany's plans was to conclude non-aggression treaties with the border states. On 7 June 1939 Estonia and Latvia finally yielded to German pressure and signed non-aggression pacts. Such treaties enabled Germany to pose as a friendly supporter of Baltic independence, but Baltic neutrality could then be used by Germany as a barrier against the Soviets: 'Due to the non-aggression pacts we have concluded . . . no agreement can be signed by the Baltic states and the Soviet Union which would automatically involve intervention by the Soviet Union.'[38] The pacts had major military advantages for Germany. First, they obviated the need to allocate resources to holding the Baltic states in check during the attack on Poland. Second, by persuading the Baltic states that there was no German threat, the agreements encouraged the Estonians and Latvians to concentrate their defence forces solely against the Soviet Union. Hitler intended to exploit anti-Soviet sentiments in the Baltic states as a cheap line of defence.[39] There was every chance of this strategy working. For a long time it had been clear that the military exerted a decisive influence on Estonian foreign policy, and that of necessity it leaned increasingly towards Germany in the absence of any other credible defence against the Soviet Union. General Laidoner was the dominant figure and his intelligence chief, Colonel Maasing, was known as the General Staff's 'foreign minister'.[40] The British were warned by the Estonians on 19 June that if they were compelled to accept Soviet assistance 'this would force every Estonian to fight on the side of Germany.'[41]

For their strategy to be fully effective, it was important for the German armed forces to become better informed about the state of Baltic military preparedness and if possible to coordinate measures for joint defence between Germany, Latvia and Estonia. In late June 1939, therefore, General Halder, Chief of the German General Staff, visited

---

37 Cited ibid, p 350.
38 Cited in Arumäe, *At the Crossroads*, p 122.
39 Ahmann, German treaties: 353.
40 Mylliniemi, *Baltische Krise*, pp 33–8.
41 Cited ibid, p 123.

Estonia and Finland. Later in the summer Estonia received a visit from Admiral Canaris, the head of the German Abwehr. These developments must be seen as more than a mere political demonstration. It is unlikely that the Soviets saw them solely in that light, particularly in conjunction with the series of alarming events reported in July by the Soviet minister in Tallinn. He detailed the arrival in Estonian waters of the German warship *Admiral Hipper* and night-time transports of Estonian military equipment to the Soviet border.[42] This intermittent activity tends to support the argument that Hitler had continuing doubts about the possibility, or indeed desirability, of reaching an understanding with his ideological foe, the Soviet Union.

In the final stages of what became a race between Germany and the West for Soviet favours, it is ironic that the French, who had been the architects of an eastern European security system after 1919, were inclined twenty years later to hand over those states to the mercies of Moscow. Conversely, Britain, still often regarded as hostile to the idea of a *cordon sanitaire*, ultimately refused to purchase an agreement with the Soviet Union at the expense of the Baltic states.[43] They went a long way towards recognising what the Soviet ambassador in London, Maisky, termed the 'Soviet Monroe doctrine in eastern Europe.'[44] However, they refused to accept a formula for 'indirect aggression' which would have allowed Soviet troops to enter the territory of the Baltic states under almost any pretext. Ultimately, they were not prepared to defeat one dictatorship by appeasing another.

This was consistent with the 'unspoken assumptions' which had guided Britain's relations with the Baltic republics since 1919. Admittedly, the British had never promised direct military suppport to the Baltic states. Yet their contribution to Baltic independence over a period of twenty years had been considerable. The initial reservations which the British had expressed about the viability of the Baltic states dwindled to insignificance after the early 1920s. By the late 1930s, even the Bank of England shared the generally positive assessment of Baltic economic prospects. What bothered the Bank was the intentions of the neighbours of Estonia, Latvia and Lithuania. Any reservations in Threadneedle Street about investing more money in the Baltic countries related largely to the fact that 'the political risks in that corner of Europe are obvious.'[45] Those problems, alas, Britain could not solve alone.

42 Ibid, p 351.
43 Crowe, *Great Britain and the Baltic States*, pp 115–18.
44 DBFP, Series 3, Vol VI, p 152.
45 Bank of England Archive, Memorandum by Gunston of 24 March 1937, 'Lithuania: Foreign borrowings,' OV 119/2 Lithuania.

The issue of 'indirect aggression' remained unresolved throughout the negotiations between Britain, France and the Soviet Union in the summer of 1939. The British could not accept the Soviet case for being able to move into the Baltic countries to meet an *expected* attack from Hitler's Germany. None the less, the British and French went on to hold military conversations in Moscow in August 1939 in an atmosphere of increasing unreality. The Soviets demanded that the western powers should occupy bases in Finland and the Baltic states, prior to handing them over to the Red Army and Navy. What was this if not another variation on the theme of indirect aggression?

Even as the Anglo-French delegation negotiated, Ribbentrop's envoys were preparing for the Reich foreign minister's dramatic flight to Moscow. The final phase of the process culminating in the signature of the German–Soviet non-aggression pact began on 15 August. By now Hitler's military timetable for the attack on Poland dictated a rapid settlement with Moscow. Ribbentrop indicated the extent to which Germany was prepared to go when he suggested on 18 August that Germany was ready to sign a special protocol regulating, 'for instance, the settlement of spheres of interest in the Baltic area, the problem of the Baltic states, etc.'[46] However, when Ribbentrop finally appeared in Moscow in person, he found that the Soviets had set a much higher price for the deal than he had expected. Whereas the Germans had hoped to retain the southern half of Latvia, the Soviets insisted on pushing the line southwards to the Latvian–Lithuanian border. This would bring their strategic frontier 200 miles further west. Such was Hitler's desperation that he conceded even this vital point. It was a decision which Ludendorff and the *Oberost* would have found hard to forgive. Hitler had abandoned Estonia and Livonia: he now relinquished Courland – 'the nation's war aim' – as well.

The arrangements were given final form in a secret supplementary protocol (unpublished in the Soviet Union until fifty years later) attached to the German–Soviet non-aggression treaty of 23 August 1939. The relevant clause was as follows:

> In the event of a territorial and political rearrangement in the areas belonging to the Baltic states (Finland, Estonia, Latvia, Lithuania), the northern boundary of Lithuania shall represent the boundary of the spheres of influence of Germany and the USSR. In this connection the interest of Lithuania in the Vilnius area is recognized by each party.

Lithuania, as so often in its history, followed a different route from its Baltic cousins. Firmly in Germany's orbit after the Reich had reincor-

46 DGFP, Series C, Vol 6, pp 121–3.

porated Klaipeda in March 1939, Lithuania did not need to be formally included as an issue in either the western or the German negotiations with Russia. After Germany's invasion of Poland on 1 September 1939 and a further visit by Ribbentrop to Moscow, a second secret protocol of 28 September 1939 consigned Lithuania, along with half of Poland, to the Soviet sphere.

The Nazi–Soviet pact is unexampled in its cynicism and callous indifference to the fate of small nations. Yet it brought no lasting advantages to its signatories. If not in 1939, then certainly by 1945, when the Reich itself was partitioned, it was only too evident that Germany had gained nothing from it. For the Soviet Union the disadvantages were for a long time concealed. Fifty years later, however, the Baltic peoples exploited the treaty to lever open the constitutional relationship between their republics and the Soviet state.

PART THREE
Eclipse 1940–85

CHAPTER SEVEN
Casualties of War

The Lithuanian dissident poet Tomas Venclova wrote of the years of the Second World War: 'I do not envy the leaders of those days to whom history presented a choice among Hitler, Stalin, and death, each choice not necessarily excluding the other two.'[1] Estonia, Latvia and Lithuania were consigned to the Soviet sphere of influence in 1939 and absorbed by the Soviet Union in 1940. They were under German rule from 1941 to 1944, when the return of the Red Army led to the reimposition of Soviet control. War brought not merely the extinction of Baltic independence but also death and deportation for hundreds of thousands of citizens who failed the tests set by the two dictators: for Hitler that of racial acceptability; for Stalin that of political reliability. The war spelt the end for two minority groups in particular, the Baltic Germans and the Jews: the former by evacuation, the latter by extermination. Both Germany and the Soviet Union took steps to ensure that independent Baltic states should never be restored. German and Soviet actions alike endorsed the view of the Baltic German Nazi ideologue Alfred Rosenberg that 'twenty years of independence have shown the absolute sovereignty of small peoples wedged between two great states to be unthinkable.'[2] Rosenberg's words were echoed by Molotov when he told a Lithuanian leader in June 1940 that 'in the present state of international politics, small nations were a complete anomaly'.[3] The war made possible the subjection of the Baltic repub-

1 Cited in V S Vardys and R J Misiunas (eds), *The Baltic States in Peace and War 1917–1945*, University Park and London 1978, p 198.
2 Cited in A Dallin, *German Rule in Russia 1941–1945*, London and New York 1957, p 184.
3 Cited in I J Vizulis, *Nations under Duress: The Baltic States*, Port Washington, NY 1985, p 49.

lics to a Soviet domination which has not yet been ended. Neither Hitler nor Stalin, however, was able to erase the national identities of the Baltic peoples.

In September 1939 the Soviet Union acted quickly to assert its control over the sphere of influence in north-eastern Europe assigned to it by the secret protocol to the Nazi–Soviet pact and the supplementary secret protocol of 28 September. After making peace with Japan in the Far East and occupying eastern Poland, the Soviets put pressure on the three Baltic states and Finland to conclude 'mutual assistance' treaties. The process began when Estonia was accused of being unable to protect its own territorial waters following the escape of a Polish submarine from Tallinn harbour on 18 September. On 24 September the Estonian foreign minister, expecting to sign a trade agreement in Moscow, was given an ultimatum by Molotov demanding the conclusion of a treaty of mutual assistance to enable the Soviet Union to occupy strategic bases on Estonian soil. In view of the military threat to Leningrad, Molotov declared, 'The *status quo*, which was established twenty years ago when the Soviet Union was weakened by civil war, can no longer be considered adequate to the present situation, nor normal.'[4] The Estonian government felt that it had no choice but to negotiate. Four days later a treaty was signed which allowed the Soviet Union to establish naval, air and military bases on two Estonian islands and at the port of Paldiski. The total of Soviet troops to be quartered there was put at 25,000 (reduced from 35,000 as a gesture of 'generosity' by Stalin). The Soviet–Estonian treaty of 28 September, to last for ten years, was the model for similar agreements with Latvia on 5 October and with Lithuania on 10 October. The latter treaty, however, made some pretence of mutual consultation. More importantly, it provided for the transfer to Lithuania of much of the Vilnius district, recently occupied by the Red Army. Thus Lithuania finally regained control of Vilnius for the sake of which it had, for a few days in early September, contemplated intervening against Poland in the German–Polish war.[5]

The treaties were clearly signed under duress.[6] Yet the Baltic states were perhaps weaker and more divided than they need have been even in the face of such overwhelming pressure. There was no consultation between Estonia and Latvia, the two states which had the

4 Cited ibid, p 27.

5 Sabaliunas, *Lithuania in Crisis: Nationalism to Communism, 1939–1940*, Bloomington, Ind 1972, pp 147–9.

6 Ibid, pp 35–7.

closest defence and foreign policy relationship. The Estonian foreign minister returned from Moscow on 26 September via Riga but did not take the opportunity to consult the Latvian government.[7]

Would Estonian, Latvian or Lithuanian resistance, against such odds, have made any difference to their ultimate fate? A commentator highly sympathetic to the Baltic cause has argued that 'probably the best course would have been for the Baltic nations to fight the Soviet troops independently from the outset.'[8] This was the course taken by Finland as a consequence of the invitation to enter into similar discussions issued by Molotov on 5 October. Negotiations lasted for weeks rather than days as a result of Finnish intransigence, and the Finns resisted fiercely when the Soviets invaded their country on 30 November. The three states which signed mutual assistance treaties to this day (late 1990) form part of the Soviet Union; Finland, which refused to sign and fought Russia in two wars in 1939–40 and 1941–44, does not. Perhaps token resistance on the part of the Baltic states would have been better than none at all. Yet it was impossible to predict how such a courageous gesture would end. What was true of Päts in Estonia was equally true of the other Baltic leaders: 'it was better to face an uncertain future with the Estonian people intact than to resort to armed resistance that would lead to the certain destruction of a significant minority of the nation.'[9]

Even today, the question of the Soviet Union's intentions in pressing for mutual assistance treaties is at very least an open one.[10] Did the treaties represent a settled attempt on the part of Stalin to destroy the independence of the border states and regain the boundaries of the former Russian empire? Or were they merely intended to establish a defensive line, beyond Soviet frontiers, against a future German (or even Anglo-German) invasion? Stalin's fears of a naval assault on Leningrad via the Gulf of Finland, expressed at length to Finnish negotiators in Moscow in October 1939, were almost certainly genuine.[11] They may have been prompted by memories of British and German intervention in the Baltic in 1918–21, as well as by the attitudes and conduct of the general staffs of the Baltic states and Finland. The treaties, though signed under duress, could have formed the basis for a durable security relationship between the Soviet Union and the border

---

7 D Kirby, The Baltic States 1940–50. In M McCauley (ed), *Communist Power in Europe 1944–1949*, London 1977, p 24.

8 Vizulis, *Nations*, p 35.

9 T U Raun, *Estonia and the Estonians,* Stanford, Calif 1987, p 142.

10 Kirby, Baltic States, p 25.

11 M Jakobson, *The Diplomacy of the Winter War*, Cambridge, Mass 1961.

states. Although Russia's action in 1940 made a mockery of the 1939 treaties (and they would in any case have lapsed in 1949), it is conceivable that they might yet form the model for a new defence arrangement between the Soviet Union and independent Baltic republics. Such a treaty was, after all, signed in 1948 by a chastened and much weakened, but still independent Finland. The Soviet Union today is free from any conceivable threat in the Baltic. In addition it has possessed since 1945 the important naval base of Kaliningrad (formerly the German city of Königsberg). As a detached enclave of the Russian republic, the status of Kaliningrad would not necessarily be affected if Lithuania became independent (although it may change as a result of pressure from its own citizens).[12]

The suggestion that the Soviet Union might have been prepared to accept Baltic independence coupled with adequate guarantees for its security seems to be supported by its conduct towards the Baltic states from October 1939 to the spring of 1940. It signed a series of trade agreements and scrupulously refrained from interfering in the internal politics of the three countries. An order to Red Army units stationed in Estonia declared that 'talk about 'Sovietization' of Estonia' conflicted 'radically . . . with the policy of our Party and government.'[13] The return of Vilnius meant that in Lithuania at least, the new relationship with the Soviet Union met with a large measure of approval.[14] More sinister intentions are, however, suggested by evidence from the archives of the former government of Latvia which have recently been opened to Latvian scholars.[15]

It now appears that as early as December 1939 the Soviets were hoping to be able to take control of Latvia by exploiting left-wing and bourgeois elements in a pretence of a popular front government. The model was the puppet government set up at Terijoki under the Finnish communist Otto Kuusinen on 30 November 1939, the day that the Red Army invaded Finland.[16] It was to be organised from Liepaja,

12 E Lucas, Kaliningrad seeks to emerge from Monster's shadow, *Independent*, 17 September 1990.

13 Cited in G Roberts, *The Unholy Alliance: Stalin's Pact with Hitler*, London 1989, p 164. For further examples of Soviet restraint see Kirby, Baltic States, p 26.

14 Ibid, p 25; Sabaliunas, *Lithuania in Crisis*, pp 153–7.

15 A Stranga, Latvian–Soviet Relations from the Molotov–Ribbentrop Pact of August 23, 1939 to the Ultimatum of June 16, 1940 (paper given at a symposium at the Centre for Baltic Studies, University of Stockholm, 12–14 October 1989).

16 For discussions of the possible functions of the Terijoki government see D W Spring, The Soviet decision for war against Finland, 30 November 1939, *Soviet Studies* **38** (1986): 207–26; T Vihavainen, The Soviet decision for war against Finland, November 1939: a comment, ibid **39** (1987): 314–17.

the largest Soviet military base in Latvia. Latvian communists – those few who had survived Stalin's purges – were called to Moscow for consultation in December; numerous NKVD officers were present in the country, their activities including among other things the collection of information on expressions of opinion hostile to the Soviet Union. The Latvians for their part had an agent in the Soviet legation in Riga and the Latvian security police, well informed about left-wing activities, rounded up communist and social democratic leaders in April 1940. Deprived of the chance to utilise genuine popular opposition to the Ulmanis dictatorship, the Soviets turned in May to the idea of direct military intervention but still aimed to use the 'Terijoki' model along with a staged border incident of the kind that had prefaced their attack on Finland. Since there was clearly no military need for such a puppet government the Soviets apparently hoped, undeterred by the embarrassing failure of the Kuusinen regime, to convince the world at large that there was popular support for a Soviet takeover.

These considerations may help to explain the change in Soviet behaviour which became evident after the end of the Soviet–Finnish 'Winter War' in March 1940 and more marked after the launching of the German offensive in the west in May. The timing, however, must have been influenced by the unexpected speed with which Germany overwhelmed France. Whatever motives may have been uppermost in Stalin's mind, Molotov's words in June 1940 for once have the ring of truth. 'It would have been unforgivable', he said, 'if the Soviet government had failed to take advantage of this opportunity, which may never recur.'[17]

A press campaign against the allegedly pro-Allied sympathies of the Baltic governments was followed in late May and early June by accusations of military collaboration between the three states against the Soviet Union and by incidents involving the Soviet garrisons in Lithuania. The Lithuanian Cabinet, the first to feel the weight of Soviet pressure, protested its loyalty but found that it was required to agree to the formation of a new government capable of enforcing the mutual assistance treaty and to permit the entry of an unspecified number of Soviet troops. On 15 June the Cabinet refused to back President Smetona in his desire to resist the Soviet demands by force but tried to put forward their own candidate for the post of prime minister. Their choice was rejected by the Soviets, who sent deputy foreign commissar

17 As reported by the Lithuanian vice-premier Kreve-Mickevicius: A Dallin, *The Baltic States between Nazi Germany and Soviet Russia*. In Vardys and Misiunas (eds), *Baltic States*, pp 108–9.

Dekanozov to take charge of Lithuanian affairs while the Red Army occupied the country.

Latvia and Estonia soon shared the same fate. Ultimatums were delivered to the two governments on 16 June and a serious incident took place (according to plan) on the Soviet–Latvian border. These were followed by the arrival of Soviet troops and further high-ranking emissaries: Andrei Vyshinsky, who had presided over Stalin's show trials, went to Latvia while Andrei Zhdanov, the Leningrad Party boss, took control in Estonia. In each country new governments were formed between 18 and 21 June on popular front lines. Composed mainly of progressive intellectuals, each had a communist in the key post of minister of the interior. They were confirmed in office by rigged elections held on 14–15 July. On 18 July 'demonstrators' in the major cities of the Baltic states called for their incorporation in the Soviet Union: three days later all three parliaments declared their countries Soviet republics and applied for membership. The formal incorporation of Lithuania, Latvia and Estonia followed between 3 and 6 August 1940.

However cynical the Soviets may have been in their promotion of popular fronts in the Baltic republics, the new governments could draw on a measure of genuine support from the left-wing and democratic forces which had been repressed under the regimes of Päts, Ulmanis and Smetona, as well as from the Jewish and Russian minorities.[18] Nor was the sovietisation of Baltic society as thoroughgoing as it was to be after the Soviets returned in 1944. Nevertheless the period saw the first mass deportations of Baltic citizens to the Soviet Union. In the summer of 1940 ministers and officials of the former regimes, including Päts and Ulmanis and their military chiefs Laidoner and Balodis, were carried off to unknown destinations. While Smetona managed to escape, his old opponent Voldemaras fell into Soviet hands shortly after returning to Lithuania from exile. Few of those deported ever returned. In many cases even their dates of death can only be guessed at.[19] A rare survivor was the Lithuanian foreign minister Urbsys, who lived to tell the story of the imposition of Soviet rule (by tape-recorded message) to a meeting of 250,000 people in

18 Kirby, Baltic States, p 30.

19 The death of Päts was eventually given by the Soviet authorities as 1956. Tönisson's date of death remains unknown. In 1977 three messages written by Päts, probably written in 1953 or 1954, reached the West. Their texts are printed in A Küng, *A Dream of Freedom: Four Decades of National Survival versus Russian Imperialism in Estonia, Latvia and Lithuania 1940–1980*, Cardiff 1981, pp 244–7.

Vilnius on 23 August 1988.[20] Far greater numbers, from a much broader social spectrum, were deported on the eve of the German invasion in June 1941. The twenty-three categories of 'enemies of the people' covered almost everyone active in public life, including local government officials, businessmen, trade unionists and clergymen. The total numbers of those deported or killed in 1940–1 have been estimated at 34,250 for Latvia, nearly 60,000 for Estonia and 75,000 for Lithuania.[21]

In such circumstances it is not surprising that many members of the majority populations of the Baltic countries welcomed the German armed forces when they crossed the frontiers of Lithuania on 22 June 1941 and pressed on into Latvia and Estonia.

Since signing the Nazi–Soviet pact the Third Reich had displayed a conspicuous lack of concern for the fate of the three republics. In the autumn of 1939 it initiated the evacuation of the Baltic German populations of Estonia and Latvia, thus bringing to an end 700 years of Baltic German history.[22] Hitler 'carried out the Baltic resettlement not for the sake of the Nazi–Soviet alliance, but in spite of it'.[23] The secret German–Soviet agreement of 28 September 1939 made provision for German nationals and ethnic Germans to migrate from areas of Soviet jurisdiction to those under German jurisdiction. There was, however, no Soviet pressure for such a move. Nor was there any concern for the welfare of the German element on the part of the Reich government. Ultimately the evacuation had more to do with Himmler's interest in correcting Germany's labour shortage by resettling ethnically reliable Germans from abroad.[24] Between October and December 1939, 13,700 Germans were evacuated from Estonia and 52,583 from Latvia. They were settled in Polish territories incorporated into the Reich. The former Jewish and Polish inhabitants had already been deported to the area of Poland known as the *Generalgouvernement*.

Germany's continuing interest in the Baltic states was, however, much greater than appearances suggested. In the first six months of 1940 secret trade agreements were signed with all three countries by

20 V S Vardys, Lithuanian national politics, *Problems of Communism* **38**, 4 (1989): 62.

21 Vizulis, *Nations*, pp 102–4.

22 For details see D A Loeber (ed), *Diktierte Option: Die Umsiedlung der Deutsch-Balten aus Estland und Lettland*, Neumünster 1973.

23 K D Hoover, The Baltic Resettlement of 1939 and National Socialist racial policy, *Journal of Baltic Studies*, **8** (1977): 79–89.

24 Ibid, p 88.

which up to 70 per cent of their total exports, including grain, butter, eggs, flax, timber and petroleum, went to Germany.[25] A Foreign Ministry economic expert warned in June 1940 that 'the consolidation of Russian influence in these areas will seriously endanger these necessary imports.'[26] Although the ministry declared that there was 'no reason for nervousness on our part' as a result of the absorption of the Baltic states, the Soviet action was one among several in the latter part of 1940 which may have led Hitler and the German general staff to question the advisability of remaining economically dependent on so unreliable an ally.[27] Other factors included pressure on Romania over Bessarabia and on Finland over the question of the Petsamo nickel mines in the far north, as well as ominous troop movements on the Soviet Union's western frontiers.[28]

Whatever motives lay behind Operation Barbarossa, the principles for the treatment of occupied Soviet territory were brutally straightforward. In May 1941 Alfred Rosenberg, entrusted by Hitler with the task of planning the 'occupation of the European East', decreed:

> The General Kommissare of Estonia, Latvia and Lithuania will take measures to establish a German Protectorate there, so that it will be possible in the future to annex these territories to the German Reich. The suitable elements among the population must be assimilated and the undesirable elements exterminated. The Baltic Sea must become an inland German lake, under the protection of Greater Germany.[29]

In reality German occupation policy was hopelessly complicated by competition among rival jurisdictions at every level: most obviously between Nazi Party and Wehrmacht, and between Rosenberg, Himmler and their respective subordinates. The Baltic states were lumped together with Belorussia for administrative convenience in the '*Reichskommissariat Ostland*'. They were ruled by the Gauleiter of Schleswig-Holstein, Hinrich Lohse, a man obsessed with bureaucratic detail who 'personally insisted on signing 'No smoking' signs and regulations for garbage collection.'[30] The Baltic area occupied a privileged position in the occupied east as the only region destined to

---

25 Memorandum by Karl Schnurre of 17 June 1940, *Nazi-Soviet Relations 1939–1941*, Washington 1948, p 153.

26 Ibid, p 153.

27 Ibid, pp 153–4.

28 H W Koch, Hitler's 'Programme' and the genesis of Operation 'Barbarossa', *Historical Journal* **26** (1983): pp 811–920.

29 Cited in Y Arad, *Ghetto in Flames: The Struggle and Destruction of the Jews in Vilna in the Holocaust*, Jerusalem 1980, pp 37–8.

30 Dallin, *German Rule in Russia*, p 186.

become a full province of the German Reich. It was, however, to be firmly under German tutelage. Rosenberg insisted that its rulers had to be German with 'a Hanseatic stamp'.[31] The other nationalities were to be treated strictly according to racial criteria.

On this point the views of German racial 'experts' differed. As leader of the Nazi Party's *Aussenpolitisches Amt* (Foreign Policy Office) in the 1930s, Rosenberg had been curiously passive in his attitude towards the Baltic states despite (or perhaps because of) his Baltic German origins.[32] His tactics fluctuated between support for the Baltic Germans and support for the majority Baltic peoples, whose nationalism was not only suitably anti-Russian but also inconveniently anti-German. Rosenberg regarded the Estonians as the 'elite' of Baltic peoples: they had allegedly been 'Germanized not only in intellect but also in blood.' About the Latvians (whom Hitler deemed 'bolsheviks'), Rosenberg was less certain. Some could be assimilated but it would be necessary to transfer 'larger groups of intellectuals, especially Latvians, into the area of Russia proper.' The Lithuanians ranked lowest in scale and were 'strongly subject to Jewish and Russian pressures.' This meant 'exiling the racially inferior groups of the Lithuanian population in considerable numbers.' No such fine distinctions were drawn in a memorandum prepared for Himmler as early as December 1938.[33] Here all three Baltic peoples – admittedly the Estonians and Latvians more than the Lithuanians – were written off as 'dying races'. Their exceptionally low birth-rates had deprived them of the right to exist as independent nations. The 'population vacuum' in the Baltic area would have to be filled by more dynamic races.

In practice, however, the main thrust of National Socialist racial policies was directed not against the majority Baltic peoples but against the Jews. There were of course very large numbers of Jews in the major cities of the Baltic republics, notably in Vilnius, where they constituted over 28 per cent of the population, Kaunas (26 per cent) and Riga (9 per cent). Mobile killing units, the *Einsatzgruppen*, swept into Soviet territory in the wake of the advancing German armies, taking the Jews by surprise and slaughtering them in their hundreds of thousands.[34] *Einsatzgruppe A*, assigned to the Baltic area, was much the most effective of the four units. By October 1941 it had killed

31 Ibid, p 184.

32 S Kuusisto, *Alfred Rosenberg in der nationalsozialistische Aussenpolitik 1933–1939*, Helsinki 1984, pp 72–5.

33 S Mylliniemi, *Die Neuordnung der baltischen Länder 1941–1944*, Helsinki 1973, pp 48–9.

34 R Hilberg, *The Destruction of the European Jews*, Chicago, Ill 1961, pp 190–208.

125,000 Jews. In Riga alone 10,600 died. With the establishment of *Reichskommissariat Ostland*, German policy shifted to one of herding Jews into ghettoes. Later, in 1943, Himmler ordered that the ghettoes be liquidated and their survivors transferred to concentration camps. A camp had already been built at Salaspils, near Riga, for Jews from the Reich and Poland as well as from Latvia. Other Jews, from the Vilnius and Kaunas ghettoes, were transferred on Himmler's orders to Estonia, for hard labour in the oil shale mines. Finally, as the Red Army advanced on the Baltic in 1944, a desperate drive was launched to kill the last surviving Lithuanian Jews. At the beginning of July 1944 about 33,000 out of Lithuania's prewar Jewish population of 250,000 still lived under German rule. By the time Soviet forces entered Lithuanian territory at the end of the month, 2,000 were left. Those who had survived on Soviet territory or elsewhere in German-occupied Europe brought the total of Lithuanian Jewish survivors to about 25,000 – 10 per cent of the prewar population.[35]

German rule exposed the ugliest instincts of some elements in the majority populations of the Baltic states. From the beginning to the end of the war, many collaborated actively in the killing of Jews. The *Einsatzgruppen* were more successful than in other parts of the occupied Soviet Union in provoking pogroms among the local inhabitants, especially in Lithuania. Here one of the leaders of the anti-Soviet partisan movement was persuaded to turn his forces against the Jews: within a few days 5,000 had been killed. At a later stage, again in Lithuania but also in Latvia and to a lesser extent in Estonia (where there were fewer Jews) the German extermination squads were given valuable assistance by local auxiliary police and militia units. Ordinary people also played their part. A Jewish partisan recalled his return to his former home in Lithuania in July 1944:

> The encounter with our former neighbours was painful. Most of the population treated us with hostility, although they took pains to conceal it. The first question we were asked everywhere was: 'How did you survive?' The question did not stem from curiosity. There was a tone of regret in their voices that we were left alive.[36]

The record of Baltic collaboration in the murder of their Jewish fellow citizens is a shameful one. Yet there is little in their previous record to suggest that it would have taken place without German instigation. All

---

35 D Levin, July 1944 – The crucial month for the remnants of Lithuanian Jewry. In M Marrus (ed), *The Nazi Holocaust: Historical Articles on the Destruction of European Jews*, Westport, Conn 1989, Vol 9, pp 447–75.

36 Y Arad, cited ibid, p 469.

three Baltic governments had a good record for their treatment of Jews between the wars. This was true even of Lithuania under the Smetona regime. Although Jews became increasingly marginalised with the growth of a native Lithuanian professional and commercial middle class, their position was certainly preferable to that of their counterparts in neighbouring Poland.[37] It can be argued, further, that in the light of the treatment of the Jews of Vilnius by successive rulers – Polish discrimination from 1920 to 1939; Soviet deportations from 1940 to 1941; German deportations and exterminations after 1941 – the brief interlude of independent Lithuanian rule over the city, from October 1939 to June 1940 at least provided a breathing space. After initial anti-Jewish riots, the Lithuanian government restored order, and Jewish political and cultural activities revived. 'Eight months of Lithuanian rule in Vilna were marked by increased Jewish activity – the final chapter in the history of 'Jerusalem of Lithuania'.'[38] There was no significant tradition of anti-Semitism in the Baltic countries. If there was resentment, it was generally directed against traditional ruling groups: German, Russian or Polish. Undoubtedly the period of Soviet rule between 1940 and 1941 brought about a change in this respect. Jews did serve the Soviet authorities and were more conspicuous than native Lithuanian collaborators (although Jews were also disproportionately represented among those deported to Siberia). Nevertheless, 'spontaneous' pogroms were not what they seemed. Brigadeführer Dr Stahlecker reported to Himmler in October 1941 that even in Lithuania, 'To our surprise, it was not easy at first to set in motion an extensive pogrom against the Jews.'[39] Pogroms 'were not self-perpetuating, nor could new ones be started after things had settled down.'[40]

For the majority populations of the Baltic countries, the best that could be said of German rule between 1941 and 1944 was that it was less harsh than the periods of Soviet rule which preceded and followed it, and less brutal than the treatment meted out by Germany to the other subject nationalities of eastern Europe. Puppet governments – the so-called Directorates – carried out certain administrative functions on behalf of the German authorities; prices for agricultural produce were higher than for the rest of eastern Europe, though lower than

---

37 I Deak, Heroism in Hell (review of Avraham Tory, *Surviving the Holocaust: The Kovno Ghetto Diary*, Cambridge, Mass 1990), *New York Review of Books*, 8 November 1990, p 55.

38 Arad, *Ghetto in Flames*, p 13.

39 Cited in Hilberg, *Destruction of the European Jews*, p 203.

40 Ibid, p 204.

those of the Reich; schools and even universities were permitted to function. But in February 1943 Hitler vetoed even the half-hearted gestures towards political autonomy proposed by Rosenberg. Nor were the Germans prepared to reverse the nationalisation measures introduced by the Soviets in 1940–1. Members of the majority Baltic populations were denied the rights to lands and businesses which they had formerly owned. Echoing the policy of the *Land Oberost* in the First World War, the authorities encouraged colonists from the Reich to settle on Lithuanian farms. There were also attempts to attract settlers from racially acceptable countries, notably Holland, Denmark and Norway, as well as projects for joint business ventures between German and Danish firms.[41] The effects of such measures on the local population were described with unusual perception by Litzmann, the General Kommissar for Estonia, in August 1942:

> Their almost total disbarment from wholesale trade, the impending dissolution of banks, the still unfulfilled desire for reprivatization on the part of the indigenous population, the tremendous number of [German] monopoly and trusteeship companies . . . which multiply daily like mushrooms, each depriving the indigenous population of further fields of endeavour, have a highly depressing effect on their morale, which must sooner or later lead to passive resistance, which in turn would seriously impair the war economy . . . The dualism of our policy – economic measures as if we were operating in a Gau reintegrated into the Reich, while leaving the population in the dark about their future – is bound to lead to tensions and have the opposite effect of what we aim at.[42]

There were indeed determined efforts to restore Baltic independence during the period of German rule. In Lithuania a large-scale revolt overthrew Soviet rule two days before the arrival of German troops in Kaunas.[43] The Germans permitted a provisional government to function until 5 August 1941, but had no serious intention of restoring Lithuanian sovereignty. In Latvia attempts were made to secure independence both through collaboration and in opposition to the German authorities. In 1941 insurrectionists seized the opportunity offered by the German invasion to attack Soviet forces, while the Latvian Directorate attempted in 1942–3 to secure a measure of genuine self-government from the occupation authorities. From 1943 onwards, when

41 Memorandum of meeting between members of Foreign Ministry and Ostministerium, 23 March 1942, DZA, AA 68319, pp 19–20.

42 Cited in Dallin, *German Rule in Russia*, pp 192–3.

43 Z Ivinskis, Lithuania during the war: Resistance against the Soviet and the Nazi occupants. In V S Vardys (ed), *Lithuania under the Soviets: Portrait of a Nation, 1940– 65*, New York 1965, pp 61–84.

increasing numbers of young Latvians were being drafted into 'volunteer' SS divisions, a Latvian Central Council was set up as an underground organisation. After its discovery and destruction by the Gestapo the Latvians again tried to work with the Germans, this time through the Latvian National Committee established in February 1945 under the leadership of General Dankers. Finally, when this too was revealed as nothing more than a Nazi propaganda exercise, an attempt was made in early May – far too late in the day – to set up a provisional government in Liepaja. Events in Estonia followed a similar path. The last legal prime minister of the republic, Professor Uluots, was rebuffed by the Germans when he proposed the restoration of Estonian independence in July 1941, but was briefly courted by Ribbentrop in October 1943 when the Germans were looking for assistance in utilising Estonian manpower. The German offer was refused and in March 1944 a secret Republic National Council was formed. Like its Latvian counterpart, the Council was soon broken up by the Gestapo but in September 1944, as German forces evacuated the country, Uluots briefly became acting president of an independent Estonian republic.

Crushed between the Third Reich and the Soviet Union, the Baltic peoples looked to the Western Allies for support. If they could make no material contribution to the cause of Baltic independence as the British had done at the end of the First World War, Great Britain and the United States might still be expected to make a moral commitment to the restoration of independent Baltic states once the fighting was over. Due to the circumstances in which they had been absorbed by the Soviet Union in 1940–1 the three republics lacked the means to plead their case in Allied capitals. They had no governments in exile; there was no Baltic Sikorski or de Gaulle. Geography made communications between the Baltic countries and the West more tenuous than those established by the other peoples of German-occupied Europe. More importantly, Baltic independence was not an issue of primary importance to either Britain or the United States. As long as the outcome of the war remained undecided and the Soviet Union was bearing the brunt of the fighting against Germany, the western powers felt obliged to go a long way towards meeting Stalin's demands. These included at very least the recognition of the Soviet Union's 1941 frontiers, as well as a sphere of influence extending substantially beyond those frontiers into eastern and central Europe. Even after the opening of the Second Front in June 1944 and in spite of the beginnings of Allied disharmony over Poland in 1944–5, there was pressure to appease Stalin so as to secure Soviet entry into the war against Japan and participation in the postwar United Nations organisation.

There were of course important differences of emphasis on Baltic questions both within and between the British and American governments. Broadly speaking, however, the Americans took their stand on 'morality', the British on 'expediency'.[44] The American attitude reflected the presence in the United States of many citizens of Baltic origin, as well as the dogmatic views on foreign affairs of secretary of state Cordell Hull and under-secretary Sumner Welles. The British, closer to Germany and with only Russia for an ally until December 1941, could not afford such sentiments. Admittedly the Northern Department of the Foreign Office was as reluctant to sacrifice Baltic interests to a Soviet alliance in 1941 as it had been in 1939. Winston Churchill, too, strongly opposed acquiescing in frontiers which had been acquired by 'acts of aggression in collusion with Hitler.'[45] However, both Sir Stafford Cripps, the British ambassador in Moscow, and, more reluctantly, the foreign secretary Anthony Eden, urged acceptance of the Soviet demands as the price for an Anglo-Soviet treaty. During protracted negotiations between December 1941 and May 1942 the British government were on the verge of acknowledging Stalin's claims, with the exception of the Russo-Polish frontier, when the Soviets suddenly agreed to a treaty which made no mention of frontiers. Their abrupt turnabout seems to have been due to a recognition of the strength of American disapproval, together with Roosevelt's offer of a Second Front in 1942 if the frontier demands were postponed.

The British government was thus 'saved by Soviet greediness' from having to forgo its principles.[46] Its behaviour was understandable: Britain was after all fighting a war for survival. Yet the opinions voiced by some British leaders were dismissive even by the standards of the habitual disdain of British officialdom for the smaller nations of Europe. In June 1941, for example, Lord Halifax, now British ambassador to Washington, confessed to Sumner Welles that 'he was rather cynical with regard to the Baltic States.'[47] He said that 'he did not think the Baltic peoples were peoples who demanded very much respect or consideration', and that Britain might go some way towards recognising Soviet claims 'in order to form close relations with the Soviet Union.'

44 D Kirby, Morality or expediency? The Baltic Question in British-Soviet relations, 1941–42. In Vardys and Misiunas (eds), *Baltic States*, pp 159–72.
45 Ibid, p 163.
46 Ibid, p 172.
47 Cited in J P Lash, *Roosevelt and Churchill 1939–1941*, London 1977, p 366.

Halifax did not accept Welles's assertion that Russia's conquest of the Baltic states was as brutal as Hitler's conquest of Holland and Belgium since 'the Baltic states for over a century had been under the domination of Russia'. When Welles objected that 'the same might be said of the Finns', the ambassador answered that 'he did not have the same respect and regard for the Baltic peoples as he had for the Finnish people'. Even Churchill's view of the Baltic question had changed by 1944. As he admitted to Eden, 'The tremendous victories of the Russian armies, the deep-seated changes which have taken place in the character of the Russian state and government, the new confidence which has grown in our hearts towards Stalin – these have all had their effect.'[48]

To some extent, no doubt, Churchill was whistling in the dark to keep up his spirits. The discovery of the Katyn massacre in 1943 and Moscow's callous conduct towards the Warsaw uprising of 1944 were already casting their shadow over relations between the wartime Allies as the war with Hitler drew to its close.[49] Yet the display of Allied solidarity was maintained through the Yalta conference of February 1945 and did not weaken visibly until the three victors met on German soil at Potsdam in July. Churchill was able to reach agreement with Stalin in October 1944 on a division of eastern Europe into spheres of influence – the famous 'percentages' deal. In early 1945 Britain and the United States showed themselves ready to write off countries like Bulgaria, Romania and Poland to a Soviet sphere of influence. They were later to acquiesce in the extension of that sphere to include Hungary, Czechoslovakia, Yugoslavia (until 1948) and the Soviet occupation zone of Germany. It is therefore not surprising that the claims of Estonia, Latvia and Lithuania were almost wholly disregarded.

Soviet control over these countries had already been established and had been given popular approval – so Stalin claimed – through plebiscites in July 1940. Although President Roosevelt chose to believe this claim, few other members of his administration can have done so.[50] Most recognised that, as a member of the State Department noted in January 1945, however much they disliked the incorporation of the Baltic republics, 'it has been done and nothing which is in the power

48 Cited in Kirby, *Morality*, p 172.
49 For the impact of these events on Churchill see M Charlton, *The Eagle and the Small Birds: Crisis in the Soviet Empire: from Yalta to Solidarity*, London 1974, pp 20–33.
50 Vizulis, *Nations*, pp 70–2.

of the United States government to do can undo it.'[51] However, the Americans did not go as far as the British in acknowledging the reality of Soviet rule. While Great Britain continued to withhold formal recognition of Soviet sovereignty over the Baltic republics but accepted it de facto, the United States refused to recognise their incorporation into the Soviet Union either de jure or de facto. Yet in practice both of the Western Allies subordinated Baltic interests to the overriding priority of remaining on good terms with Stalin. The inclination to view the Baltic question as part of the 'Russian question' thus reasserted itself as it had done after 1917 and was to do so again in the glasnost era with the western reluctance to encourage separatist tendencies which might unseat Gorbachev and end his reform programme.[52]

To an even greater extent than the other nations of eastern Europe the Baltic peoples had been deprived of the means to articulate their demands. The circumstances in which the Second World War ended were much less favourable to the interests of the smaller nationalities than had been the case in 1918. The dominance of the two emergent superpowers was much greater than that of Britain, France, Italy and the United States at the end of the First World War. Even a country as large as France, under a leader as determined as de Gaulle, could not arrest the growing bipolarity of the postwar international order. In 1918 the collapse of the German, Russian and Austro-Hungarian empires and the conversion of Germany into a democratic republic had left a vacuum which could be filled by the emergent nation states of central and eastern Europe. Germany's defeat in 1945 left a vacuum which was filled by the victorious Red Army. Nor, with the onset of the Cold War, was there any equivalent of the Paris peace conference at which Baltic leaders could lobby and thus internationalise their cause. In any case such leaders no longer existed. Baltic elites had been decimated and the isolation into which their countries had been plunged after 1939 had been intensified with the reimposition of Soviet rule in 1944.

If the whole of eastern and much of central Europe was to become part of the Soviet empire, what chance of escape had the Baltic republics? One state, tantalisingly close, did escape. Finland was not absorbed into either the Soviet Union or the postwar Soviet security system in eastern Europe. Despite drastic territorial losses and a heavy reparations burden, Finland survived as a neutral, western-oriented

51 Cited ibid, p 72.
52 Cf N Hawkes, Let the Baltic States drift offshore, *Observer*, 7 January 1990.

capitalist democracy. Perhaps, as was suggested earlier in this chapter, the Finns gained Stalin's grudging respect through their tough fighting in 1939–40 and 1941–4. Certainly, too, they possessed geographical and historical advantages which were not shared by the Baltic republics. Finland had enjoyed considerably greater autonomy within the Russian empire than had the Baltic provinces; after independence it had constructed a 'Scandinavian' cultural and political identity which the Baltic states had not been able to emulate; geographically, Finland posed less of a risk to the security of Leningrad than did the territories of the three Baltic republics.

To this extent the Finns were luckier than their Baltic neighbours. Yet the Finnish position at the end of the war was still highly precarious. Expanding Finland's freedom of manoeuvre *vis-à-vis* the Soviet Union required considerable political skill. In their first postwar presidents, Mannerheim and Paasikivi, they had leaders who could bring Finnish society intact through the traumas of war and reconstruction and forge a new relationship with the Soviet Union on the basis of the 1948 treaty of friendship and reconstruction. Yet that treaty implied a measure of subservience to Soviet foreign policy interests, as critics of 'Finlandisation' were not slow to argue. Nor were the Soviets averse to utilising native communists to destabilise Finnish politics in the late 1940s.[53] Finland therefore managed to distance itself from the Soviet Union after 1948 and establish its credibility as a neutral only with great difficulty, in a process lasting at least until the early 1960s. The Finnish case was simply unique. As President Kekkonen of Finland was fond of arguing, Finlandisation was not for export. Until the breakdown of the Soviet empire Finlandisation was not a plausible model for Russia's former satellites, still less for constituent republics of the Soviet Union.

The Baltic republics were the only members of the League of Nations not to be restored to full sovereignty after the Second World War. Written off by the West, they were subjected for nearly fifty years to a Soviet state determined that they should never regain their independence.

---

53 K Devlin, Finland in 1948: the lessons of a crisis. In T T Hammond (ed), *The Anatomy of Communist Takeovers*, New Haven, Conn and London 1975, pp 433–47.

CHAPTER EIGHT
Soviet Winter

In the years between 1945 and 1985 the Soviet Union came closer than any past rulers to extinguishing the national identities of the Estonian, Latvian and Lithuanian peoples. It did so not so much through direct attacks on Baltic culture, religion and freedom of expression, though these were at times drastic enough. The effect was achieved rather as an indirect consequence of economic modernisation, Soviet style. Large-scale industrialisation, whatever its economic merits, had three consequences of profound significance for the development of postwar society in the Baltic republics. First and perhaps most seriously, it shifted the ethnic balance of Baltic society through the large-scale immigration of industrial workers from other parts of the Soviet Union, especially the Russian federal republic. Second, industrialisation, as in other advanced societies, brought social pressures which undermined family life: divorce rates in Estonia and Latvia were among the highest in the Soviet Union. Finally industry inflicted severe damage on the environment, whether in the oil shale mining districts of Estonia or on the shores of the Baltic Sea.

The results varied widely among the three republics. On the whole the effect was to accentuate the deep-seated differences between Estonia and Latvia on the one hand and Lithuania on the other. Lithuania industrialised more rapidly than the other two republics but remained less advanced and did not experience so massive an influx of immigrants from outside its borders. In Latvia, by contrast, the point had been reached by the 1980s where ethnic Latvians were on the verge of becoming a minority in their own republic. Nor did Lithuania experience social and environmental damage on the same scale as that of Estonia and Latvia. Such variations go a long way towards explaining why each republic responded to the challenges of glasnost at a different pace and with differing emphases. The societies of Estonia and Latvia were the most 'modern' and in many ways the most sophisticated in their responses, but at the same time nationalist politicians had to take more account of the interests of other ethnic groups. Lithuanian society remained less developed and for this very reason was able by 1990 to mount a more direct challenge to the authority of the Kremlin.

It would be easy to assume that, while the social and environmental consequences were unintended, the demographic shift was part of a deliberate attempt to stifle Baltic national identities. Moscow's motives in promoting the rapid industrialisation of Lithuania were, it has been argued, 'of a purely political nature':

> Moscow aims to unite Lithuania permanently to the Russian sphere in an economic union and to colonise Lithuania demographically – in short, to russify and assimilate it. These efforts are conducted under the pretext of improving the national economy, in order to escape giving the appearance of straightforward colonisation.[1]

Other commentators, equally sympathetic to the Baltic predicament, have, however, refrained from making such a claim.[2] It has been suggested that in the case of Estonia industrialisation 'probably does not reflect a purposeful, centrally directed technique of russification.'[3] Soviet policy towards the Baltic republics must be placed in perspective. First, Baltic encounters with the dictates of Moscow are not unique. Some national groups, notably the Volga Germans, the Jews and the Tatars, suffered even more at Stalin's hands in the late 1940s and early 1950s. All of the non-Russian republics have undergone a similar process of modernisation combined with russification even though only one, Kazakhstan, has experienced a more radical demographic shift than Latvia.

Nor have the consequences of modernisation been wholly negative. The three Baltic republics enjoy the highest standards of living in the Soviet Union. They remain distinctly 'western' in culture and outlook, a fact that places them at an advantage in the Soviet context. They are still able to fulfil their historic role as mediators between Russia and

---

1 P Zunde, Lithuania's economy: introduction of the Soviet pattern. In V S Vardys (ed), *Lithuania under the Soviets: Portrait of a Nation, 1940–65*, New York 1965, p 169.

2 A Küng, *A Dream of Freedom: Four Decades of National Survival versus Russian Imperialism in Estonia, Latvia and Lithuania 1940–1980*, Cardiff 1981, pp 185–6.

3 E Järvesoo, The postwar economic transformation. In T Pärming and E Järvesoo (eds), *A Case Study of a Soviet Republic: The Estonian SSR*, Boulder, Col 1978, p 139.

the West. Estonia in particular, owing to its small size and the political, intellectual and cultural sophistication of its society, enjoyed a unique position as a kind of laboratory where the study of technological, managerial and cultural change could proceed with little fear for the repercussions in the rest of the country. 'After all, except for 1 million Estonians, no one in the Soviet Union understands Estonian'.[4] Even Baltic nationalism received a measure of acceptance on the part of the Soviet authorities who perhaps realised that a policy of outright repression would be counter-productive. It was, until recently, 'to Moscow's advantage to tolerate certain Estonian idiosyncracies, so long as performance levels remain high and political or ideological deviance remains low.'[5] Thus it was, paradoxically, the social and economic advances of the Baltic republics since 1944 together with their privileged position within the Soviet Union which enabled them to articulate their demands so effectively in the glasnost era.

None of these positive developments can disguise the ruthlessness and brutality with which Soviet rule was reimposed on Estonia, Latvia and Lithuania after 1944.

Sovietisation met with determined resistance in all three Baltic republics. Guerrilla formations operated in Estonia and, on a larger scale, in the Latvian and Lithuanian countryside until the early 1950s.[6] 'The most long-lived and heroic guerrilla struggle in postwar Europe' went largely unnoticed in the West except, unfortunately, among the intelligence community.[7] Between 1949 and 1955 MI6, the British secret intelligence service, sent numerous Latvian and Lithuanian émigrés back to their countries where they became victims of the KGB, which had prior knowledge of the entire operation. Some were killed; some were imprisoned; one returned to Britain in 1990 to visit his old haunts.[8] The Baltic partisans were nothing if not tenacious. A Lithuanian guerrilla leader was reported killed in action in 1965, while an Estonian partisan was executed as late as 1976.[9]

---

4 Ibid, p. 11; V S Vardys, The role of the Baltic republics in Soviet society. In R Szporluk (ed), *The Influence of East Europe and the Soviet West on the USSR*, New York 1975, p 158.

5 Parming and Järvesoo (eds), *The Estonian SSR*, p 11.

6 V S Vardys, The Partisan movement in postwar Lithuania. In Vardys (ed), *Lithuania under the Soviets*, pp 85–108.

7 Küng, *Dream of Freedom*, p 16.

8 T Bower, *The Red Web*, London 1989; T Bower, Back from the dead, *Independent Magazine*, 22 September 1990: 32–4.

9 Küng, *Dream of Freedom*, p 202.

For the Soviet authorities the elimination of opposition and the transformation of the Baltic economies went hand in hand. Deportations were a key instrument of Soviet policy. They both deprived partisans of support among the rural population and removed the chief opponents of the collectivisation of agriculture. Carried out between 1944 and 1952, the deportations involved much larger numbers and represented a more deliberate attempt to reshape Baltic society than those of 1940–1. After the initial Soviet takeovers in 1940, agricultural land had been confiscated and distributed among landless peasants and smallholders, with only a limited amount of voluntary collectivisation taking place. Now the process became compulsory. Thousands of 'kulaks' were evicted from their farms and sent to labour camps in Siberia. In Estonia as many as 80,000 people were deported in 1949 alone. The total numbers deported in 1944–52 have been estimated at 124,000 for Estonia, 136,000 for Latvia and 245,000 for Lithuania.[10] Although deportees were allowed to return after Khrushchev's de-Stalinisation speech of 1956, many did not survive the years in Siberia.

Deportations represented the largest population losses for the Baltic republics but they were not the only ones. Many members of the majority populations had already died either at the hands of the German occupation authorities or in their service. Perhaps 6,000 Estonians were executed by the Germans between 1941 and 1944, and another 25,000 may have died either as conscripts or volunteers in German military units.[11] The war had brought the destruction of the Baltic German communities of Estonia and Latvia and the Jewish communities of all three republics. The few thousand Estonians of Swedish origin, who had mostly lived as fishermen and farmers on the offshore islands, were evacuated to Sweden in 1943–4. Large numbers of the majority Baltic populations fled westward in the face of the invading Soviet forces in 1944. Those who survived eventually helped to found important émigré communities in such countries as Sweden, Great Britain and the United States. Even the boundaries of the Baltic republics were altered. While Lithuania's control of the Vilnius and Klaipeda regions was confirmed by the Soviet Union, both Estonia and Latvia were obliged to cede part of their territories to the Russian federal republic. Estonia lost 5 per cent of its prewar territory and 6 per cent of its prewar population; Latvia's territorial and population

10 I J Vizulis, *Nations under Duress: The Baltic States*, Port Washington, N Y 1985, p 107.
11 T Parming, Population changes and processes. In Parming and Järvesoo (eds), *The Estonian SSR*, p 26.

losses amounted to about 2 per cent. In both cases the areas lost were inhabited predominantly by Russians.

Estonia and Latvia underwent more radical demographic change than Lithuania not merely through wartime losses but also through the impact of postwar industrial development and urban growth. These two republics bore the brunt of the large-scale immigration from other parts of the Soviet Union which resulted from the rapid programme of industrialisation pushed through by the Soviet authorities in the Stalinist era. Soviet policy brought about the reintegration of the Baltic economies into the larger Russian economic sphere from which they had been detached in the period of independence. The very large capital investments made by the Soviet Union in the postwar era were an indication of the importance attached by economic planners to the Baltic region as a source of energy resources and a wide range of industrial and agricultural products.[12] They could draw on the technical and managerial skills, together with the high levels of education, which had been inherited from tsarist times and the period of independence and which had not been entirely eradicated during the war. There were also industrial plant and a transport infrastructure which were advanced by Soviet standards despite wartime depredations. Nevertheless the Soviet contribution to postwar reconstruction should not be underestimated. 'While the uninterrupted development of the prewar economy would probably have led to a higher standard of living than currently exists . . . the recovery of the war-destroyed economy probably would not have been faster without Soviet rule.'[13]

It must always be kept in mind, however, that the Baltic peoples had to pay a high price for the forms of modernisation favoured by their Soviet masters. The initial priorities of Soviet economic policy in Estonia were the reactivation of manufacturing industry and the expansion of the oil shale industry. The latter had been one of the most successful industrial enterprises of independent Estonia. After the war it was 'developed forcefully and wastefully' by the Soviets, mainly as a source of energy for Leningrad.[14] Initially utilising German prisoners of war, the Soviets soon came to rely almost entirely on immigrant Russian labour. The oil shale region of north-eastern Estonia saw some of the most rapid urban growth in the entire republic, with the former villages of Kohtla-Järve, Sillamäa and Kivioli accounting for 11 per cent of the country's urban population by 1959. It also saw some

12 Järvesoo, Postwar economic transformation, p 141.
13 Parming and Järvesoo (eds), *The Estonian SSR*, p 10.
14 Järvesoo, Postwar economic transformation, p 164.

of the worst pollution.[15] Traditional industrial centres such as Tallinn and Narva also experienced rapid population growth, again largely through immigration, so that by 1970 Estonia was the most urbanised of the Baltic republics with 65 per cent of its population living in cities. In addition to energy the Estonian economy specialised in the production of chemicals and cement, as well as in textiles for which Narva had been a major centre since tsarist times.

Industrial development in Latvia followed a similar pattern, but with an emphasis on the production of steel, agricultural machinery and motor vehicles – the kinds of heavy industry for which cities like Riga had been important before 1914. The republic's population was 62.5 per cent urban in 1970, with Russians concentrated in all the major cities. By 1979 ethnic Latvians constituted only 38.3 per cent of the population of their own capital, Riga. Of the seven largest cities only Jelgava had a bare majority (52 per cent) of Latvian inhabitants.[16] The postwar industrial development of Lithuania, though very rapid, began only in the 1950s. Lithuania remains less industrialised and less urbanised than the other two republics: in 1970 only 50.2 per cent of its population lived in towns or cities. Soviet economic policy in Lithuania concentrated on the establishment of very large plants such as the power station at Vievis, constructed in the early 1960s and then the largest in the Soviet Union, which used raw materials from outside the country and served the needs not only of Lithuania and the other Baltic republics, but also of neighbouring regions such as Kaliningrad and Belorussia.[17]

In all three republics manufacturing industry was initially developed at the expense of other sectors of the economy, notably agriculture and housing. The rural economy of course suffered not only from lack of investment but also from the disruption brought about by collectivisation. In Estonia agricultural production did not regain the 1938–9 level until the early 1960s – ten years later than manufacturing industry. From that point onwards there was a greater investment in fertilisers and mechanisation, as well as in agricultural education. By the 1970s Estonian agriculture was among the most efficient in the Soviet Union. Significantly, a large proportion of Estonian production came, as in every other Soviet republic, from the 'private sector' – the small plots and livestock owned by individual collective farmers and others. Even on collective farms, however, labour productivity in Estonia was

15 M Taagepera, Ecological problems in Estonia, *Journal of Baltic Studies* **14** (1983): 307–14.

16 J Dreifelds, Latvian national rebirth, *Problems of Communism* **38** (1989): 79.

17 Zunde, Lithuania's economy, pp 160–2.

higher than in any other Soviet republic and well ahead of both Latvia and Lithuania. Productivity in the latter republic was held back in part by the much larger proportion of the population that remained on the land. Housing suffered even worse neglect than agriculture in the early years of Soviet rule. Baltic towns and cities were extensively damaged during wartime fighting and housing losses were not made up in Estonia until 1955. New construction was often of poor quality and limited in space. Although the situation improved after the early 1960s, the shortage of housing and cramped living conditions were among the chief causes of tension within families. Housing was also a source of ethnic tension since allocation policies favoured Russian immigrants at the expense of locals.

The demographic changes experienced by the two most industrialised Baltic republics have been dramatic. According to the 1970 census ethnic Estonians constituted 60 per cent of their republic's population against over 88 per cent in 1934. In Latvia ethnic Latvians amounted to 57 per cent in comparison with a prewar figure of over 75 per cent. By 1989 the proportion of Latvians had fallen to 50.7 per cent – a bare majority. In Lithuania, by contrast, the proportion of ethnic Lithuanians still stood at 80 per cent of the total population – only 4 per cent less than the figure for 1923. They had even managed to increase their share of the population of Vilnius to 43 per cent by 1970.[18]

The absence of large-scale Russian immigration provides only part of the explanation for Lithuania's demographic resilience. The war had a less devastating impact on the Lithuanian population than on those of Estonia and Latvia. The Lithuanians managed to prevent the German authorities from drafting their young men into the German armed forces; fewer Lithuanians fled to the West at the end of the war. For the Polish and Jewish inhabitants of prewar Lithuania, on the other hand, the war had a devastating impact. The virtual elimination of these important minorities left Lithuania more ethnically homogeneous than before the war, and left a space which could be filled by immigrant Russians without seriously affecting the predominance of ethnic Lithuanians. The Catholic Church is still strong in Lithuania and the birth-rate remains high.

---

18 Population figures for Vilnius in the interwar period were grossly distorted by both Poles and Lithuanians. The Polish census of 1931 gave a figure of barely 1 per cent for the Lithuanian population; in 1941 the Lithuanians told the Germans that the figure was 30 per cent. Y Arad, *Ghetto in Flames: The Struggle and Destruction of the Jews in Vilna in the Holocaust,* Jerusalem 1980, p 27.

Birth-rates among Latvians are the lowest in the world; the Estonians come next, followed by the Swedes.[19] To some extent these represent cultural patterns of low marriage rates and a high average age of marriage for females which date back to the eighteenth and nineteenth centuries, and which were already a source of anxiety between the wars.[20] They reflect, too, different patterns of religious belief. Low birth-rates are also a product of the way in which modern industrial society has developed in Estonia and Latvia. Many of its features, such as high divorce rates, the increase in female employment and the widespread use of contraception, are familiar throughout the industrialised world. However, very high divorce rates have a disproportionate effect on population growth when marriage rates are low. The prevalence of abortion reflects the unavailability of other birth-control devices but is also a sign of social and familial pressures. In a study conducted between 1967 and 1969 'the reason most frequently cited by women as to why they were resorting to abortion was the smallness of their living quarters; for women who already had one or more children, this became the overriding consideration.'[21]

The Estonian and Latvian majority populations, with their low natural rates of increase, are ageing populations. In the three recent years for with official data are available (1980, 1985 and 1987) more Latvians died than were born.[22] They confront an immigrant population composed predominantly of Russians but also of other Soviet nationalities among all of whom, again for reasons that have to do with cultural patterns and age profiles, birth-rates are much higher. Moreover immigration continues even though it is no longer centrally directed. The Baltic republics, with their high living standards and 'western' life styles are attractive to Russian tourists and settlers. 'Coming here is like going abroad', one Moscow student explained to a western correspondent.[23] In 1987 nearly 136,000 individuals moved into Latvia while 117,000 left for other areas. In that year immigration accounted for 65 per cent of Latvia's total population growth.[24]

The turnover rate among the Russian populations of the Baltic republics is high: perhaps fifty leave for every hundred new arrivals.[25]

19 Küng, *Dream of Freedom*, p 182.

20 Parming, Population changes, p 43; S Mylliniemi, *Die baltische Krise 1938–1941*, Stuttgart 1979, p 15.

21 Parming, Population changes, p 49.

22 Dreifelds, Latvian national rebirth, p 79.

23 Cited in Vardys, The role of the Baltic republics, p 159.

24 Dreifelds, Latvian national rebirth, p 79.

25 R Taagepera, Baltic population changes, 1950–1980, *Journal of Baltic Studies* **12** (1981): 45.

Many such people feel little attachment to the area and are particularly resented by the majority populations for their refusal to adapt. However, 'those Russians who have lived there since the period of independence or who know the local language are regarded as a special group of 'local Russians' with whom relations are much better.'[26] It is not surprising that the Latvians in particular have often seen their future in apocalyptic terms. The playwright Mara Zalite warned a meeting of the Writers' Union in 1988 that 'Latvians are presently on the threshold of extinction' and asked her colleagues whether they were prepared to go on living with the thought that 'we are the last generation of intellectuals of a disappearing nation.'[27]

Between the late 1940s and the mid-1980s the Baltic republics were largely isolated from the outside world. Sealed off from virtually all contact with the West during the Stalinist era, they remained closed to western journalists until the 1960s and to western television for much longer. Even tourists were confined mainly to Tallinn, Riga and Vilnius: much of the countryside and coastline remained off-limits. Postal correspondence was subject to censorship and information about dissent could be smuggled out only with great difficulty and at considerable personal risk. Soviet sensitivity about the Baltic region was due not merely to the suspect loyalties of much of the population but to its military importance. Admittedly the Baltic had become something of a backwater in the nuclear era and the Red Navy's most important naval base was the Arctic port of Murmansk. In the Baltic itself the Soviet Union's strategic frontier had been pushed as far west as the East German border and the headquarters of the Soviet Baltic fleet were at Kaliningrad, an enclave of the Russian federal republic, rather than in the Baltic republics themselves. Nevertheless the supply lines to Kaliningrad ran through Lithuania and numerous military installations were located on Baltic territory. They contained many surveillance centres, valuable as listening posts on the West. The large Estonian islands of Hiiumaa and Saaremaa were given over almost entirely to military purposes, while the expansion of the submarine base at Liepaja and the discovery of Soviet submarines in Swedish waters in the early 1980s were indications of the extent to which the Red Navy regarded the Baltic as its own preserve.

The information reaching the West provided ample evidence of the rigour with which Moscow suppressed all overt criticism of the 'sys-

---

26 R Karklins, *Ethnic Relations in the USSR: The Perspective from Below*, Boston, Mass 1986, p 54.

27 Cited in Dreifelds, Latvian national rebirth, p 79.

tem' in the Baltic republics. Throughout the postwar period courageous individuals and groups expressed their dissent by a variety of means. Although the experience of independence and the manner in which the three republics had been annexed in 1940 gave a special edge to Baltic dissent, opposition to the regime was not confined to the majority populations, nor was it motivated by nationalist considerations alone. Many aspects of Soviet policy provoked resistance, notably the regime's attacks on religion. The Catholic Church in Lithuania and the Lutheran Churches in Estonia and Latvia were the main targets, although the Orthodox Church was not spared. Just as the church of St Casimir in Vilnius became a museum of atheism and the Lutheran cathedral in Riga a concert hall, so the Orthodox cathedral in Riga became a cinema and café. The Catholic clergy of Lithuania were as resolute in their resistance to religious persecution as their predecessors were to the russification of the tsarist era.

More generally Baltic dissidents, like their counterparts elsewhere in the Soviet Union, took their stand on the issue of human rights. In the late 1960s the Democratic Movement in the USSR, which demanded that the Soviet Union should respect the UN Declaration of Human Rights and the Soviet constitution, found support within the Estonian intelligentsia and even among officers of the Baltic fleet (most of whom were not of Baltic origin).[28] A better known case was that of the letter from seventeen long-serving Latvian communists which reached the West in 1972 and sharply criticised Soviet policy for its betrayal of the principles of Marx, Engels and Lenin.[29] A new wave of dissent was provoked by the Soviet government's signature of the Helsinki declaration on human rights in 1975. A Helsinki monitoring group was established in Lithuania in 1976 and the republic 'produced more dissident publications per capita than any other Soviet republic' in the 1970s and 1980s.[30] Members of the minority nationalities were also active in campaigns for civil rights. Jewish dissidents were as vocal in the Baltic republics as elsewhere, particularly in Latvia and Lithuania: indeed it has been argued that in Riga 'opposition and dissent are essentially Jewish activities'.[31] Their demands concerned the right not merely to emigrate but to practise their religion and their culture, long suppressed by the regime. Germans from Estonia and Latvia were prominent in the campaign to win the right to emigrate for the Soviet

---

28 Küng, *Dream of Freedom*, pp 204–7.

29 Ibid, pp 169–70.

30 V S Vardys, Lithuanian national politics, *Problems of Communism* **38** (1989): p 54.

31 D Kirby, The Baltic States 1940–50. In M McCauley (ed), *Communist Power in Europe 1944–1949*, London 1977, p 32.

Union's 2 million citizens of German origin: four were imprisoned in 1974 for 'illegal demonstration' and 'slandering the Soviet state.'[32]

Frequently, of course, national, religious and human rights demands merged into one another. In the 1970s democratic and nationalist underground organisations joined forces to issue appeals to the outside world. To an increasing extent, too, dissidents cooperated with groups in neighbouring republics. Two appeals were addressed to the Secretary General and General Assembly of the United Nations in 1972 by the Estonian National Front and the Estonian Democratic Movement, while in 1975 'Representatives of the Estonian and Latvian Democrats' issued an appeal to the governments participating in the Helsinki conference. Nationalism and religion inspired the tragic protest of the nineteen-year-old worker Romas Kalanta in Kaunas in 1972. His self-immolation, following the example of Jan Palach in Czechoslovakia four years earlier and a failed attempt in Latvia in 1969, led to demonstrations and riots by thousands of young Lithuanians which had to be suppressed by paratroops from Central Asia.[33]

All such demonstrations, to the extent that they became known outside the Baltic republics, helped to remind people elsewhere in the Soviet Union and in the West of the plight of the Baltic peoples. Andrei Sakharov and other Moscow dissidents issued a statement in support of the Baltic demand for self-determination in 1975.[34] The death in 1981 of the imprisoned Estonian scientist and human rights protester Juri Kukk, as a result of a hunger strike, prompted French colleagues to call for a boycott of scientific relations with the Soviet Union. The European Parliament passed a resolution in 1982 supporting the declaration issued by citizens of the three Baltic republics on the fortieth anniversary of the Nazi–Soviet pact in 1979.

Western governments were not, on the whole, so ready to identify themselves with the Baltic cause. None formally recognised the Soviet annexations of 1940 but few were as forthright or as consistent in their support for the Baltic peoples as the United States.[35] 'The Swedish position comes closest to a de jure recognition of the Soviet annexation although the Swedish Government has never officially confirmed it.'[36] Finland, too, refused formal recognition although the question

32 Küng, *Dream of Freedom*, p 220.

33 Ibid, pp 212–15. At least four other Lithuanians, two of them in their sixties, attempted to emulate Kalanta's example. Three of them were successful.

34 Vizulis, *Nations under Duress*, pp 161–76.

35 Ibid, pp 153–7; 176–9.

36 W J H Hough, III, The annexation of the Baltic States and its effect on the development of law prohibiting forcible seizure of territory, *New York Law School Journal of International and Comparative Law* **6** (1985): 440.

was not publicly discussed and the Soviet government chose to view a visit by President Kekkonen to Estonia in 1964 as a sign of de jure recognition. The Australian Labour government did actually give formal recognition in 1974 but its decision was reversed by the incoming Liberal administration in 1975.[37] The attitude of Great Britain was also disturbingly ambivalent. In 1967 the British government reached an agreement with the Soviet Union on the question of the gold reserves deposited for safe keeping with the Bank of England by the Latvian and Estonian governments in 1940.[38] The Baltic gold, valued at around £7 million, was used to settle long-standing claims of British individuals and companies against the Soviet Union. Although the British government had continued to accord recognition to the surviving diplomatic representatives of the Baltic states in London, it refused in 1974 to recognise a successor to the Estonian envoy, who had died in 1971. This was in contrast to the attitude of the United States government, which agreed in 1980 to permit the current Baltic chargés d'affaires to name their successors in office, provided they held Baltic citizenship.[39] A final blow was delivered in 1982, when the British government withdrew the tax concession previously enjoyed by the Estonian legation as a diplomatic residence and treated it as commercial property instead.

If they had only a limited impact on the outside world, dissident activities undoubtedly did much for Baltic morale. Information passed quickly from one republic to another despite the efforts of the authorities. It is doubtful, however, whether such activities had any effect on official policy apart from making it more repressive. After Kukk's death, for example, the regime became more determined to suppress Estonian dissent and had arrested nearly all open dissidents by 1983.[40] Efforts to preserve Baltic national identities or to modify the nature of Soviet rule therefore had to be carried out by less overt means. In the absence of mutual trust between rulers and ruled, the latter turned to their only remaining resources: their culture, enterprise and religious beliefs – everything that made them different from the system in which the Baltic republics had been enveloped.

In doing so they used the ostensibly non-political weapons that had underpinned the national awakenings of the nineteenth century: edu-

---

37 E Dunsdorfs, *The Baltic Dilemma: The Case of the de jure Recognition by Australia of the Incorporation of the Baltic States into the Soviet Union*, New York 1975.

38 Ibid, pp 412–24.

39 Ibid, p 412.

40 R Taagepera, Estonia's road to independence, *Problems of Communism* **38**, 6 (1989): 15.

cation and culture. Here they were aided, paradoxically, by the 'striking ethnic pluralism' maintained and even encouraged by the Soviet Union alongside its efforts to impose greater uniformity. The Soviet authorities have been persistent in their efforts to russify the education systems of the Baltic republics: indeed a new wave of russification began in the late 1970s as part of a renewed attempt to create a 'Soviet' national identity.[41] On the other hand 'most Western countries do not, either in domestic or colonial policies, maintain such an extensive cultural and educational apparatus, not to mention scientific activity, in languages other than that of the dominant group.'[42] Although Estonian, Latvian and Lithuanian children have to learn Russian, their entire education is conducted in their native languages. Schools in the Baltic republics have, furthermore, retained eleven years of schooling rather than the ten to which the rest of the Soviet Union was reduced in 1965. In many respects intellectual life and scientific research are strikingly advanced by Soviet standards. Estonia led the field in computer technology with the establishment of the Cybernetics Institute of the Estonian Academy of Sciences in 1960, while the University of Tartu retained its pre-eminence in the natural sciences: in the 1960s Professor Endel Lippmaa became a figure of international importance in the field of molecular biology.[43]

Other aspects of intellectual life were, however, more ideologically sensitive. In literature and the visual arts the Soviet authorities remained vigilant in their search not merely for open expressions of dissent, but for any deviation from the official line of socialist realism. Leading writers were deported to labour camps in the 1940s and 1950s, some to die in captivity. Despite some liberalisation in the 1960s, the 1970s saw renewed attacks on freedom of expression. Music proved more difficult to control. The great song festivals in Estonia, Latvia and Lithuania remained a means for national self-expression as they had been in tsarist times. Although the programmes made token gestures towards Soviet uniformity, the greatest applause was reserved for traditional patriotic songs. The Soviet authorities, however, showed their disapproval for other musical forms, notably rock music and jazz, and even classical music. Estonia's greatest modern composer, Arvo Pärt, was subjected to criticism for his receptivity to foreign influences.

41 R J Misiunas and R Taagepera, *The Baltic States: Years of Dependence 1940–1980*, Berkeley, Calif 1983, pp 202–4.

42 T Parming, Roots of nationality differences. In E Allworth (ed), *Nationality Group Survival in Multi-Ethnic States: Shifting Support Patterns in the Soviet Baltic Region*, New York 1977, p 42.

43 H Susi, Selected aspects of scientific research; R Türn, Computers, computer sciences, and computer applications, in Parming and Järvesoo (eds), *The Estonian SSR*.

Restrictions were placed on Pärt's travel abroad until he finally received permission to emigrate permanently in 1979, the same year as his compatriot Neeme Järvi, who had already established an international reputation as a conductor.[44]

The vitality of Baltic culture and national identities placed the political leadership of the Baltic republics in a dilemma. The Communist Parties of Estonia, Latvia and Lithuania had been the key instruments of Soviet rule but had been unable to ignore the aspirations of the Baltic peoples. In all three republics individual communists had persistently shown themselves unwilling to act merely as agents of the central authorities. This was, of course, very far from what Stalin had in mind when communism was imposed on the Baltic republics in the 1940s. Communism had attracted support in all three countries since pre-revolutionary times, and Baltic communists were prominent among the founders of the new Soviet state after 1917. The purges of the 1930s, however, decimated both the leadership and those members of the rank and file of the Baltic Communist Parties who had fled to the Soviet Union to escape the attentions of the bourgeois regimes of the interwar period. Many other communists died during the war, often at the hands of a populace which regarded them as collaborators with the Soviets. The new regimes established in 1944 could draw to some extent on native communists who had fought with the Red Army: members of the Estonian Rifle Corps formed in 1942 represented a significant proportion of Estonia's postwar political and intellectual elite.[45] However, the Soviets also had to rely heavily on Russians and upon people of Baltic origin who had been born or educated in the Soviet Union. In Latvia, for example, nearly 100,000 such people, known by the locals as 'latovichi', were imported to fill political, administrative and managerial posts. 'The fact that the 'latovichi' lacked Latvian language skills, had minimal knowledge of local practices, and were shunned by the indigenous population turned them into a generally intolerant, exaggeratedly pro-Russian, and heavily sovietised force.'[46] The important post of second secretary of the local Communist Parties was almost invariably held, as in other Soviet republics, by a Russian or a member of another Slavic nationality.[47]

Nevertheless 'national communism' was a persistent deviation in all three Baltic Communist Parties. The Estonian Party was purged in

44 Misiunas and Taagepera, *Baltic States*, pp 170, 232.

45 J Pennar, Soviet nationality policy and the Estonian Communist elite. In Parming and Järvesoo (eds), *The Estonian SSR*, pp 114–15.

46 Dreifelds, Latvian national rebirth, p 78.

47 J Fleming, Political leaders. In Allworth (ed), *Nationality Group Survival*, p 138.

1950 for its failure to stem 'bourgeois nationalism'. The then first secretary Nikolai Karotamm was replaced by Johannes Käbin, born in Estonia but Russian educated and Moscow trained. However, during his long tenure of the post up to 1978, Käbin gradually abandoned his Stalinism and his preference for the Russian language (expressed, for instance, in his use of the Russian version of his name, Ivan Kebin). He showed 'increasing tolerance towards ethnic Estonian idiosyncracies', apparently because this aided the republic's economic performance, and in the Khrushchev era he was known to have disregarded the occasional 'incoherent or inapplicable all-union directive'.[48] Ethnic Estonians also came to play a larger role in the Party. Even so the Estonian-born Vaino Väljas was passed over for the post of first secretary in 1978, despite his strongly pro-Moscow stance. The job went instead to 'Siberian-born Karl Vaino, whose chief distinction was his inability to learn his ancestral Estonian during a 40-year residence in the country.'[49]

Käbin's longevity in office was greatly exceeded by that of Antanas Snieckus in Lithuania. He actually became first secretary of the Lithuanian Communist Party in 1936 and held the post until his death in 1974. Active underground against the prewar Lithuanian government, Snieckus held on to his position through the vicissitudes of war and the postwar party upheavals by avoiding involvement in Moscow power struggles. Even the purge of Lithuanian 'national communism' which took place in 1959 was mild by comparison with comparable purges in Estonia and Latvia and did not affect the position of the first secretary.[50] 'Snieckus preferred to be number one in his own country instead of trying to be number two in the Kremlin.'[51] There were more native communists in the Lithuanian Communist Party than in any other republic apart from Armenia and Georgia. Although the price of greater autonomy was less influence in Moscow it was one which Snieckus and other Lithuanian communists were prepared to pay. After his death the Party leadership 'fell into the hands of mediocre *apparatchiks*': first Petras Griskevicius, who was regarded as a compromise choice between Moscow-oriented and nationally–oriented communism and then, following Griskevicius's death in November 1987, Ringaudas Songaila.[52]

48 Pennar, Soviet nationality policy, p 123.

49 Taagepera, Estonia's road to independence, p 14.

50 T Remeikis, The administration of power: the Communist Party and the Soviet Government. In Vardys (ed), *Lithuania under the Soviets*, p 140.

51 Küng, *Dream of Freedom*, p 155.

52 Vardys, Lithuanian national politics, pp 54–5.

While both the Estonian and the Lithuanian Communist Parties chose a gradualist approach in their pursuit of greater autonomy, their Latvian counterparts directly challenged Moscow's authority in the late 1950s. The then first secretary, Janis Kalnberzins, was elderly and ineffectual; the republic was facing an influx of Russian immigrants. In 1958 a faction of 'national communists' led by the deputy prime minister Eduards Berklavs gained control of the Party and attempted to stem the tide of russification and centralisation. Khrushchev reacted vigorously, appointing the Moscow-trained Arvids Pelse as first secretary with the task of carrying out a purge of the Party. Berklavs was deported from Latvia in 1959 and hundreds of other Party members were purged. The accusations against them were revealing. It was claimed that

> out of false fear that the Latvian Republic could lose her national character, some comrades tried to artificially hinder the objectively determined process of population resettlement. In their speeches, they repeatedly asserted that one could, for example, not allow the mechanical growth of the population of Riga even by one person.[53]

There are striking parallels between the events in Latvia and better known manifestations of 'national communism' in eastern Europe: the return of Gomulka to power in Poland in 1956; the Hungarian revolution of the same year and the 'Prague spring' of 1968. Pelse reaped the rewards for acting as Latvia's Kadar or Husak. He was elected a full member of the Politburo in 1966, the first Baltic communist to reach that position. Latvian communists were also better represented on the Party's central committee than were those of Estonia or Lithuania. Under the leadership of Augusts Voss after 1966 the Latvians remained the most subservient to Moscow of the three Baltic Communist Parties. That 'national communism' had not been eradicated was shown, however, by the letter of the seventeen Latvian communists in 1972. Nevertheless the experience of 1959 has weighed heavily on Latvian minds in the glasnost era, making them more cautious than the Estonians and Lithuanians in their bid for greater self-determination. It was heartening when Berklavs re-emerged from obscurity, as Dubcek was to do in Czechoslovakia in 1989. But the distinguished poet and Popular Front leader Janis Peters warned in 1988 that if the process of recovery were to fail, 'we will not rise a second time.'[54]

---

53 Cited in Karklins, *Ethnic Relations in the USSR*, p 52.
54 Cited in Dreifelds, Latvian national rebirth, p 79.

Those Baltic communists who went on to adopt the cause of autonomy or independence in the glasnost era cannot, therefore, be dismissed merely as opportunists. They stood in a tradition of Communist Party defence of local interests. Their integrity came to be recognised both by the Baltic Popular Fronts, whose candidates eventually often stood down in their favour, and by the electorates at large.

Yet in the last resort the Baltic Communist Parties were – at that stage – answerable not to the people but to Moscow. The people had, furthermore, a readily available standard of comparison with which to measure communist performance since the memory of independence made them 'quite aware that they were then able to govern themselves and to maintain a relatively high standard of living without foreign supervision.'[55]

By the beginning of the 1980s the Baltic peoples were doing well by all measurable Soviet standards. They had also been remarkably successful in preserving their cultural identities. There was on the other hand worrying evidence of the negative consequences of economic growth: social problems, unchecked immigration and damage to the environment. The growing problems of the Soviet economy as a whole were also having their effect, with shortages of food and consumer goods becoming evident after 1975. Yet there was no prospect of an end to Soviet rule. In the declining years of the Brezhnev era the regime showed itself more than ready to stamp out all expressions of dissent. In these circumstances the Baltic peoples discovered affinities with other citizens of the Soviet Union, though not in ways that would have met with the approval of the authorities. The Kirghiz writer Chingiz Aitmatov's novel *And the Day Lasts Longer than a Hundred Years* (1981) 'had a unique resonance in the Baltic area which is entirely remote from Central Asia culturally as well as geographically.'[56] Its central image was that of the 'Mankurt' – a person forcibly deprived of memory:

> In unofficial Lithuanian circles the term 'mankurtization' spread, meaning russification, departure from one's native language and religion, the forgetting of national history, the creation of mixed families, and similar processes. . . This, without doubt, is a good example of the interchange of ideas between Soviet nationalities 'over the heads of Russians' – although the Russian language indeed played the role of mediator.[57]

55 Fleming, Political leaders, p 125.
56 T Venclova, Ethnic identity and the nationality issue in contemporary Soviet literature, *Studies in Comparative Communism* **21** (1988): 327.
57 Ibid, p 327.

Western observers detected a growing acceptance of the 'system' on the part of the majority Baltic peoples.

> For an increasing number of Balts, the independence period was receding into a past beyond that crucial personal watershed between the contemporary and the historical: one's own date of birth. . . . In this sense time was definitely on the Soviet side. However, the new generation also lacked the obeisance which had been beaten into their elders by Stalinist terror. [58]

Moreover, the republican Communist Parties were themselves becoming vehicles for native aspirations to a greater voice in political decision-making. This was an unintended byproduct of the Brezhnev era, which saw the advance of non-Russians at the expense of Russians in the Party bureaucracies. New generations of Party members emerged, particularly in Estonia, who had been entirely brought up in the postwar republics and were not tainted by the 'Russian' associations of their predecessors. Through Party membership they 'gained the right to work within the most powerful, and only legal, political organisation in the USSR.'[59]

As the majority Baltic nationalities gained in self-confidence they presented a new and potentially profound challenge to the Soviet system. The new nationalism, in the Baltic republics as elsewhere, was characterised by an 'intense competition for jobs and resources among elites of various national groups rather than simple attachment to tradition.'[60] Increasingly well-educated majority populations found their paths to employment and promotion blocked by Russians. On the other hand the fact that they had been obliged to learn Russian in school made them better able to compete with Russians for jobs. 'As more non-Russians became qualified for jobs held by Russians, both groups tended to invest the situation with ethnic meaning, especially in the case of failure.'[61] To an increasing extent, in fact, it was the native Baltic peoples who comprised the intellectual elites of the three republics. This was particularly true of Lithuania, where the Jews, Poles and Germans who made up most of the prewar educated class had disappeared, and the new Russian immigrants were mainly manual workers. 'That the native elements are at the top of the social scale in

58 Misiunas and Taagepera, *Baltic States*, p 200.
59 Fleming, Political leaders, p 144.
60 P A Goble, Gorbachev and the Soviet nationality problem. In M Friedberg and H Isham (eds), *Soviet Society under Gorbachev: Current Trends and the Prospects for Reform*, Armonk, NY 1987, p 77.
61 Ibid, p 91.

Lithuania and in the rest of Eastern Europe is indeed one of the most important social developments in the region's recent history.'[62]

By the 1980s there was therefore much latent social and political tension both within the Baltic republics and between the Baltic republics and Moscow. Under these conditions Gorbachev's policies, with their emphasis on efficiency at the expense of ethnicity, represented a challenge to all of the non-Russian republics.[63]

---

62 I Deak, Heroism in hell (review of Avraham Tory, *Surviving the Holocaust: The Kovno Ghetto Diary*, Cambridge, Mass 1990), *New York Review of Books*, 8 November 1990, p 52

63 Goble, Gorbachev, pp 94–9.

PART FOUR
Reawakening

CHAPTER NINE
Baltic Spring

After the death of Brezhnev in 1982 the crisis of the Soviet system could not be long delayed. Gorbachev, who came to power in 1985, was the first Soviet leader to acknowledge the existence of such a crisis. It was an opportunity of which the Baltic peoples took full advantage. Glasnost and perestroika were primarily a response to the breakdown, above all economic, of the Soviet system. Gorbachev was in historic company in attempting reform from above to avoid revolution from below. His prime concern was always in reality to preserve the Communist Party's monopoly of power through *managed* change. This was always likely to be a gamble in view of the ethnic tensions within the Soviet Union. Of all the nationalities the Baltic peoples were the most determined and the best placed to exploit the new conditions. In this sense Gorbachev's reforms *occasioned* rather than caused the remarkable contemporary reawakening of the Baltic republics.

The changes which Gorbachev proposed to Brezhnev's constitution of 1977 were fundamental to that reawakening. Central to the new constitutional order – approved after heated debate early in December 1988 – was the proposed Congress of People's Deputies, comprising 2,250 members. This was to be elected by secret ballot, providing for the first time a choice of candidates for the Soviet voter. The Supreme Soviets in the various republics, hitherto largely rubber stamps of the central administration, were to receive enlarged powers. The vast Congress of People's Deputies – sitting only briefly each year – was in turn to select a smaller central Supreme Soviet to function as a parliament for eight months of the year and to elect a head of state with wide-ranging authority.

Many of the seats in the proposed Congress were earmarked for selected organisations and in 385 constituencies there was only one candidate on the ballot paper. Moreover the Communist Party still dominated the central and republican apparatus of government and controlled the media. Opportunities for ensuring the success of favoured candidates abounded. Nevertheless, if the intention of the central Soviet authorities had been to cloak the one-party system in democratic guise, the reforms promised an historic election for March 1989. Most voters would face a choice of anything from three to twelve candidates. Western observers rightly insisted that the elections would accelerate changes in East Europe, where Poland, Hungary and the Baltic republics were seen as testing a 'still mysterious limit' to what was possible under Gorbachev's rule.[1]

The importance of the Baltic republics in exploring this limit can hardly be exaggerated, precisely because the Baltic area had assumed such a central strategic and economic significance for the USSR following the Second World War. The three Baltic republics, as we have stressed, protected the Soviet Baltic seaboard. Assuming that the withdrawal of Soviet troops from elsewhere in East Europe was a matter of time, the Baltic countries were inevitably regarded by the Soviet military leaders as a vital buffer zone inside the Soviet borders.[2] Economically, as we have seen, the Baltic republics had also been locked into the Soviet system. If the Baltic republics were to develop as a showcase under perestroika it was desirable from Moscow's viewpoint that they remained within the Soviet state. Politically, Gorbachev became obsessed about the precedent which might be created if the Baltic republics were to leave the USSR. Here it is not necessary to accept the validity of Gorbachev's thinking; only to draw attention to the obstacles placed on the Baltic road to independence.

The argument, repeatedly advanced in the West, that Gorbachev was unaware of the forces he was 'unleashing', appears to underestimate the degree of pressure on the Soviet leadership which had generated reformist policies in the first instance. In professing to encourage enterprise to lift the Soviet 'command economy' from the doldrums perestroika necessarily provided incentives to regional managers. Sooner or later tensions were likely to arise between these and the ossified central apparatus of control into which the Soviet economy had for so long been locked. Centrifugal forces, beginning to operate

1 E Steen, Soviet elections set to speed pace of East European reform, *Independent*, 29 March 1989.

2 M Nicholson, Soviet military fights to defend its Baltic strongholds, *The Times*, 30 March 1990.

at once at an economic level under perestroika, were inevitably compounded by a resurgence of political enterprise, as it were, in what western analysts described as the peripheral areas of the 'Soviet Empire'. In the Baltic republics, where memories of their enforced incorporation into the USSR in 1940 were never far below the surface, the habits of submission practised after fifty years of Soviet rule were rapidly dropped after 1987. Estonia, Latvia and Lithuania each again took on 'the psychology of an occupied country . . . vigorously and persistently reasserting their national culture and reclaiming their national identity'.[3]

Economic and ecological considerations were already radicalising political life in the Baltic republics during the 1980s. Major protests in Riga about the environment in November 1986 had been followed by similar demonstrations in Tallinn in spring 1987. The latter successfully blocked the plans of the Soviet central authorities to begin phosphate mining in north-eastern Estonia, already a major ecological disaster area. Such small but significant steps towards organised protest encouraged key individuals within the government establishments in the three Baltic republics to contemplate reform more seriously as glasnost began to take root. This was less true of Latvia, where Russians and other immigrants with a predominantly dogmatic view made up the majority of Party membership and state bureaucracy, than it was of Estonia and Lithuania. Here, in the course of 1988, the monolithic unity of the Communist Party crumbled and the hard-liners, largely Russian, were opposed by a reform wing comprising above all native Baltic peoples. By the end of 1988 the reform wing had gained the decisive positions in the state and Party leadership of the Baltic republics.

The Baltic cause was furthered by the development of the so-called Popular Fronts which came into being in Estonia, Latvia and Lithuania during 1988. These were not political parties but coalitions of reformist and populist forces, including communists outside and within the governing republican establishments. *Sajudis*, as the Lithuanian Popular Front was termed, was formed in the summer of 1988 primarily as a ginger group for reforms. Its growth was rapid and by the time of its formal founding congress on 23–4 October 1988 its leaders' speeches seemed 'less platforms for change than torrents of pent-up nationhood.'[4] In Estonia a 'Popular Front for the Support of Perestroika' was

---

3 R Taagepera, Estonia's road to independence, *Problems of Communism* 38, 6 (1989): 11.
4 R Cornwall, The rebirth of a proud nation, *Independent*, 24 October 1988.

proposed by Edgar Savisaar, a former planning committee official. He had been involved in drafting proposals for economic autonomy in Estonia since the end of 1987 and is now (1990) Estonia's prime minister. On 2 October Estonia's Popular Front was formally constituted.[5] On the 9th Latvia too 'slipped the Kremlin leash' by instituting its own Popular Front. The foundation of the Popular Fronts, together with the resurgence of national emblems in the same year (badges as well as flags), the massive song festivals and the revival of the Churches, added up to a display of national self-awareness which obsessed the world's media. The confrontational imagery favoured by the West to describe Baltic developments tended to obscure the fact that the Popular Fronts concentrated largely on calls for autonomy rather than independence, notwithstanding individual voices demanding secession, and that they based their appeal on the continuation of the reform processes launched under Gorbachev. In short, their premise was that under the new conditions further instalments of change could be agreed with the central authorities.

Nevertheless, their demands by autumn 1988 included, as well as a desire for more control over their economic affairs, calls for cuts in immigration from the other Soviet republics and for greater cultural and ecological self-determination. The question had already been posed as to how far the Communist Party in the three Baltic republics could work with rather than against the popular movements as the latter grew bolder with success. The ruling Communist Party in Estonia, under its new first secretary from June 1988, Vaino Väljas (passed over for the post ten years earlier), had better relations at that stage with Estonia's Popular Front than was the case in either Latvia or Lithuania. Indeed, Väljas had delivered a warm address at the founding congress of the Estonian Popular Front. Moreover, alongside the Popular Fronts more radical, if unofficial, independence movements were also active. These focused from the outset on disputing the legality of the events of 1939–1940. They argued that it was futile even to contest the elections to the new Congress of People's Deputies since it was the concern of a 'foreign state'. At the other extreme, each of the three republics contained substantial Russian immigrant communities which had largely settled there after 1940 and which had a vested interest in the USSR remaining centralised.

Of the three republics, Latvia and Estonia had by far the largest proportion of Russian immigrants. The percentage of Russians in Estonia at the time of the 1979 census was 27.9 per cent. For Latvia the

5 Taagepera, Estonia's road, p 18.

figure was 32.8 per cent and for Lithuania 8.9 per cent. The rising Russian share of the population of Estonia and Latvia after 1945 can be set against the relative decline of Estonians and Latvians as a percentage of total population noted in the last chapter.

It is an oversimplification to depict *all* Russians in the Baltic republics as obstructing *all* reform after 1987. There were and are the deeply intransigent. They include, for example, the workers in the heavy concentrations of large-scale industry, especially in north-east Estonia, or at the Ignalina/Snieckus nuclear generating station in Lithuania, as well as the large military element in the Baltic. On the other hand Russian intellectual elements have been more flexible. This applies also to the technical intelligentsia involved in the industrialisation of the Baltic republics after the Second World War. A study of these in Lithuania found many of them sceptical but not hostile to the idea of Lithuanian independence.[6] In Latvia a number of Orthodox believers who adhered to the Old Church could recollect their Church flourishing during the period of Latvian independence, in contrast to Russia. Other Russians, particularly those who had lived in the Baltic republics for a long time, showed sympathy for the Popular Fronts. Nevertheless, the Soviet policy of settling Russians in the Baltic republics provided perhaps the major cause of political tension. The Russian settlers constitute the majority in some towns and regions; the ignorance of such settlers on the subject of the language, culture and history of the Baltic peoples, combined to make the nationality conflict more intractable still. Not surprisingly, there was a hostile Russian reaction to the language laws passed by the Supreme Soviet of the Estonian SSR on 18 January 1989, which made Estonian the state language again and demanded that within four years officials and sales personnel should be able to work in both Estonian and Russian. Similar legislation was passed in Latvia in the same month and in Lithuania in June. The relationship between the Baltic governments and the Russian minorities was further strained when declarations 'about sovereignty' were made by Estonia on 16 November 1988, Lithuania in May 1989 and Latvia on 28 July 1989.

The ambiguity of the phrase 'about sovereignty' was not accidental. Yet the tentative declarations represented an attempt to give substance to a term which had hitherto been largely symbolic in the Soviet context. When Lithuania affirmed its sovereignty on 18 May 1989 it insisted that the only laws in force in the Lithuanian SSR were those

6 D Cuplinkskas, Ethnic minorities: diversity and rootedness, *Lithuanian Review*, 2 March 1990.

adopted by its Supreme Soviet or after a referendum. It went beyond Estonia's declaration by referring to Lithuania's independent past and to its illegal incorporation into the Soviet Union in 1940. Latvia, under a more cautious leadership, was less explicit. Estonia reserved the general right to halt or limit federal laws of the USSR if they infringed Estonian sovereignty.[7] When the Estonian parliament voted on 16 November 1988 to give itself the right to veto laws of the central Supreme Soviet it was also reacting against suspected attempts by Moscow to limit the rights of secession from the Union under the proposed new constitution. Although the article giving that right, article 72 of the old Soviet constitution, was not abolished, the constitution envisaged the new Congress of People's Deputies having power to 'take decisions on questions of the composition of the USSR'.

The subsequent stalemate on this issue, after the Presidium of the USSR Supreme Soviet condemned the Estonian legislation on sovereignty as unconstitutional and Estonia in turn reaffirmed its stance, was to prove typical over the following two years. It has been said that the sovereignty declarations were already chipping at 'the legal cement holding the Soviet Union together.'[8] At first, however, the republican declarations about sovereignty envisaged gaining more republican authority within a federative USSR, rather than complete independence from Moscow.

Within this context the historic Supreme Soviet elections in the USSR took place on 26 March 1989. The fact that multi-candidate choice was available for the first time encouraged the Popular Fronts and other radical groups to organise and to spread their own electoral message, with no small success even though there was still only one legal *party*, the Communist Party, and most of the candidates were members of it. Party members fought the campaign as individuals, however, because of the Communist Party's growing unpopularity as an organisation. Where individual communist candidates were liked – Brazauskas in Lithuania being perhaps the most well-known example in the West – *Sajudis* was prepared to leave the field open. Similarly, in Estonia, CP members like Väljas, Arnold Rüütel and Indrek Toome were all endorsed by the Popular Front. In Latvia, by contrast, the unpopular Communist Party leader, Vagris, was opposed by the Latvian Popular Front.

7 D Bungs, A comparison of the Baltic declarations of sovereignty, *Radio Free Europe Research*, Baltic Area SR 8, 11 September 1989.

8 R Cornwall, Estonia calls the shots in a war of nerves, *Independent*, 21 November 1988.

In other words candidates who had not readily identified with the reawakening of the Baltic peoples found themselves with a struggle on their hands. The Party was obviously dividing along nationalist lines; under popular pressure the native Baltic political leaders were increasingly responding as Estonians, Latvians and Lithuanians rather than as Party men. The Russians in the Baltic republics felt compelled to react to the electoral threat by organising 'international fronts' in the three republics. The Interfront movement in Latvia and Estonia, coming into existence late in the summer of 1988, coordinated with the pro-Moscow organisation of Russians, *Yedinstvo* (Unity), formed in Lithuania in November of that year.[9]

The elections ultimately had a profound impact on relations between the Communist Party in the three republics and their Popular Fronts, particularly in Estonia and Latvia. Popular Front-backed candidates, communist or otherwise, emerged as winners at the poll, with limited success for the smaller nationalist groups but relatively poor showings for Interfront hopefuls. Although the Communist Party in the three Baltic republics continued to wield the power derived from Moscow, the Popular Fronts had strengthened their position and could afford to be more confident in relation to the Party. It was of course now easier in Estonia for reformist CP leaders to align themselves with the Popular Front, but the latter had been confirmed as the clear favourite with the Estonian electorate. The next significant step forward was taken in convening the first assembly of all three fronts, meeting in Tallin on 13–14 May 1989. The assembly resolved:

> To coordinate joint policies of the biggest popular movements of the
> Soviet Baltic countries and to make the general public of the Soviet
> Union and the World at large aware of the democratic aspirations pursued
> by the Baltic popular movements.

Once again, there was no call for political independence but economic independence from Moscow was demanded by 1990. At the same time there was much discussion of a possible 'bloc' of between eighty and ninety like-minded deputies from the Baltic republics acting together in the Congress of People's Deputies. Lauristin, the Estonian Popular Front leader, predicted that such a grouping would constitute the first faction in the USSR's new parliament.[10]

The captive nation theme of the Tallinn meeting of Popular Front delegates was echoed soon afterwards in the Estonian Supreme Soviet,

9 V Ivanov, Soviet Lithuania forever, *Lithuanian Review*, 13 April 1990.

10 J-T Dahlburg, Baltic nationalists press demands for freedom, *Independent*, 15 May 1989.

where on 18 May the secret clauses to the 1939 Molotov–Ribbentrop pact were condemned.[11] The commissions set up by the Supreme Soviets of the three Baltic republics to examine the events of 1939/40 indicated just how far the Party leadership was running with the popular mood. In June the Congress of People's Deputies had also appointed a twenty-six-man commission under Yakovlev, one of Gorbachev's closest collaborators and a Politburo member, to examine the political and legal implications of the 1939 pact. On it were a number of Baltic delegates, including the president of the Estonian Popular Front, Savisaar. Ultimately, the Baltic republics and the central commission were at one in finding the secret protocol illegal. At the same time the split vote on the Yakovlev commission (whose report was accepted by a vote of 14 to 12) indicated how reluctant many were to draw the further conclusion that the elections of 1940 were also illegal, and thus to reject the Kremlin line that the Baltic states had been voluntarily incorporated into the Soviet Union.[12] That fiction was of course duly rejected by the Baltic Supreme Soviets, which during November 1989 condemned the 'military occupation' of the Baltic republics and declared their incorporation into the Soviet Union null and void.[13]

A dramatic verdict against the 1939 pact and its secret protocol had in any case long since been delivered on 23 August 1989. The fiftieth anniversary of the Nazi–Soviet pact was marked by a human chain linking hands across the three republics. Notwithstanding Latvia's more cautious path towards independence, Riga formed the heart of the demonstration, with its Freedom Monument, the tall column marking Latvian independence between the wars.[14] A joint statement from the three Popular Fronts, 'The Baltic Way', pointedly emphasised the peaceful, parliamentary methods to achieve Baltic statehood in contrast to the 'criminal and unlawful' agreement of 1939. The fervour and sheer organisation behind the human chain – which could hardly have been constructed without government complicity – stung Gorbachev into making the first official statement hostile to the Baltic republics since becoming General Secretary of the Communist Party of the So-

11 P Conradi, Estonians lead the Baltic wave, *Independent*, 19 May 1989.

12 Molotov–Ribbentrop Commission Conclusions, *Radio Free Europe Research*, Baltic Area SR 8, 11 September 1989.

13 B Meissner, Die staatliche Kontinuität und völkerrechtliche Stellung der baltischen Länder. In Meissner (ed), *Die baltischen Nationen: Estland, Lettland, Litauen*, Cologne 1990, pp 207–9; A Këëpna, U Lepp, X Lindpere, L Meri, E Truuvali, *1940 god v Estonii. Dokumenti i materiali*, Tallin, 1989.

14 T Fishlock, Human chain links the three Baltic republics, *Daily Telegraph*, 24 August 1989.

viet Union (CPSU). His diatribe against 'nationalist excesses', delivered on television on 26 August, warned the Communist Party leadership in the Baltic against giving way to nationalist forces and thus damaging perestroika. He included the threatening remark that 'the state of the Baltic peoples is in serious danger.'

The clear implication was that perestroika had to be managed at all costs by the Party. Evidently, Baltic reformism had been tolerable to Gorbachev for just so long as it remained unequivocally loyal to a unitary state. That premise was clearly open to doubt once the August demonstration had placed the whole question of the events of 1939–40 so much more publicly on the current agenda. In retrospect it is difficult to imagine a tactically more inept warning than that delivered by Gorbachev after the celebrations of 23 August. His strictures against the Party hierarchy in the Baltic republics certainly failed to consider the positive aspects of encouraging closer CP ties with the Popular Fronts, the better to manage change. Instead, those ties were tightened in reaction *against* Moscow's heavy hand. The CP leaders of Latvia, Estonia and Lithuania – Vagris, Väljas and Brazauskas – admitted mistakes but also attacked the conservative forces in the Soviet Union and reaffirmed the Party's support for autonomy. In the words of Brazauskas, 'A Lithuania without sovereignty is a Lithuania without a future.'[15] The Baltic Communist Parties' replies to Gorbachev indicated, moreover, a degree of coordination between the three republican governments.

Gorbachev's attack confirmed how difficult it had become for the Party leaders in the Baltic to keep Moscow's trust while at the same time not alienating the hugely influential Popular Fronts. The Party leadership in Tallin, Riga and Vilnius had certainly refused to be intimidated by the thunder from the Kremlin, insisting as they did on continuing movement towards greater autonomy and a review of the 1939 pact. Leaders and led had already achieved a large measure of agreement in reacting against Moscow's control – even though, it has been suggested:

> For the Soviet leadership in these republics, this . . . means enhanced republican sovereignty within the framework of the USSR; for many Estonians, Latvians and Lithuanians the ultimate goal is . . . independence outside the borders of the USSR.[16]

15 R Cornwall, Baltic republics coordinate their reply to Moscow, *Independent*, 30 August 1989.
16 *Radio Free Europe Research*, Baltic Area SR 8, 11 September 1989.

It is difficult to resist the conclusion, however, that from August onwards a stronger conviction also took root amongst many at government level that perestroika would not itself result in substantial autonomy for the Baltic peoples. That perception was probably also partly the result of the experience of preparing plans for the economic autonomy of the Baltic republics, accepted in general terms by Moscow on 27 July 1989. In keeping with the historical memory of free enterprise in the independent Baltic states, recognition came much more quickly in Tallinn, Riga and Vilnius than in Moscow, that any successful liberalising of the economy would entail a loosening of Party control.

Until the early autumn of 1989, neither the Baltic governments nor the Popular Fronts had unequivocally staked a claim to full independence, although the word was in the air as a result of the August demonstrations and the investigations of the events of 1939–40. The threat that Gorbachev detected to his own plans for a revamped Soviet federation from Baltic developments can be seen only too clearly in his meeting with the Baltic governments on 13 September. Here he insisted on a federal solution to the nationality conflicts, as well as equality of treatment for the different nationalities. Earlier in the summer, the law concerning local elections passed by the Estonian Supreme Soviet, which linked voting rights to minimum lengths of residence in Estonia, had produced a wave of strikes from Intermovement and bitter recriminations from the Russians in Estonia. Significantly, Gorbachev was against any idea of breakaway Communist Parties being formed in the Soviet republics, insisting on the unity of the Party. Few proposals could have been better calculated to circumscribe the freedom of movement of the Baltic Party leaders, precisely at a time when the popular mood was intensifying and they were trying to manage it to the best effect. What is more, Moscow's intransigence over key issues was having the affect of nourishing more radical approaches towards the restoration of statehood. The question was becoming more insistent by the autumn, as to whether any further progress towards greater independence *could* be made by Baltic governments and legislatures which sprang from the existing Soviet structures.

Admittedly in Lithuania the demographic mixture generally made for a much more ready identification between the Communist Party of Lithuania (CPL) and the cause of independence. This close identity of interest helped to account for the massive personal popularity of the head of the CPL, Brazauskas. Nevertheless, the latter was unhappy with the Lithuanian Supreme Soviet's endorsement in October 1989 of the idea that the Soviet Union was illegally occupying the country as a result of 1939–40. It seems highly likely that Brazauskas' preference at that stage was for independence for Lithuania *within* a renewed Soviet federation. On 19 December 1989, however, a special congress of the Lithuanian CPL expressed its determination not to be outstripped by the popular mood (with local elections looming) in declaring itself by 855 to 160 votes in favour of the CPL becoming independent of the Communist Party of the Soviet Union. Not only did the delegates reject a compromise formula referring to a 'sovereign CPL within a renewed CPSU'; they also provisionally adopted a resolution committing the CPL to creating 'an independent, socialist Lithuanian state and a democratic society.'

By then the CPL was facing a range of embryonic 'parties' embracing the common goal of independence. *Sajudis*, from whose ranks many of the new formations sprang, had more than fulfilled its original aim to act as a ginger group. Some of the leaders of the new formations promised to surrender their CP cards when their parties were properly registered and up and running. The remaining obstacle to genuine multi-party elections had in fact already fallen with the Lithuanian Supreme Soviet's earlier deletion of Article 6 from the republic's constitution. The CPL's primacy had been based on that article. While the CPL still had the edge over the other parties in terms of organisation, offices and expertise, it could hardly be said to be in full control of events. The pace quickened dramatically shortly before Christmas, when the Lithuanian Supreme Soviet set up a commission to explore in more detail the legal path to independence.

Shortly afterwards Moscow pronounced the breakaway of the CPL from the main Communist Party of the Soviet Union illegal. Brazauskas was criticised sharply on the grounds that one of the pillars of the federal state was the 'single, unitary structure of the Communist Party of the Soviet Union.'[17] But Gorbachev's dilemma was by then acute. The use of force to restore a hardline CPL would bring almost certain humiliation for the Party in the Lithuanian elections, due in February 1990. If the split passed unheeded, on the other hand, it would signal encouragement to other republics. In the background there was already considerable pressure coming from radicals within the Congress of People's Deputies to topple Article 6 throughout the Soviet Union. Gorbachev's preference for calling a vote of each of the 200,000 Party members in Lithuania would probably only have produced support for

17 R Cornwall, Gorbachev caught on the horns of the Lithuanian dilemma, *Independent*, 27 December 1989.

Brazauskas. The latter was now convinced, however, that CPL could remain a force in Lithuania only on the basis of its support for independence. Doubtless Gorbachev saw the force of this argument for himself during his historic visit to Lithuania in January 1990, when he stated that his fate was linked to that of the Baltic republics. He departed from Vilnius with a promise that a new law of secession would be worked out over time, so that 'certain mutual obligations' could be resolved before any 'divorce' of Lithuania from the Soviet Union.

For *Sajudis* leader Vytautas Landsbergis, Gorbachev's promise of a new law was a 'cheap lie' directed at the western media and in any case irrelevant to the Baltic states which were not legally part of the Soviet Union. A month later, at the elections to the Lithuanian Supreme Soviet on 24 February, *Sajudis*-backed candidates, including pro-independence Communists, easily secured the necessary two-thirds majority of the 141 seats.[18]

Sajudis' own 'parliament', the *Seim*, promptly demanded that the new Lithuanian Supreme Soviet 'pass lawful acts on the continuation of the Lithuanian state and restore the rights to statehood which have been violated or suspended'. On 11 March 1990 the Lithuanian Supreme Soviet demonstrated conclusively its wish 'to live in the European common home but in a separate apartment.'[19] With 124 votes in favour, none against and 6 abstentions, the Lithuanian Supreme Soviet declared Lithuania's independence. The Lithuanan SSR changed its name to the Republic of Lithuania and appointed Landsbergis as its president and Kazimiera Prunskiene as prime minister.

Latvia and Estonia lagged behind at that stage. The Popular Fronts in both republics admittedly came out with unambiguous declarations in favour of independence before Christmas. Yet if the Estonian and Latvian Supreme Soviets were to be the instruments of change, the large and obstructive Russian minorities represented there would have to be won over. Although Lithuania had also made great efforts to placate its own minorities and to reassure them about their future in an independent state, the Popular Front movements in Estonia and Latvia had a far more formidable task of education and persuasion on their hands.[20] At the same time, the tactics of the Popular Front were also coming under increasing pressure. The spread of the so-called citizens'

18 For full breakdown of results see *Lithuanian Review*, 2 March 1990.
19 V Berzins, Lithuania on the road to freedom, *Atmoda*, 25 January 1990.
20 Cf article on the Association of National Cultural Societies in Latvia, *Atmoda*, 1 September 1989.

committees in the last part of 1989 was a logical outcome of the radical conviction that independence could never be restored legally by organs of the occupying power, that is to say the Supreme Soviets. Instead, the citizens' committees argued, priority should be given to asserting the case in international law for the continuity of existence of the prewar republics of Estonia and Latvia. On this argument only 'citizens' of the independent Republics of Estonia and Latvia, or their descendants, were qualified 'voters'. Between late 1989 and early 1990, therefore, 'citizens' registered themselves in preparation for wholly non-Soviet 'elections'. The polls to elect Citizens' Congresses in both republics were planned to take place at or near the time of the Supreme Soviet elections in Latvia and Estonia in March 1990. Meeting objections about excluding non-Baltic peoples, the citizens' committee movement intimated that citizenship could be earned, not least by acknowledging the illegality of the 1940 annexations.

There is little doubt that, in part at least, the Popular Fronts themselves were impelled towards more unambiguous statements about independence by the activities of the citizens' committees. These managed to organise the registration of over 700,000 individuals in Estonia and some 500,000 in Latvia by early 1990. Conflicts over strategy between citizens' committees and the Popular Fronts marred the run-up to the municipal elections in the Baltic republics in December 1989. The municipal elections involved thousands of offices at various levels of local government. The Congress movement's view was that such elections were a matter for the 'Empire' and of little concern to citizens of legally independent republics. By contrast, the Latvian Popular Front stressed the need to infiltrate and use state offices to wrest control from the Communist Party, still exercising that power formally.

> We should not build serious political ideas on a legal base. We must fight for this independence with the help of newly elected local government officials.[21]

In practice there was collaboration between the congress movement and the Popular Fronts, marked by the formation of election unions spanning both organisations for the December local elections.[22] Such unions included candidates of the by then numerous small parties. These could not be legally registered until the deletion of Article 6

21 J Skapars, The opinion of the Popular Front on the coming municipal and Supreme Soviet elections, *Atmoda*, 19 December 1989.

22 Electors have a choice of candidates and a boycott, *Homeland*, 6 December 1989.

from the constitution. The formal end to the leading role of the CP in Latvia came through the Latvian Supreme Soviet's decision on 11 January 1990, although the same step was not taken in Estonia until after the Supreme Soviet elections of March 1990. Meanwhile, however, the election unions provided them with a vehicle to contest the municipal elections. The latter thus became genuinely multi-party affairs. They resulted in an overwhelming majority for pro-independence candidates who in Latvia, for example, secured three-quarters of the 14,000 contested offices.

At the turn of 1989/1990, Latvian and Estonian politicians were stressing the need to follow a different route from that taken by Lithuania. In fact the unfavourable demographic balance in Latvia forced it to lag behind Estonia too in the early part of 1990. 'If you kick a bear in the belly', the Latvian Popular Front foreign affairs spokesman said in January 1990, emphasising the need for patience in view of the large numbers of Russians in Latvia, 'you are dead.'[23] The congress movement in Latvia was also fractionally more cautious than that in Estonia and it was in Tallinn that the impact of the citizens' committees on the political debate could be seen most plainly.

The strategy favoured by the congress movement exploited more systematically the declaration of the USSR Supreme Soviet of December 1989, that the Nazi–Soviet pacts were null and void. Congress spokesmen pushed this argument to its logical conclusion by insisting therefore on the 'calm restoration' of the old (legally still existing) state of Estonia. In refuting the idea that a new state needed to be set up, the non-Soviet citizens' committees were also rejecting any suggestion that they were creating a precedent for the breakdown of the Soviet Empire by leaving it.[24] Estonia and Latvia could not 'leave' something they had never joined.[25] That this strategy had spread beyond the congress movement was shown at an important assembly convened in early February 1990, for all Estonian elected representatives, at local and Supreme Soviet level and including Estonian delegates to the Congress of People's Deputies.

The assembly voted to open talks with Moscow to restore its lost independent statehood on the basis of the Treaty of Tartu 2 February 1920, when the Soviet Union had recognised Estonia's independence. The Chairman of the Estonian Supreme Soviet, Arnold Rüütel,

23 E Lucas, The Latvian way is not to kick the bear in the belly, *Independent*, 16 January 1990.

24 J Kaza, Estonians may take different route, *Independent*, 13 March 1990.

25 E Lippmaa, How to regain Estonia's statehood, *Homeland*, 21 February 1990.

presided over the assembly. He had already informed Gorbachev of the planned events and that the Estonian goal was full independence. The unprecedented agreement between Estonian political groups about the significance of the Tartu agreement was evidence enough against the Moscow line that only the 'extremists' in Estonia wanted independence.

In Latvia, plans for 'elections' to the citizens' Congress were deferred until after the Supreme Soviet poll.[26] Estonia's Congress 'elections' were, however, deliberately staged before voting to the Supreme Soviet was due to start. The 700,000 citizens who had registered for the elections gave the 499 member Congress, meeting on 11–12 March 1990, a popular mandate which no other body had. The fact that it was wholly non-Soviet was, according to one of its key founders, Tunne Kelam, its major strength. The Congress elected a seventy-one-member Council of Estonia under Kelam's chairmanship. At the same time the Congress voiced criticism of key Communist Party officials and insisted that, after the elections to the Estonian Supreme Soviet, the latter should join with the Congress to form a joint body to begin independence negotiations with Moscow. The Congress remained determined that the cause of independence should not be captured and perhaps even subverted at the last moment by any hostile forces hoping to operate through the existing Soviet structures.

The municipal elections, in so far as they gave independence-minded candidates the opportunity to participate in and control local executive power had, however, at least worked against manipulation by the central apparatus. In that sense they vindicated the 'parliamentary way' of working through the Supreme Soviets favoured by the Popular Fronts. They also ensured similar approaches to the Supreme Soviet elections in Estonia and Latvia on 18–20 March. In any case the continuing decline of the Communist *Party* as a distinct force in Estonia was all too evident. One in four candidates supported by the Popular Front was a CP member and several of these were pledging themselves willing to hand in their Party cards after the election. As in Lithuania, so in Estonia and Latvia, there were also now numerous small parties. In spite of a close race, with some four contestants per seat, the Estonian Popular Front secured 43 out of the 105 seats in the new Soviet, with the Russian loyalists of the Intermovement bloc gaining 27. The other 30 seats were shared between other pro-independence parties. One of these, Free Estonia, was felt to have been

26 J Kaza, Estonians pick a team to lead them to independence, *Independent*, 14 March 1990.

formed as a vehicle to get Communists returned without having to campaign under the CP banner. In Latvia, too, the Popular Front candidates took a majority of the seats in the new Supreme Soviet. Shortly afterwards Latvia's Congress was also 'elected' by the voters who had duly registered as citizens.

In important respects it is misleading to talk of a duality of power between the Congresses in Latvia and Estonia and the respective Supreme Soviets of the two republics from March 1990, although substantial differences were to continue to develop. In the first place there was an overlap in the membership of the non-Soviet and Soviet bodies. Some forty members of the Congress of Estonia, for instance, were also sitting as members of the new Supreme Soviet.[27] Moreover it was envisaged by some that the roles of the Congress on the one hand and the Supreme Soviet on the other, would be complementary. Congress representatives regarded themselves as having the sole right to represent the Baltic nations abroad, as direct descendants of the independent Baltic states. The Supreme Soviets, on the other hand, were in practice the only channel of communication to Moscow, where sooner or later negotiations would have to take place.[28]

Congress movements and Supreme Soviets alike had the common goal of independence. On 30 March 1990 the new Estonian Supreme Soviet, with a new prime minister, Edgar Savisaar, made its own declaration of independence. More exactly, it declared the annexation of 1940 to be illegal and resolved to begin a 'transition period' towards the 'reformation of the constitutional institutions of the Republic of Estonia'. During the interim period Soviet law would continue to apply providing it did not conflict with Estonia's sovereignty.[29] By 4 May 1990 the Latvian Supreme Soviet had in turn made a similar declaration, reinstating in the process the Latvian constitution of 1922. On paper at least the republics of Lithuania, Estonia and Latvia had reappeared, dropping their 'Soviet' appellations in the process. The resistance to the Estonian and Latvian declarations shown by the pro-Moscow loyalists in both Supreme Soviets was a reminder, however, of how much still remained to be done.

It must be remembered that the above events took place against the background of the Lithuanian crisis. As a result of the republic's declaration of independence on 11 March, Gorbachev threatened a blockade

27 Estonia elects a pro-independence Supreme Soviet, *Homeland*, 28 March 1990.

28 Congress of Estonia lays down path to independence, *Homeland*, 21 March 1990.

29 Transition period to end Moscow's rule in Estonia, *Homeland*, 4 April 1990.

and ultimately imposed it on 17 April. At the time the West tended to portray Lithuania as headstrong and the other two republics deliberately sought a less confrontational route to independence by providing for 'transitional' periods. Gorbachev did not of course apply a blockade to Estonia or Latvia, although one was threatened in the case of the former. Nor did the military adopt such a high profile as it did in Lithuania, with its 'controlled displays' of force, although there were also troop demonstrations in Riga in May and a brief display of rather badly organised intimidation in the government buildings in Tallinn. In other respects, however, Gorbachev's reactions to all three declarations were almost equally hostile.

Furthermore, all three republics proceeded to draft laws which were unwelcome to Moscow, including proposals for alternative military service enabling Baltic recruits to fulfil their service obligations on Baltic territory. For Gorbachev, recently armed with new powers as the Soviet Union's first executive president, it had therefore become imperative to revamp the Soviet federation before the rot went too far. This was all too obvious from the tough secession laws Gorbachev promised in March, demanding that two-thirds of the population of any given republic approve secession by referendum and that final approval be dependent on the full Soviet parliament after a five-year transition period. It was consistent with this approach that Gorbachev refused negotiations with Lithuania throughout April and May. 'Negotiations', he insisted, could take place only with a foreign state. There were dark hints of imposing presidential rule on Lithuania under the Kremlin's new emergency powers. Yet by mid-June Moscow had in fact moved from its insistence on a 'respectful dialogue'. The term 'negotiations' was used for the first time , when all three Baltic states were urged to 'freeze' their declarations of independence so that talks could begin.

There were a number of reasons for this change of tactics. First, Lithuania itself had suffered from the blockade and Prunskiene in particular had intimated that although rescinding the declaration of independence was impossible, a freeze – eventually set at 100 days – might be introduced once talks started. A vote to this effect was passed in the Lithuanian parliament on 29 June 1990, although Landsbergis insisted that only the bills passed since 11 March would be suspended.[30] Second, the international mood, while not as supportive of Lithuania as it might have been, registered genuine alarm at Gorbachev's policy to-

---

30 I Karacs, Lithuanian PM hails beginning of end of crisis, *Independent*, 30 June 90. For text of the resolution see *ELTA Information Bulletin*, August 1990.

wards the Baltic republics. There were some indications of possible economic disadvantages for the Soviet Union if it failed to resolve its conflicts with the Baltic republics. Most important was the success of Yeltsin in the elections to the Supreme Soviet of the Russian federal republic. The republic's proclamation of sovereignty in June provided Gorbachev with a new and potentially far more worrying challenge than he faced in the Baltic. As if to underline this, Yeltsin promptly condemned the blockade of Lithuania. He had already made it clear to an Estonian delegation in early June that 'were the Baltic states to finally opt for independence, Russia would be the first to sign treaties with them.'[31] It was hardly surprising that on 12 June, Gorbachev met representatives of the Baltic republics in Moscow and spoke of the urgent need to transform relations between the fifteen republics of the Soviet Union. He was reported as offering the Baltic republics a special status within a renewed Soviet federation. Ironically, such an idea had come from the Baltics in the autumn of 1988. By now it was a case of too little, too late. The proposal, actually voiced from Moscow in mid-April 1990 for the first time, had already been refused by Estonia and Latvia.

In reality, the Soviet federation was inexorably transforming itself without the benefit of a master plan from Gorbachev. Economic talks between Estonia and the Russian federal republic and with Leningrad took place from June onwards and led to direct trade agreements between Estonia and Leningrad on 27 July. The Estonian government even convened a meeting in the last week of September for the prime ministers of all the Soviet republics, thus neatly making the point that there was no longer a 'centre of power' in Moscow.[32] The move was all the more pointed in that the Baltic republics eventually refused to take part in the talks which Moscow was holding to hammer out a new shape to the Soviet Union in the Federation Council, the body supposedly uniting the fifteen republics. Irrespective of Gorbachev's continuing strictures against the Baltic leaders, the Estonian parliament went ahead with its plan to form a negotiating team for independence talks with Moscow.[33] By 23 August Moscow had agreed that high-level joint talks could take place with Estonia. Two teams of negotiators were scheduled to meet every Thursday until 18 October, when it was hoped that an agreement would be reached. Meanwhile, Savisaar's government was launching a number of initiatives to open a

---

31 Yeltsin seen as partner for Estonia, *Estonian Independent*, 6 June 1990.

32 Congress criticizes, *Estonian Independent*, 15 August 1990.

33 V Pettai, Estonian parliament firm on independence, *Estonian Independent*, 15 August 1990.

dialogue with the Russian military in Estonia and with the Soviet Ministry of the Interior as part of the slow process of restoring Estonia's control over its own affairs. Yet although Estonia began to assume a leading practical role in the cause of Baltic independence, it is important to stress the growing coordination between Tallinn, Riga and Vilnius.

Paradoxically, this was in part due to the blockade of Lithuania. Gorbachev's action stimulated a show of solidarity in March between the three Popular Fronts, through their coordinating body, the Baltic Council, which called on Moscow to end threats of military force.[34] In spite of their reservations at the outset of the Lithuanian crisis about the wisdom of Lithuania's early declaration of independence, the Latvian and Estonian governments were also soon doing what they could, at least to ease the entry of essential supplies to Lithuania. Together the republican government spokesmen termed Gorbachev's new secession law a 'law against secession'. On 12 May 1990 the presidents of Latvia, Estonia and Lithuania, meeting in Tallinn for the first of such summits for fifty years, signed a joint declaration renewing the Baltic Entente of 1934. At the same time the Council of Baltic States was restored, whereby the presidents of the republics and the top officials could consult on a regular basis. Although there was no insistence on joint moves, President Rüütel of Estonia argued that the Baltic problem should be treated as a process rather than as something pursued by the republics individually.[35] At the second summit, on 13 June, this time in Riga, the three presidents sent a telegram to Gorbachev asking for a joint meeting to agree a timetable for negotiations. Apart from economic talks the summit discussed lobbying for membership of the Helsinki Conference on Security and Cooperation in Europe. The Riga meeting closed with the setting up of a secretariat for the Council of Baltic States in Vilnius.[36]

The year 1990 had begun with references to Lithuania's intransigence, and fears in European capitals about destabilising the Soviet Union, not least in the interests of preserving the superpower conference in Washington in June. Yet the Baltic governments made giant steps in internationalising the Baltic problem during and after the Lithuanian crisis. Even though unreserved support for independence was

---

34 Baltic states stand together but roads to independence differ, *Homeland*, 4 April 1990.

35 V Pettai, Baltic summit revives state relations, *Estonian Independent*, 16 May 1990.

36 V Pettai, Second Baltic summit strengthens freedom drive, *Estonian Independent*, 13 June 1990.

not forthcoming from the major powers, sympathy for Estonia, Latvia and Lithuania had grown and Gorbachev's own position was viewed more sceptically. It was precisely the growing apprehension that western governments might soon recognise the existing Baltic governments which disturbed the Congress leaders in Estonia and Latvia. Yet their complaints about being ignored by the government seemed increasingly tetchy; their insistence on independence through the non-Soviet route more difficult to sustain as the ruling Baltic governments, although of Soviet origin, took one practical step after another towards independence. Nor was it easy to see what was to be gained from the call by Congress spokesmen for public trials of former communist officials by an international tribunal named 'Nuremberg 2'.[37] The relentless decline of the Communist Party in all three republics has reduced even further the remote possibility that the Baltic parliaments can be hijacked and coerced into a new union under Moscow's terms.[38]

Major problems remain to be resolved, not least that of the Russian minorities, which are still disruptive within the Estonian and Latvian parliaments and form intractable centres of influence in key areas of the economy. Yet the history of the Baltic republics as independent states gives some cause for optimism that minority problems will be tackled sensibly once independence is achieved. In the meantime, at least some Russians must have been sympathetic to the Baltic cause to produce the election results of February and March 1990. Others wish to stay in the Baltic republics, independent or not. This applies, for example, to between 80 and 85 per cent of Soviet immigrants in Estonia, according to a poll conducted by the Estonian Heritage Society in April 1990.[39] Economic inducements might also be used to lessen Russian resistance to independence. The assertion of sovereignty by the Russian federal republic must change the terms of reference in important respects. Many non-Estonians are also disenchanted with Moscow loyalists.[40] Nor is disillusionment with Gorbachev lacking among the Russians in the Baltic republics.

By September 1990 direct consultations had started only between Moscow and Estonia. The significant feature of the document setting out the proposals for talks was that it sidestepped the issue of whether

37 V Pettai, Estonian opposition toughens stand, *Estonian Independent*, 30 August 1990.

38 V Pettai, Reformed communists preach cautious line, *Estonian Independent*, 6 September 1990.

39 No Estonian please, we are Soviets, *Homeland*, 4 April 1990.

40 L Oll, Estonian leaders enjoy firm support, poll says, *Estonian Independent*, 6 September 1990.

Estonia is legally a republic of the Soviet Union. The words 'Republic of Estonia' were used in the Estonian language version while the Russian version referred simply to 'Estonia'. Doubtless, Moscow's agreement to the talks reflected its mounting fears about the Russian Federation's negotiations with Estonia, which by 23 August had reached the stage where a basis for mutual political recognition was being sought. Admittedly difficulties disrupted the third session of the talks between the Soviet Union and Estonia. The head of the Soviet delegation, Gritsenko, insisted that only consultations, not negotiations could take place, since Estonia was both de jure and de facto a Soviet republic. Sceptics had warned that the Kremlin had only used the talks to send signals to the West that all was well in the Baltic. At that time neither Latvia nor Lithuania were engaged in dialogue with the Kremlin. On 2 October 1990, however, a high-level Kremlin meeting led by Lithuanian President Landsbergis and Soviet Prime Minister Ryzhkov began to discuss a timetable for talks and a framework of problems to be considered.

Real negotiations on independence have yet to begin but it is difficult not to view these recent exchanges as yet another step forward. Gorbachev may cling to the hope that a new Treaty of Union will overtake the exchanges but it is now impossible to envisage the Baltic republics accepting this under any circumstances. By conceding the illegality of the Hitler–Stalin pact the Soviet Union has placed a large question mark over the elections of 1940 and any 'negotiations' will leave Moscow on shaky ground.[41] In any case, it is now questionable whether there is any 'central' authority with which the Baltic governments can negotiate.

41 T Tammerk, Germany, Moscow and the Baltics – talks break down, *Estonian Independent*, 13 September 1990.

CHAPTER TEN
Planning to Leave

Economic imperatives played a central role in the Baltic drive for independence. The growing disenchantment in the Baltic with the pace of economic reform in the Soviet Union as a whole was a vital factor in turning opinion from the idea of autonomy within a revamped federation towards full independence. Moscow's own failure to facilitate the practical implementation of regional self-management, a principle which it had agreed in general terms as early as July 1989 and which was formally accepted by the Supreme Soviet of the USSR in November 1989, fuelled the mounting resentment in Tallinn, Riga and Vilnius. During 1990, therefore, the emphasis in Baltic planning shifted perceptibly towards preparing the ground for an economic existence outside the framework of the USSR.

In practice there was no real prospect of effecting the changeover to self-financing for the republics by January 1989, as many had hoped. Moscow's anxiety was evident enough from its warning in November 1988, that the proposed switch to regional self-financing would never mean 'national and territorial isolationism' and that economically the USSR had to develop as a 'united entity'.[1] To this end Moscow proposed to retain control of heavy industry, fuels and raw materials, while allowing the constituent Soviet republics greater latitude over food and consumer products. This insistence was maintained throughout the summer of 1989 and prior to the formal acceptance on 27 November by the Supreme Soviet of the USSR, of the law granting economic self-management to the Baltic republics. The time lag

---

1 R Cornwall, Moscow tells Republics not to hope for separatism, *Independent*, 7 November 1988.

between the approval of the principle in July and the final passage of the law barely concealed the struggle for and against the changes.

The first assembly of the Baltic Popular Fronts had already made clear, in calling on 14 May 1989 for economic independence from Moscow by 1990, that the Baltic republics should be free to select appropriate models of socio-economic development, including capitalism.[2] This implicit criticism of Moscow's plan to retain key elements of the 'command economy' found a particularly strong echo in the Estonian Supreme Soviet, where a draft programme for an economically independent Estonia (*Ise-Majandav Eesti* – IME) was thrashed out and eventually accepted in May. It covered, among other things, general principles of ownership, taxation, prices, social and cultural policy, investment, citizenship and relations with other Soviet republics. In addition a separate currency was mooted. Many separate legislative acts were of course required for the implementation of the whole reform package by early 1991. But it 'was not' – the head of the Estonian state-planning committee drily remarked – 'compatible with the Soviet five-year plans.'[3] The Estonian version of self-management exposed the gulf between central Soviet and Baltic conceptions of practical economic reform.

Arguments concerning the ultimate control over Union (Moscow-managed) industries situated on Baltic soil and a separate currency for the Baltic republics were coloured by the growing mood in favour of political independence for the Baltic republics in the second half of 1989, although IME was predicated on perestroika and the principle of economic change in the Baltic being carried out in conjunction with Moscow.[4] It was consistent with Gorbachev's determination to anchor the Baltic republics to the larger cause of a revamped Soviet federation that he used his personal influence to push through a vote on the final draft of the law on economic self-management for the Baltic republics in its entirety. A detailed and acrimonious debate on each separate article of the bill would have badly exposed the rift between diehards in the Supreme Soviet, whose fear was the imminent collapse of the Soviet Union, and radicals who felt it did not go far enough to guarantee economic autonomy.[5]

2 J Dahlburg, Baltic nationalists press demands for economic freedom, *Independent*, 15 May 1989.

3 J Lloyd, Estonians test the limits of liberalisation in the Soviet Union, *Financial Times*, 7 May 1989; *Konseptsia IME proyekt*, Tallinn, 1988.

4 P Värv, Economic autonomy sanctioned after heated debates, *Homeland*, 6 December 1989.

5 Ibid.

The law's passage thus allowed Gorbachev to perpetuate a little longer the fiction that the USSR had taken 'a good step forward in our strivings to introduce a radical reform' and that Baltic interests were being accommodated. In reality, the vagueness of many of the clauses in the Bill gave grounds for concern, as the Estonian deputy prime minister, Rein Otsason, showed in his analysis of the likely effects on Estonia. There was, he pointed out, still no clear procedure for transferring Moscow-run industries on Estonian soil to the republic; the requirement that in key budgetary matters Estonia would remain bound by 'Soviet law' meant that unpredictable budgetary decisions could still be taken by the central authorities, perhaps leading to unexpected increases in Estonia's contributions to the Union budget.[6] Indeed, only weeks after the legislation formally came into effect reports began to appear in the Baltic press of action taken by the central authorities against the spirit of the law, notably when the USSR's Foreign Economic Bank closed down its foreign accounts on Estonian soil. Thereafter Finnish banks were forced to go via Moscow and to abandon for the time being their direct operations in Estonia, with resultant slowdowns of business. Otsason rightly characterised this – many weeks before the overt Soviet action against Lithuania – as 'an attempt at an economic blockade.'[7]

Such fiscal pugilism fuelled political discontent and deepened the conviction of progressive economists that economic advance for the Baltic republics would never come with perestroika, precisely because of its now all too evident purpose in shoring up the federation as a whole. The latter was in a dire economic condition and Gorbachev's glaring failure to put together an effective reform package during 1990 was becoming tinged by high farce. His repeated insistence in March, shortly after he gained his new presidential powers, that 'demonopolisation of the economy brooks no delay', was followed by news that the Soviet leader and his advisers were backing away from radical therapy to the economy.[8] Subsequent talk of reforms was overlaid by references to discussions of 'concepts' of reforms; the buzzword of a 'planned market economy' gave way to that of a 'regulated market economy'.[9] At the end of May announcements were being made about the government favouring a slow, steady package of reform

---

6 Ibid.

7 Moscow's undeclared financial war, *Homeland*, 21 February 1990.

8 See R Cornwall, Gorbachev promises 'breakthrough', *Independent*, 16 March 1990; *The Times*, 11 April 1990.

9 R Cornwall, Kremlin poised before economic abyss, *Independent*, 30 April 1990.

when Yeltsin's electoral success in the Russian federation injected a new note of urgency into the proceedings.[10] With the undisputed popular backing that Gorbachev lacked, Yeltsin *was* able to contemplate radical and rapid reform.

In this sense at least his cause was converging with that of the governments of Estonia, Latvia and Lithuania, newly installed after the Supreme Soviet elections in February and March. The new Estonian prime minister, Edgar Savisaar, who had worked on IME but who had been dismissed as economics minister on 23 February 1990, had earlier criticised Indrek Toome's government for not defending Estonia's right to economic self-management more actively. He had hinted darkly that the Soviet elections would further force the issue of 'whether Estonian communists are helping to restore independence or are secretly working against it.'[11] Savisaar, along with the other newly elected leaders, finding themselves on a sinking ship in sight of the coast, and a captain merely entreating them not to leave, were much more inclined after March 1990 to strike out for the shore on their own.

Just as the concept of regional self-management was predicated on the notion of economic reform in conjunction with the Soviet federation, so the declarations of Baltic independence in the spring of 1990 made it necessary to move more rapidly towards economic planning for life after IME. The Soviet blockade of Lithuania forced Vilnius first to confront its economic future outside the Soviet Union, but all three Baltic republics were soon engaged with this harsh and ultimately most decisive challenge.

The deliberate enmeshing of the Soviet and Baltic economies after 1945 under Stalin and his successors created a formidable economic obstacle to independence for Estonia, Latvia and Lithuania. By the early 1980s almost 90 per cent of industrial concerns in the Baltic were run solely or jointly by All-Union authorities.[12] Moscow will not lightly abandon its well-entrenched economic positions inside Baltic territory, as the sharp contrast between the promise and the practice of 'regional self-management' made all too clear. Not only have fifty years of being locked into the Soviet economy bequeathed to the Baltic republics massive practical tasks in reorientating their economies towards independence, but also they have deepened the scepticism of

10 Cf Gorbachev reforms on a knife edge, *Independent*, 12 June 1990.
11 Moscow dictating the pace of self-management, *Homeland*, 7 March 1990.
12 V Vincentz, Ohne prallen Geldbeutel keine Eigenverantwortung, *Die Welt*, 20 April 1990.

the outside world about the ability of the Baltic peoples with their 'tiny states' to *survive* outside the Soviet Union. In that respect one of the purposes of sovietisation after 1945 has been achieved all too well. The almost universal response in the western media to the Lithuanian crisis in March and April 1990 was to cast doubt on Lithuania's ability to survive economically on its own.

This was founded in part on the misconception that Lithuania, and indeed the other two Baltic republics, had derived more benefit than harm from their integration in the economy of the USSR. Superficially, there was something to be said for this. Baltic industries, in comparison with the Russian Federation for example, were modern because of the recent and relatively rapid nature of industrial expansion. The speed of economic growth may be judged from Lithuania's example, where by 1989 the index of net material product was 26 per cent higher than it had been in 1985.[13] The Baltic republics also developed important areas of specialisation. Obvious examples were the manufacture of radio and television sets, electric trains and telephone exchanges. In comparative terms, the Baltic republics were generally over represented in Soviet production of other consumer durables, such as tape recorders, motor bikes, sewing machines, refrigerators, textiles and shoes. The diversity of consumer goods produced by the Baltic republics was and is a major source of their economic strength, even though their total production was put at about 3.5 per cent of that of the Soviet Union as a whole.[14]

In Soviet terms at least, agriculture also proved to be a success story in the Baltic republics after 1945. Their intensively farmed acres yielded fodder for extensive stock breeding and expanding food production. Over 12 per cent of the meat produced in the USSR comes from the Baltic. The achievement of Baltic agriculture even under sovietisation was seen more clearly in the West during the blockade of Lithuania. The outside world became more aware of the republic's capacity to feed itself and of its ability to export surplus meat, milk, fish, fruit and vegetables. Other economic indices appeared to confirm the benefits for the Baltic republics of life within the USSR. The average per capita income in the Baltic republics was higher than that in the Soviet Union as a whole; there was more space per inhabitant in the Baltic region and a lower child mortality.

During the Lithuanian crisis Moscow's strategy was to intensify the

13 M Kaser, Prosperity under Moscow's rule and the price of intimate linkage, *Financial Times*.

14 Vincentz, Ohne prallen Geldbeutel.

172

West's scepticism about the economics of Baltic independence by stressing the massive costs which Vilnius would incur through 'secession'. The shutdown of oil and gas supplies to Lithuania during the Soviet blockade in the spring of 1990 made the point graphically enough. Although in terms of electricity Lithuania exported over twice as many kilowatts as it received, making it difficult to switch the republic out of the national electricity grid, it was heavily dependent on the USSR for its coal and gas (below world prices) for domestic heating. During the crisis Lithuanian industry was of course shown to be equally reliant on Soviet supplies and equipment, construction machinery and power plant. Soviet calculations based on figures for 1988 suggested that, were Lithuania to be forced to trade in normal terms for its supplies, it would have a deficit of 3.5 billion roubles.[15] In March 1990 the Kremlin mentioned the alarming figure of 21 billion roubles, which it claimed Lithuania owed the Soviet Union for its economic investment in the ungrateful republic.[16] Within a week or so the figure had risen to 50 billion roubles expended since 1940.[17]

In responding to the charges that independence would be economically disastrous for their republics Baltic governments pointed to the omission from the Soviet balance sheet of the losses caused by their annexation to the USSR since 1940. In general terms the Baltic republics all stressed the costs inflicted on them by the loss of life through execution and deportation since 1940 and by the tremendous pollution problems which the vast Union-controlled industries created in the Baltic area. Of these, the industries of the densely industrialised Virumaa area in north-east Estonia were legendary. Some forests in Estonia were ruined by the emissions from the oil-shale-fuelled thermal power stations near Narva. The vegetation in the region of the cement industry at Kunda is still grey. Tales of children losing hair are far from uncommon. Vast, once fertile areas have been turned into wastelands by the cheap but ecologically disastrous open-cast mining of the region. Hills of ash 'like skyscrapers' emit radioactivity.[18] To such environmental costs must be added the social burdens of enforced im-

15 Kaser, Prosperity under Moscow's rule.

16 J Rettie, Lithuanians break with the Soviet Union, *Guardian*, 12 March 1990.

17 J Lloyd, *Financial Times*, 17 April 1990. For further details on Lithuania see V Samonis, One step forward and two steps back: the effects of sovietization on the Lithuanian economy, Research Paper prepared at the Centre for Russian and East European Studies, University of Toronto, 1990.

18 See The Virumaa Foundation, *Homeland*, 13 December 1989; Oil shale for five more decades, *Homeland*, 27 December 1989. Cf an article on Estonia in *National Geographic* **147** (1980): 507.

migration which, far from providing a cheap solution to labour shortages, brought with it the hidden expense of settling the workers and
their families.[19]

Such ecological and social burdens were not easy to quantify, particularly since the central Soviet authorities controlled statistical information. It proved difficult even to disaggregate overall figures on
foreign trade so that a clearer picture could be given of Baltic contributions to the Soviet economy. But above all the Baltic republics
resorted to history to demonstrate that any assessment of alleged economic gains from the Soviet Union had to begin with the destruction
of the functioning Baltic economies which existed in 1940, and that
the period after 1945 had to be compared with that of Baltic independence between the World Wars.

To charges levelled by Moscow that Lithuania, for example, was
underdeveloped before sovietisation, Lithuanians replied: underdeveloped in comparison with which country? An interesting analysis was
made at the beginning of 1990 by Valdas Terleckas, an economist
from Vilnius University and head of the working group for the creation of an independent monetary and credit system, set up by the
Lithuanian Council of Ministers. Between the wars, Terleckas argued,
the USSR was the richest country in the world in terms of arable land
and resources yet in the first half of 1940 Lithuania produced per
capita 1.9 times more meat, 2.8 times more milk, 2.7 times more pigs.
During the twenty-two years of its independence Lithuania doubled its
industrial production. Estimates put the annual growth rate of the Lithuanian economy between 1928 and 1936 at about 10 per cent per
annum. If Lithuania's industrialisation lagged behind that of the USSR,
it was neither forced nor paid for by the inhuman price exacted by
Stalin. Moreover these achievements had be seen against the fact that
Lithuania was forced to build its economy after the losses caused by
the First World War and German occupation. These costs may have
been as high as 5 billion litas, or more than three times Lithuania's
national income in 1924.[20] The other two Baltic republics suffered
similar ill effects from being wrenched from the small corner of the
world markets which they had been able to occupy by 1940. In the
case of Estonia enforced integration with the Soviet economy meant
that the USSR's share of Estonian exports soared from 4.5 per cent in
the 1920s to 98 per cent in the 1980s. To make matters worse, Esto-

19 E Tiit, Immigration: for Estonians a matter of life and death, *Homeland*, 17 April
1990.
20 V Terleckas, Lithuanian economic dependence: fact or fiction?, *Lithuanian Review*, 15 February 1990.

nia was also made to sell much of that produce at below world market prices and some of its agricultural products even below cost price.[21]

Yet the assumption behind the determined Baltic efforts to draw up a fair balance sheet of gains and losses under sovietisation is not that in future the independent Baltic republics will have nothing to do with the Soviet Union. On the contrary, current planning strategies in all three Baltic republics are predicated on future strong economic ties with the other Soviet republics, but on the basis of sound business principles. The grossly unfair current arrangements, which violate the principles of regional self-management to which the central Soviet authorities themselves agreed, will have to be abandoned. Thus Estonia was suddenly asked to pay 340 million roubles to the central Soviet budget for 1990, compared with the 168 million roubles it paid in 1989.[22] Equally, popular opinion was alienated in Latvia by the way in which manufacturing branches in the Soviet Union simply began forming Union-wide 'Associations'. Since these functioned as cartels, exerting pressure on relevant enterprises in the Baltic republics to join, they again effectively frustrated self-management.[23]

As a blockade of Lithuania loomed in March 1990 the *Lithuanian Review* published an article entitled 'How will an independent Lithuania's economy function?'.[24] It was based on the work of the Lithuanian Supreme Soviet Commission for the re-establishment of Lithuanian independence. Full recognition was given to the fact that because of 1940 the economic structure to sustain a sovereign state no longer existed. The largest single problem to overcome concerned energy provision. The assumption was that instead of the 28 roubles per 1,000 cubic metres of natural gas which Lithuania paid for Soviet imports a world price of 97 dollars would be likely. A deficit of 700 million dollars was predicted if oil alone had to be bought at world market prices. The alternative strategies to offset dependence on Soviet sources were all expensive. They included gaining access to North Sea gas via the German, Dutch or Danish systems and developing facilities at Klaipeda to import foreign oil by tanker instead of through the pipeline from the USSR. At the same time the document stressed the need to evaluate Lithuania's own potential – the limited natural gas

---

21 A Kuddo, Can Estonia make it alone?, *Homeland*, 28 March 1990.

22 A Kuddo, *Homeland*, 31 March 1990.

23 B Apanis, What belongs to Latvia and what belongs to the imperialistic syndicates?, *Atmoda*, 25 January 1990.

24 How will an independent Lithuania's economy function?, *Lithuanian Review*, 2 March 1990.

reserves in the Klaipeda area and the anticipated oil reserves, including those in Lithuanian territorial waters and on the Baltic shelf. As to electricity, Lithuania's production was rated at 29.1 billion kWh, of which it consumed only 17 billion kWh.

Yet the optimum economic scenario for Lithuania, as for the other Baltic republics, remained one where they continued for a transitional period to receive relatively cheap energy imports from the Soviet Union, rather than substituting, for example, Polish steel or coal from the eastern part of Germany.[25] In return the Baltic economies could increase exports of consumer goods to the Soviet Union, through an increased input of western technology and capital investment in Estonia, Latvia and Lithuania. This message was also propagated outside the Baltic republics through business briefings involving Baltic economists.[26] The implication that the Soviet Union could have more to gain than to fear from regenerated Baltic economies was, however, only rarely recognised in media comment in the West, notably in proposing that the Baltic republics could become a 'Hong Kong of the north'. The notion of special economic zones in the region, as well as the proposed key role for the Baltic republics in mediating trade between East and West, is certainly fruitful; it is rooted in history. Of course, time would be needed for the Baltic republics to develop specialised skills to break back into world markets, for example in biotechnology, cybernetics, chemistry and laser technology, where Estonia in particular has much promise.[27]

The importance of an interim period, during which the Baltic republics would gradually move towards paying world prices and using clearing systems to settle accounts with other Soviet republics, on the lines of the Finnish–Soviet agreements of 1947 and 1948, was stressed in the Lithuanian planning exercise referred to earlier. In the last resort, however, economic rationalisation in the Baltic, the development of tourism, the diversification of small-scale industry and the running down of environmentally damaging giant enterprises, all depend on the outcome of the political struggle for independence. Without border controls of some sort, the Baltic republics could not hope to carry out successfully the necessary price rises and fiscal policies which are part of their plans for moving towards a market economy. The

25 D Johnson, Take the brake off the Balts, *The Times*, 20 January 1990.

26 Cf paper presented by the Professor of Business Studies at Vilnius University, S Vaitekunas, at a conference organised by Bradford University's Baltic Research Unit and Worldwide Information, The Baltic: Opportunities and strategies for the '90s, 29–30 March 1990, London.

27 A Kuddo, Can Estonia make it alone? (part two).

example of Estonia, regarded by many observers as the driving force for the Baltic republics since the spring of 1990, illustrated key aspects of the movement towards restoring the infrastructure on which the planned market economy must eventually rest.

Estonia was the first republic to grasp the nettle of currency reform. Without its own currency it was argued that Estonia would not be able to control prices nor bring these gradually in line with world levels. It would not in short reap the rewards of reform without its own currency and exchange rate against the rouble.[28] The Bank of Estonia, formed at the end of 1989, under Rein Otsason, had no substantial assets yet planned to issue its own currency. The mere expectation of the prewar Kroon reappearing was enough to trigger a flood of roubles towards Estonia from other parts of the Soviet Union in the early part of 1990. This, incidentally, illustrated the republic's vulnerability to other Soviet consumers. The desire for a new currency was not unconnected with the wish to restrict the purchases of Estonian goods by visitors from other Soviet republics, although not all shortages of goods in Estonia could be blamed on the Soviet shopper.[29] In fact plans for minting Estonia's own currency were repeatedly held up. Moscow acknowledged the threat to its own plans for a revamped federation by refusing to recognise any of the three Baltic banks.

None the less, the three bank presidents met in Tallinn for two days in late August 1990 to coordinate their strategies. In September the Bank of Estonia prepared for a November sale of loan certificates, to Estonian residents, of 100, 500 and 1,000 roubles, paying an annual rate of 5.5 per cent and redeemable after 1 January 1991.[30] As well as soaking up some of the savings iceberg of 2.8 billion roubles, it was planned to use the proceeds to buy physical assets in the other Soviet republics, particularly machinery and property. The fact is that Estonia has a high level of banking expertise and it is in this republic that commercial banking has also made most progress. The continuing failure of the State Bank of the USSR to recognise the Bank of Estonia made it difficult for the latter to prepare the legal framework of banking, which is its responsibility under the Estonian banking law adopted in Tallinn in December 1989. Otsason has, however, already

---

28 *Independent*, 7 November 1988.

29 U Hou, Empty stores: any remedy?, *Homeland*, 7 February 1990.

30 V Pettai, Bank of Estonia to issue loan certificates, *Estonian Independent*, 13 September 1990.

shown his concern that the operations of the ten or so commercial banks existing in Estonia in 1990 should not be allowed to damage the Republic's overall interests and fiscal strategy. Some of the private banks began to operate remote control accounts in Scandinavia; Estonian exporters persuaded their foreign customers to pay hard currency into foreign accounts, using the reserves to buy raw materials and technology. The newest and largest of the commercial banks, the Union Baltic Bank set its charter fund at 400 million roubles.[31]

The banking sector in Estonia is a good example of the way in which the long-dormant infrastructures of private enterprise pushed their way to the surface once more after 1988. Continuing intransigence by the central Soviet authorities could not prevent this process entirely, frustrate it as they might. Under Savisaar, the Estonian government immediately sought to push through changes concerning prices, local government, farming (decollectivisation) as well as banking. Plans were also made for private ownership and taxation. His economics minister, Jaak Leimann, was committed to radical reform and to working towards the introduction of a market economy. The government's thinking was incorporated in the first Estonian economic programme for fifty years, discussed in early June 1990. Steps to reduce the state's involvement and release the Estonian economic infrastructure to private enterprise were planned initially to occur in the service industries and state distribution networks. Attention was directed towards compensation mechanisms of some sort for former owners of industries nationalised by the Soviets, although the government recognised clearly that full market-value compensation was impossible. In sum, with the possible exception of the utilities, mining, railroads and communications, most of Estonian industry was to be privatised.

Although the disposal of heavy industry cannot take place until central Soviet control has been relinquished as a result of independence talks, the slogan 'Estonia goes up for sale' is not inappropriate.[32] With the estimates of the value of state enterprises in Estonia varying between 10 and 20 billion roubles and Estonian private savings of only 2.3 billion roubles, sales were clearly likely to be open to foreigners too. Not surprisingly, the Savisaar package was fiercely debated by the Estonian parliament, where former prime minister Toome stressed for example the huge difficulties Estonia would incur if it took over full

---

31 V Pettai, New bank rivals Bank of Estonia, *Estonian Independent*, 25 April 1990.

32 A Mikk, Privatisation: Estonia goes up for sale, *Estonian Independent*, 13 June 1990.

control of the economy, together with the responsiblity for its upgrading.[33] Nevertheless, Savisaar's determination may be seen from the detailed consideration which his government continued to give to various forms of privatisation. Proposals included selling state firms to employees or to their current directors. The first option contained the risk of inexperienced therefore defective management and the second that of corruption; Communist Party officials had already used their positions to prepare for comfortable positions in the new private sector.[34]

As well as laying the groundwork for the privatisation of enterprise, the Estonian government began to impose price rises for basic goods and services in the summer of 1990. The costs of fish, newspapers, beer and cigarettes went up, as did the cost of fares. Further huge price increases, of up to 300 per cent, came into effect on 15 October following the reduction of government subsidies on dairy products and meat.[35] The fact that only 50 per cent of Estonians and 16 per cent of non-Estonians supported the increases helps to explain the government emphasis on the need to pay attention to social welfare and to relief for pensioners, students and large families. With its adherence at the same time to the principle of low taxes, Savisaar's programme was aptly termed as representing a 'radical shift to the West'.[36]

The regional dimension of Estonian economic planning is a vital one, underlining a basic and growing communality of economic interest between the three republics. Thus in mid-April 1990, the three Baltic prime ministers, Savisaar, Prunskiene and Bresis, announced plans during a meeting in Vilnius for a 'common economic complex of the Baltic republics'. All three professed their belief in intervention 'first of all through the instruments of the market economy'. Proposals were drawn up for the elimination, commencing in 1990, of barriers to the flow of goods and services between the three republics and for the establishment of direct trade links between individual enterprises. Pledges were made about the creation of individual Baltic currencies, common customs policies and the institution of most-favoured-nation status in commercial relations between the republics. The idea of an

33 Choosing an economic system, *Homeland*, 28 March 1990.

34 Mikk, Estonia goes up for sale.

35 A Mikk, Food price hikes start off reform, *Estonian Independent*, 18 October 1990.

36 Government programme seeks radical shift to the West, *Estonian Independent*; L Oll, Prime Minister Savisaar for low taxes, free enterprise and privatisation, *Estonian Independent*, 16 May 1990.

executive commission loosely modelled on the Brussels-based EC was mooted. The Vilnius meeting claimed that 'From the moment of rati-fication, the contracting parties proclaim the creation of the Baltic market and declare it is open for the participation of the USSR, its republics and foreign countries on an equally profitable basis.'[37]

The economic agreements signed between the three Baltic republics in Riga on 12 April were ratified by the Baltic parliaments in the following month. Confirming the shared aim of restoring inde-pendence and promoting cooperation, the Baltic governments envis-aged the 'Baltic common market' being achieved in two stages. In the first phase, 1990–1, the basic legislative acts and regulations would be laid down, covering finance, prices, the exchange of information tech-nology and so forth. In the second phase the market mechanism would be refined and improved on the basis of annual contracts. In addition a monetary fund was proposed for the Baltic republics, as well as a Baltic investment bank to coordinate policy within and outside Baltic markets. The agreements would, however, permit the Baltic re-publics to issue their own national currencies, bring in common cus-toms policies and in general coordinate trade policy.[38]

In their proposals to promote cooperation through divisions of la-bour and economic integration the projected plans of 1990 showed a distinct awareness of the shortcomings of the Baltic league discussions in the 1920s, when economic cooperation was blighted by the great similarity between the economic structures of the three states, Latvia and Estonia in particular. A degree of rationalisation will be all the more vital in that the Baltic republics will almost certainly not be able to base their future prosperity on agricultural exports to the West, as they did in the 1920s and 1930s. The prospects of such regional econ-omic collaboration are, however, increased in so far as there exists today a greater degree of good will towards the Baltic republics in Scandinavia than there was before 1940. Furthermore this is now coupled with a Scandinavian readiness to help and advise far in ad-vance of that of the major western European powers.

Even in the West, however, there has been a shift of emphasis. In-itial responses to the Baltic crisis seemed to see economic development in the Baltic as a sort of substitute for independence. A lofty *Guardian* editorial argued, for example:

37 P Conradi, Baltic states agree common market plan, *Independent*, 14 April 1990.
38 Agreement on Baltic economic cooperation ratified, *Estonian Independent*, 23 May 1990.

Independence may be a rallying call but the realistic goal must be
substantial political devolution and genuine economic reforms bringing
new investment and the creation of new markets.[39]

As it transpired genuine economic progress proved impossible without
political advance in the Baltic. Of late it has been better understood in
Europe that there need be no necessary conflict between political independence for the Baltic republics and the economic well-being of
the Soviet Union. Thus, in heading what was the highest-level British
delegation to visit the republics since 1940, David Owen recognised in
September 1990 that the introduction of a market economy and a true
democracy in independent Baltic republics would bring positive benefits to the Soviet Union.

This reality was acknowledged by Boris Yeltsin, who not only
urged that 'the stronger the republics the stronger will be our union',
but also helped to shift the Baltic question to a new level by promising
to develop direct economic relations between the Baltic republics and
Russia, with its massive resources.[40] It may well be that both Gorbachev and Yeltsin have merely been playing the 'Baltic card' in their
political struggles with each other, yet the effect of the process proved
helpful rather than harmful to the Baltic cause. As a result of Savisaar's
meeting with the chairman of Leningrad city council, Sobchak, in late
June 1990, top Leningrad officials concluded a direct trade agreement
with an Estonian delegation at the beginning of August. Significantly,
this initial step towards a full-scale trade treaty envisaged not only
economic cooperation but also joint studies of the transition to a market economy.[41] By mid-October a customs border had been set up
between Estonia and the Russian federation, a major step in securing
effective execution of economic policy and price rises. By then Latvia
and Lithuania – who had also signed economic agreements with the
Russian Federation – had also commenced customs checks along their
borders with Russia and Belorussia.[42]

It is also possible that such direct relations between the Baltic republics and Russia will allow the Baltic governments to broaden the
range of instruments that can be employed to lessen the resistance of
Russians inside the republics. One interesting initiative relates to the

39 *Guardian*, 24 August 1988.

40 H Womack, Yeltsin sets Russia on collision course, *Independent*, 31 May 1990.

41 T Tammerk, Estonia to open direct ties with Leningrad, *Estonian Independent*, 4
July and 1 August 1990.

42 V Pettai, Customs border triggers opposition in Narva, *Estonian Independent*, 18
October 1990.

Savisaar government's proposal to counteract Russian resistance in Narva (where the Estonian population is a mere 4 per cent) by raising the idea of the city becoming a free enterprise zone. The hard currency which could be earned in this way could, it was suggested, help solve some of the economic and ecological problems of the region.[43]

From the vantage point of late 1990, it would be foolish to predict an easy passage towards independent Baltic republics, let alone a smooth transition to a market economy. The obstacles are formidable indeed. The ingenuity with which the Baltic republics, Estonia in particular, have prepared the legislative framework for the move towards a market economy has been more than matched by the sheer tenacity of Gorbachev's drive to conjure up a new, streamlined and somehow more acceptable federation for the USSR as a whole. And Moscow retains considerable power to frustrate, on the ground and at every turn, Baltic attempts to make the management of their own economic life a reality.

At the same time it is virtually impossible to see the Baltic republics willingly accepting any permanent new federal arrangement for the USSR, although the mere continuation of the present ambivalent constitutional relationship is enough for the moment to deter the sort of extensive western commitments to the Baltic economies which their geographical position and experience otherwise so richly merit. The economic imperatives are now difficult to stop. By 25–7 October the presidents of the Estonian, Latvian and Lithuanian central banks were meeting the first deputy chairman of the Russian central bank to begin working out common accounting procedures for their systems, revealing a growing determination to resist central control. Significantly, observers at this Tallinn meeting came from Georgia, Moldavia, the Ukraine and Belorussia, even though the last four had not yet formed their own central banks.[44]

Such direct discussions between the republics – expressed in the very reappearance of customs borders in the Baltic in October 1990 – illustrate the new reality rising alongside Gorbachev's dying vision of a federation revamped on Moscow's terms. The Estonian minister for social affairs, Arvo Kuddo, summed up the state of play in 1990 by insisting:

43 One way to make friends, *Estonian Independent*, 15 August 1990.

44 V Pettai, Baltic and Russian banks to continue their own way, *Estonian Independent*, 1 November 1990.

Russia is in a bad shape but it would be unfair to blame it on the republics. It is the fault of the system that was established in Russia in 1917 and imposed on the Baltic republics in 1940.[45]

The system of 1917 has now gone and that of 1940 must surely follow.

---

45 A Kuddo, Can Estonia make it alone? (part two), *Homeland*, 4 April 1990.

PART FIVE

Conclusion

CHAPTER ELEVEN
A European Necessity

'I do not feel that the independence of the Baltic States is a European necessity.' This sentiment was expressed by a member of the British Foreign Office in December 1941.[1] As we hope we have made clear in our book, it is a sentiment with which we emphatically disagree. Yet the West remains ambivalent towards Baltic aspirations to self-determination. As 1990 drew to a close, the West appeared bemused in the face of the momentous changes taking place in the Soviet Union and eastern Europe and distracted by events in the Gulf.

The Baltic peoples were not slow to point to the close parallels between Iraq's attack on Kuwait in 1990 and the Soviet absorption of the Baltic republics in 1940. There seemed little hope, however, of any dramatic western initiative in support of the Baltic cause. On the contrary, the Baltic republics were alarmed by the German–Soviet treaty of September 1990, which appeared to freeze their present status by recognising the territorial borders of Europe as inviolable. Despite reassurances that to 'honour' borders did not rule out the possibility of peaceful change, the Estonian parliament and foreign minister detected the 'ghost of 1939' in the diplomacy of the new Germany.[2] There was further evidence of western schizophrenia during one week in mid-November. On the one hand, President Landsbergis of Lithuania was received by the British prime minister at 10 Downing Street; on the other, the three Baltic republics were excluded from the Conference

---

1 Cited in D Kirby, Morality or expediency? The Baltic Question in British–Soviet relations, 1941–42. In V S Vardys and R J Misiunas (eds) *The Baltic States in Peace and War 1917–1945,* University Park and London 1978, p 168.

2 T Tammerk, Estonian parliament sees ghost of 1939, *Estonian Independent*, 27 September 1990.

on Security and Cooperation in Europe (CSCE) in Paris which brought a formal end to the Cold War.

Yet as the Soviet Union slides closer to the brink of catastrophe, Estonia, Latvia and Lithuania are all giving ample demonstrations of their will and capacity to survive outside the Soviet framework. The lack of international support is nothing new. The Baltic states had to fight for their independence at the end of the First World War: they are quite capable of doing so again in circumstances which, even at their worst, can scarcely be any more desperate than those of 1917–21.

If we have shown anything in this book it is that 'small' states are viable. Many such states have flourished in western Europe: there is no reason why independent Baltic states should not flourish too, just as they did between the wars. The experience of independent statehood offers other lessons for the future. Among the most vital is the need to take account of the interests of Russia. Whatever political, social and economic structures emerge from the Soviet crisis, Russia in some form will remain. It will be a powerful neighbour even if no longer a superpower. It will also be a country in urgent need of economic contact with the rest of the world – and here the Baltic states will be able to fulfil their historic mediatory role between East and West.

There is another and in some respects more disturbing lesson from the past. Baltic societies have always been multi-ethnic societies. For much of their history the various peoples inhabiting the Baltic region – Russians, Germans, Jews and Poles as well as Estonians, Latvians and Lithuanians – have shown an enviable capacity for mutual coexistence. The minority legislation of the interwar period did much to anchor those traditions of tolerance both in law and in everyday practice. However, there have also been racial friction and intolerance – and these traits too have at times been institutionalised. Today more than ever, the Baltic republics are ones in which the various nationalities will have to live and work together in order to survive. In Estonia and Latvia the native peoples are now in a much smaller majority than they were before 1940, and will have to find ways of reconciling the Russian minority to a new social, political and economic order. Lithuania, by contrast, is less ethnically mixed than it was before the Second World War. Here too, however, circumspection must be the order of the day.

These counsels of perfection are presumptuous, coming as they do from citizens of a society which has not been conspicuously successful in meeting the challenge of ethnic diversity. But for the Baltic republics anything much less than perfection will not be enough. They remain vulnerable societies in a world which is unlikely to do much for their interests, even if it is not actively hostile. The Baltic republics cannot afford to make too many mistakes. It is in the interests of other European countries to ensure that they do not.

Postscript

The main part of this book was completed during a period of stale-mate in relations between the Baltic republics and Moscow at the close of 1990. Shortly afterwards, as the world knows, a dramatic at-tempt was made to break the deadlock. As a result of the military crackdown, first in Lithuania and then in Latvia during the month of January 1991, unarmed Baltic civilians were once again killed in the streets of Vilnius and Riga. These events took place against a back-ground of economic collapse and a mounting right-wing backlash in the Soviet Union, led by such figures as the Latvian Viktor Alknis, referred to by former foreign minister Shevardnadze as 'boys in col-onels' epaulettes'. Whether the initiative came from the central auth-orities or from the increasingly beleaguered hard-line communists in the Baltic republics (and the former explanation seems the more plaus-ible), it looked as though the ground was being prepared for a take-over.[1] 'National Salvation Committees' emerged, offering an ominous reminder of the events of 1940 in the Baltic. Indeed they followed the depressingly predictable pattern of every other Moscow- inspired coup, successful or otherwise, over the last seventy years. The governments elected by popular majorities in 1990 were, it appears, to be desta-bilised and then to be swept aside.

It was no coincidence that the Gulf crisis was reaching its cres-cendo. If the Soviet central authorities and their local allies expected to profit from the West's distraction in order to teach the troublesome Baltic – and indeed other soviet republics – a lesson, they were to be disabused. On the very eve of war, Baltic spokesmen pushed Saddam Hussein from the front pages of the serious press and the lead stories of the television news coverage.

1 Cf J Laber, 'The Baltic revolt', *New York Review of Books*, 28 March 1991, 58–62.

It is true that in the case of America the response seemed at first disappointingly muted, as Bush sought to keep Gorbachev within the allied coalition against Iraq. Britain, however, was remarkably robust in its condemnation of the Baltic crackdown. It may be purely coincidental, but the departure of Thatcher from power appears to have had a liberating effect on Britain's policy towards the Baltic problem. The warm treatment of Estonian and Lithuanian representatives coming to London just prior to the crackdown contrasted markedly with the rather grudging reception which had been afforded to Mrs Prunskiene on her earlier visit to Downing Street.

There was still no question of the western powers insisting on recognition of Baltic independence but the case for it was now clearly being listened to with greater attention. This was shown by official comment, as well as by the editorials of the leading British dailies. As anger on behalf of the Baltic peoples grew, so sympathy for Gorbachev dropped sharply. If the Soviet leader was really behind the military action against defenceless Baltic citizens, he was not the man for the West to deal with. If he was unable to control events in Riga and Vilnius, then he and his government were not *worth* dealing with. John Major's visit to Moscow in March 1991 confirmed the sea change which had taken place in official British attitudes. Not only did he meet Baltic representatives in Moscow before talking with the Soviet leader, but he spoke to Gorbachev in unusually frank terms about the need to find an acceptable solution to the Baltic issue.

To an historian, it is almost as if Major were feeling his way back to the curiously dogged concern which the British showed for the welfare of the Baltic states up to 1940. The tradition of appeasing the Soviet Union, maintained by British leaders from Anthony Eden to Margaret Thatcher, seems at last to have been broken.

As a result of western condemnation and threats to withdraw economic aid packages, as well as the determination of the Baltic peoples to defend their democracies – literally – on the barricades, the Baltic republics appeared by March 1991 to have won another breathing space. Where do they go from here? It is worth quoting the words of the Estonian prime minister, Edgar Savisaar, speaking on his country's independence day on 24 February:

> We know we will not leave the Soviet Union through war. We will not buy ourselves out of the Soviet Union with money. We can only manoeuvre free from the union by wisdom and cunning.[2]

2 Cited in H Womack, 'On tiptoe towards a discreet revolt', *Independent on Sunday*, 3 March 1991.

The latter qualities are much in evidence. Faced with Gorbachev's attempt to remould the Soviet Union – and perhaps to win a mandate for a more authoritarian solution to its problems – by forcing through a national referendum, the Baltic republics held their own referendums in February and March. The results effectively refuted the claims of the pro-Moscow National Salvation Committees to speak for the majority of the non-Baltic inhabitants of the three Baltic republics. The question was squarely put as to whether people wanted fully independent republics. The turnout for the voting was exceptionally high and the large majorities in favour of independence indicated that many Russian citizens would opt for life without the Soviet Union.

The inconclusive and contradictory results of the 'national' referendum held on 17 March did not provide Gorbachev with a mandate to push through the changes which he desired. He may yet resort to an authoritarian solution, which may in turn require the further use of force – assuming that there will be wholly reliable armed forces at the disposal of the central authorities. If Gorbachev is pushed aside, the attempt may be made by his successors. Yet, as we have seen, this is an option which is unlikely to quell the Baltic spirit. Stalin was unable to do so. Can Gorbachev?

John Hiden and Patrick Salmon
March 1991

Bibliographical Essay

No attempt has been made to list all the sources cited in our footnotes. These provide plentiful guidance for the specialist. Here we confine ourselves to books published in English, together with a few important English-language articles.

Part I: Awakening

For the medieval period the best general survey of Baltic history is Eric Christiansen, *The Northern Crusades: The Baltic and the Catholic Frontier 1100–1525*, London 1980. Christiansen vividly evokes the hardships and terrors of life on the northern margins of medieval Christendom. Until recently there were few general books dealing with Baltic history in the period between the middle ages and the nineteenth century. This lack has been rectified by the appearance of the first part of David Kirby's two-volume history of the Baltic world, *Northern Europe in the Early Modern Period: The Baltic World 1492–1772*, London 1990. On the Baltic provinces in the Russian empire in the eighteenth and nineteenth centuries, see Edward C Thaden's magisterial *Russia's Western Borderlands, 1710–1870*, Princeton, N J 1984.

For more detail on the individual Baltic peoples and their history, there are a number of older books which can still be consulted with profit. Many of these were written by the first generation of Baltic émigrés. Although inevitably coloured by their authors' experiences, they are based on a profound knowledge of Baltic sources. They include: A Spekke, *A History of Latvia: An Outline*, Stockholm 1957; A Bilmanis, *A History of Latvia*, Princeton, N J 1951; A Blodnieks, *The Undefeated Nation*, New York 1960 (on Latvia); E Uustalu, *The History of the Estonian People*, London 1953; R Jurgela, *History of the Lithuanian Nation*, New York 1948. A welcome recent addition to the literature is Toivo U Raun, *Estonia and the Estonians*, Stanford, Calif 1987.

Insights into the nationality questions of the nineteenth century are provided by: E C Thaden (ed), *Russification in the Baltic Provinces and Finland, 1855–1914*, Princeton, N J 1981; A Henriksson, *The Tsar's Loyal Germans. The Riga German Community: Social Change and the Nationality Question, 1855–1905*, Boulder, Col 1983; A Loit (ed), *National Movements in the Baltic Countries during the 19th Century*, Uppsala 1985. There are a number of useful articles, including: A Plakans, 'Peasants, intellectuals and nationalism in the Russian Baltic provinces, 1820–1890', *Journal of Modern History* 46 (1974): 445–75, which concentrates mainly on Latvian nationalism; C Lundin offers a readable and highly informative account of the shifting mood in the Baltic German camp, 'The road from Tsar to Kaiser: changing loyalties of the Baltic Germans, 1905–1914', *Journal of Central European Affairs* 10 (1950): 223–55. The question of the relationship between nationalism and social democracy was posed most acutely in Lithuania. It is discussed by Leonas Sabaliunas in *Lithuanian Social Democracy in Perspective, 1893–1914*, Durham, NC 1990.

The Baltic area became a major theatre of war after 1914 and has generated an enormous literature, chiefly concerning the war aims of Imperial Germany. The book which originated this discussion is still well worth consulting: Fritz Fischer, *Germany's Aims in the First World War*, London 1967. The eastern dimension of the 'Fischer debate' is summarised in W H Maehl, 'Germany's war aims and the East 1914–17: status of the question', *The Historian* 34 (1972): 381–406. The German High Command played a major part in formulating Baltic policy. Martin Kitchen offers a readable study of its activities in *The Silent Dictatorship: The Politics of the German High Command under Hindenburg and Ludendorff*, London 1977.

Part II: States of Europe 1918–40

Indispensable for the history of the independent Baltic republics is Georg von Rauch, *The Baltic States. Estonia, Latvia, Lithuania: The Years of Independence 1917–1940*, London 1974. A collection of essays covering many important themes from the same period is: V S Vardys and R J Misiunas (eds), *The Baltic States in Peace and War 1917–45*, University Park, Pennsylvania and London 1978. Still unrivalled as a source of detailed information and analysis is *The Baltic States*, a survey produced by the Royal Institute of International Affairs (RIIA), London 1938.

On the Baltic provinces at the time of the Russian Revolution see: A Ezergailis, *The Latvian Impact on the Bolshevik Revolution: The First Phase, September 1917 – April 1918*, New York 1983. For the emergence of Baltic independence, S W Page, *The Formation of the Baltic States*, Cambridge, Mass 1959 (reprinted 1970) is still of interest and makes good use of the published Russian and German materials that were available at the time. A E Senn, *The Emergence of Modern Lithuania*, Morningside Heights, NY 1959, charts the tortuous path of one of the three republics to independence. A good discussion of the Paris peace conference and its implications for the smaller nations of Europe is G Schulze, *Revolutions and Peace Treaties 1917–1920*, London 1974. For information on Allied views on the Baltic and eastern Europe at the peace conference see Harold Nelson, *Land and Power: British and Allied Policy on Germany's Frontiers 1916–1919*, London and Toronto 1963, and Olavi Hovi, *The Baltic Area in British Policy 1918–21*, Helsinki 1980. The question of international recognition of Estonia and Latvia is discussed in volumes 3 and 4 of M W Graham, *The Diplomatic Recognition of the Border States*, Berkeley, Calif 1939–41.

A number of memoirs give a vivid picture of events in the Baltic at the time of the German and Allied military intervention of 1918–20. They include H de la Poer Gough, *Soldiering On*, London 1954; H A Grant-Watson, *An Account of a Mission to the Baltic States in 1919*, London 1957; Sir Stephen Tallents, *Man and Boy*, London 1943; Walter Duranty, *I Write as I Please*, London 1935. More generally, the atmosphere of the new Baltic republics is conveyed in a number of contemporary surveys. Among the best of these are John Buchan (ed), *Baltic and Caucasian States*, London, n.d. (*c.* 1923) (section on Estonia and Latvia written by W F Reddaway; section on Lithuania by T F Tallents); Owen Rutter, *The New Baltic States and their Future*, London 1925; J Hampden Jackson, *Estonia*, London 1941 (2nd edn 1948). There are some entertaining travellers' accounts, notably A McCallum Scott, *Beyond the Baltic*, London 1925, and John Gibbons, *Keepers of the Baltic Gates*, London 1939.

There are very few accounts in English which deal adequately with the internal politics of the independent Baltic states. For Estonia Tönu Parming comes to the rescue of English readers with his concise and thoughtful study, *The Collapse of Liberal Democracy and the Rise of Authoritarianism in Estonia*, London and Beverly Hills, Calif 1975. Interesting on the ideology of authoritarian rule in Lithuania but weak on the international dimension is L Sabaliunas, *Lithuania in Crisis: Nationalism to Communism 1939–1940*, Bloomington, Ind and London 1972. There is nothing comparable on Latvia.

Turning to the Baltic region's involvement in the international system between the wars, general bibliographical guidance and discussions of economic and foreign policy issues are to be found in J W Hiden and A Loit (eds), *The Baltic in International Relations between the Two World Wars*, Stockholm 1988.

Some studies of the policies of the major European powers are clearly relevant. For British policy in the 1920s too many books have been concerned with the period of intervention and British–Soviet relations: they often have little regard for the 'lands between'. A welcome exception is M-L Hinkkanen-Lievonen, *British Trade and Enterprise in the Baltic States 1919–25*, Helsinki 1984, not least because of its fluent English style. An entertaining autobiography, indispensable because the author was once head of the Northern Department of the Foreign Office, is J D Gregory, *On the Edge of Diplomacy: Rambles and Reflections*, London 1928. Kalervo Hovi offers a view of French alliance policy after 1919 which touches on the Baltic in *Alliance de revers: Stabilisation of France's Alliance Policies in East Central Europe 1919–21*, Turku 1984. Regrettably, the English is tortuous.

On Germany, in spite of countless books on Weimar–Soviet relations, there has been relatively little consideration of the three republics lying between the two great Baltic powers. As far as German-language works are concerned, the situation has improved in recent years. In English see J W Hiden, *The Baltic States and Weimar Ostpolitik*, Cambridge 1987. For the Soviet side there is not much in the way of balanced discussion, in English at least. A usable older book is A N Tarulis, *Soviet Policy towards the Baltic States 1918–40*, Notre Dame, Ind 1959. There is Baltic material in P S Wandycz, *Soviet–Polish Relations 1917–21*, Cambridge, Mass 1969.

On the efforts of the Baltic states to construct regional alliance systems see: B J Kaslas, *The Baltic Nations – The Quest for Regional Integration and Political Liberty*, Pittston, Pa 1976; H I Rodgers, *Search for Security: A Study in Baltic Diplomacy 1920–1934*, Hamden, Conn 1975, which, despite its title, concentrates almost exclusively on Latvia.

For the 1930s there is of course a massive literature on international relations and war origins, most of which takes little account of the Baltic. An exception, which also concentrates on the connection between foreign policy and trade, is D E Kaiser, *Economic Diplomacy and the Origins of the Second World War: Germany, Britain, France and Eastern Europe, 1930–39*, Princeton, N J 1980. M-L Hinkkanen-Lievonen and P Salmon have written English-language articles on the Baltic States and Scandinavia in the 1930s in M-L Recker (ed), *Von der Konkurrrenz zur Rivalität. Das britisch-deutsche Verhältnis in den Ländern der europäischen Peripherie 1919–39*, Stuttgart 1986. H Arumäe, *At the Crossroads: The Foreign Policy of the Republic of Estonia in 1933–1939*, Tallinn 1983, offers valuable insights despite the ideological constraints under which it was written.

For the immediate origins of the Second World War we are now fortunate to have D C Watt's magisterial *How War Came*, London 1989, one of the few accounts which takes adequate notice of the Baltic dimension in the final crisis. For more detailed attention to the Klaipeda (Memel) crisis in 1938–9, see C Thorne, *The Approach of War 1938–1939*, London 1967. The Baltic takes centre stage in a forthcoming essay collection edited by J W Hiden and T Lane, *The Baltic and the Origins of the Second World War*, Cambridge 1991. The important work of Rolf Ahmann is mostly in German but is represented in a recent article, 'The German treaties with Estonia and Latvia of 7 June 1939: bargaining ploy or an alternative for German–Soviet understanding?', *Journal of Baltic Studies* 20 (1989): 337–64.

Part III: Eclipse 1940–85

The equivalent of Rauch's book on the interwar period is, for the war and postwar period, R J Misiunas and R Taagepera, *The Baltic States: Years of Dependence 1940–80*, Berkeley, Calif 1983. Like Rauch's volume, this study is a central reference point for all those who work on the history of the Baltic republics. The Estonian-Swedish journalist Andres Küng has produced a work of passionate commitment which is especially informative on dissident activities: *A Dream of Freedom: Four Decades of National Survival versus Russian Imperialism in Estonia, Latvia and Lithuania 1940–1980*, Cardiff 1981. Slightly more up to date but disappointingly thin in some respects is I J Vizulis, *Nations under Duress: The Baltic States*, Port Washington, NY 1985. For individual countries there are two important essay collections: V S Vardys (ed), *Lithuania under the Soviets: Portrait of a Nation, 1940–65*, New York 1965; T Parming and E Järvesoo (eds), *A Case Study of a Soviet Repub-*

lic: The Estonian SSR, Boulder, Col 1978. Again, there is no comparable work on Latvia.

For the Second World War Vardys and Misiunas (eds), *The Baltic States in Peace and War*, mentioned above, contains some important essays, especially those by A Dallin and D Kirby. Kirby has also written a concise account, 'The Baltic States 1940–50', in M McCauley (ed), *Communist Power in Europe 1944–1949*, London 1977. Sabaliunas, *Lithuania in Crisis* (above), is useful for the 1939–40 period. On German occupation policy Alexander Dallin, *German Rule in Russia 1941–1945*, London and New York 1957, is still of value although English readers should be aware that its section on the *Ostland* has been largely superseded by Seppo Mylliniemi's *Die Neuordnung der baltischen Länder 1941–1944*, Helsinki 1973. For the fate of the Jews in the Baltic area see Ezra Mendelsohn, *The Jews of East Central Europe between the World Wars*, Bloomington, Ind 1983; Avraham Tory, *Surviving the Holocaust: The Kovno Ghetto Diary*, Cambridge, Mass 1990; Yitzhak Arad, *Ghetto in Flames: The Struggle and Destruction of the Jews in Vilna in the Holocaust*, Jerusalem 1980.

With its 570 footnotes and 13 appendixes, a recent article by W J H Hough, III, is as authoritative a statement of the status of the Soviet annexations of 1940 in international law as one could hope to find: 'The annexation of the Baltic States and its effect on the development of law prohibiting forcible seizure of territory', *New York Law School Journal of International and Comparative Law* 6 (1985): 300–533. Connoisseurs of the genre will note that footnote 514 runs to more than ten closely printed pages.

For the Baltic republics since 1944 (as well as for earlier periods of Baltic history), the *Journal of Baltic Studies*, published by the Association for the Advancement of Baltic Studies, is consistently informative. A number of works dealing with Soviet nationality problems touch on the Baltic republics. They include: R Karklins, *Ethnic Relations in the USSR: The Perspective from Below*, Boston, Mass 1986; and, for the early Gorbachev years, P A Goble, 'Gorbachev and the Soviet nationality problem', in M Friedberg and H Isham (eds), *Soviet Society under Gorbachev: Current Trends and the Prospects for Reform*, Armonk, NY 1987. For more recent developments see Graham Smith (ed), *The Nationalities Question in the Soviet Union*, London 1990. Highly informative and devoted exclusively to the Baltic republics is E Allworth (ed), *Nationality Group Survival in Multi-Ethnic States: Shifting Support Patterns in the Soviet Baltic Region*, New York 1977

Part IV: Reawakening

A number of surveys of the Gorbachev era are now available. One which devotes more space than most to Baltic affairs is Richard Sakwa, *Gorbachev and his Reforms 1985–1990*, London 1990. *Lithuania Awakening*, Berkeley, Calif 1990, by the distinguished Baltic scholar Alfred E Senn, covers events in that republic since 1988.

Those wishing to keep abreast of current events can rely not merely on western publications but also, to an increasing extent, on English-language material published in the Baltic republics themselves. Among British newspapers the *Independent* stands out for the breadth and quality of its coverage of day-to-day events in the Baltic. Radio Liberty's *Report on the USSR* contains up-to-date material and expert analyses. In recent years *Problems of Communism* has featured a number of lengthy analyses by Baltic experts. Of the Baltic republics, Estonia offers the most consistent source of information in the *Estonian Independent* (formerly *Homeland*), a four-page weekly newspaper. The Latvian equivalent, *Atmoda*, appears at more irregular intervals, as does the *Lithuanian Review*.

Maps and Charts

St Petersburg

ST PETERSBURG

NOVGOROD

Tallinn (Reval)

ESTLAND

LAKE PEIPUS (PEIPSI)

LAKE ILMEN

DAGÖ

Pärnu (Pernau)

Tartu (Dorpat, Iurev)

Pskov (Pleskau)

ÖSEL

LIVLAND

PSKOV

• Ventspils (Windau)

• Riga

KURLAND

• Jelgava (Mitau)

VITEBSK

Liepaja (Libau)

Dünaburg

Vitebsk

KOVNO

Klaipeda (Memel)

MOGILEV

Kaunas (Kovno)

Vilnius (Vilna)

Mogilev

• Tilsit

VILNA

Insterburg

• Königsberg

Minsk

EAST PRUSSIA (GERMANY)

• Suwalki

MINSK

• Allenstein

Grodno

POLISH PROVINCES

GRODNO

Pinsk

0		50 mls
0		100 km

• Bialystok

Brest-Litovsk

• Warsaw

• Sjedlaz

VOLHYNIA

Map 1 Provinces of the Russian Empire in 1914

203

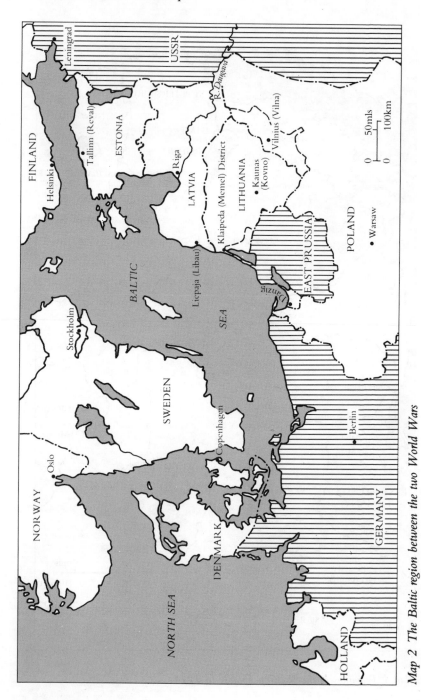

Map 2 The Baltic region between the two World Wars

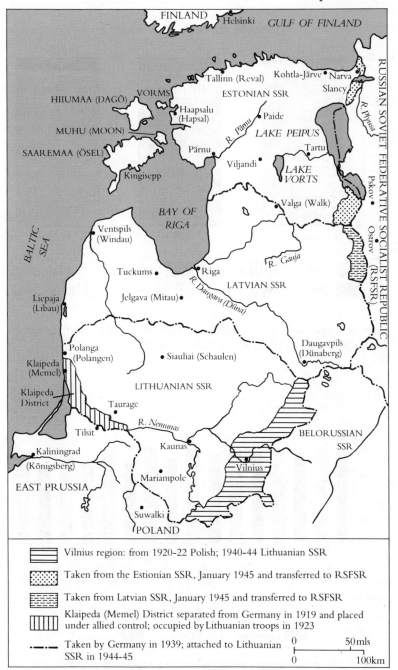

FINLAND
Helsinki
GULF OF FINLAND

Tallinn (Reval) Kohtla-Järve Narva
Slancy

RUSSIAN SOVIET FEDERATIVE SOCIALIST REPUBLIC (RSFSR)

HIIUMAA (DAGÖ) VORMS ESTONIAN SSR

Haapsalu
(Hapsal) Paide

MUHU (MOON)

R. Pärnu

LAKE PEIPUS

SAAREMAA (ÖSEL) Pärnu

Viljandi Tartu

LAKE
VORTS

Kingisepp

R. Plyusa

BAY OF
RIGA

Valga (Walk)

Pskov

Ventspils
(Windau)

Ostrov

BALTIC
SEA

R. Gauja

Tuckums Riga

LATVIAN SSR

Liepaja
(Libau)

Jelgava (Mitau)

R. Daugava (Düna)

Daugavpils
(Dünaberg)

Polanga
(Polangen) Siauliai (Schaulen)

Klaipeda
(Memel)

LITHUANIAN SSR

Klaipeda
District Taurage

BELORUSSIAN
SSR

R. Nemunas

Tilsit

Kaliningrad
(Königsberg) Kaunas

Vilnius

EAST PRUSSIA Mariampole

Suwalki

POLAND

Vilnius region: from 1920-22 Polish; 1940-44 Lithuanian SSR

Taken from the Estonian SSR, January 1945 and transferred to RSFSR

Taken from Latvian SSR, January 1945 and transferred to RSFSR

Klaipeda (Memel) District separated from Germany in 1919 and placed
under allied control; occupied by Lithuanian troops in 1923

Taken by Germany in 1939; attached to Lithuanian
SSR in 1944-45

0   50 mls
0   100 km

Map 3 The Baltic Republics after the Second World War

205

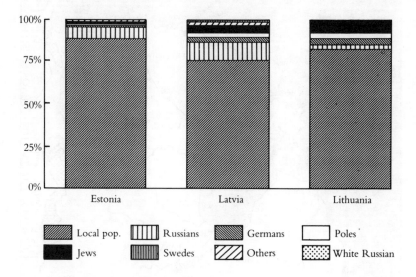

Chart 1 Ethnic groups in the Baltic, 1934 (Estonia, 1934 census; Latvia, 1935; Lithuania, 1932/4; data includes Memel)

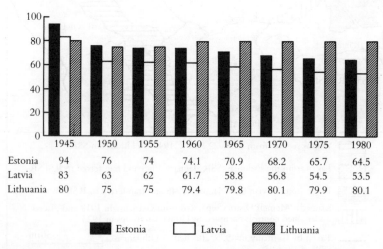

	1945	1950	1955	1960	1965	1970	1975	1980
Estonia	94	76	74	74.1	70.9	68.2	65.7	64.5
Latvia	83	63	62	61.7	58.8	56.8	54.5	53.5
Lithuania	80	75	75	79.4	79.8	80.1	79.9	80.1

Chart 2 The Baltic States: population percentage belonging to the Republic Nationality

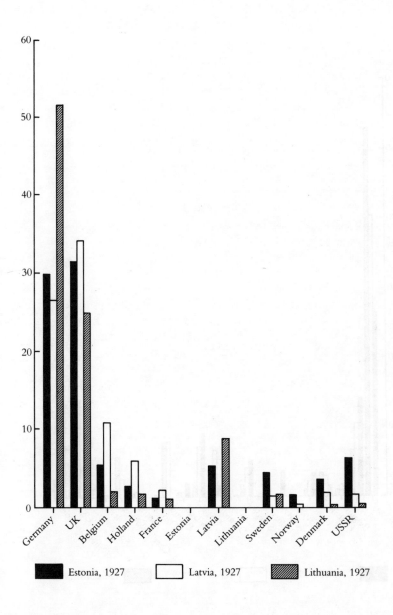

Chart 3 Distribution of the foreign trade of the Baltic countries: exports as percentage of the total value

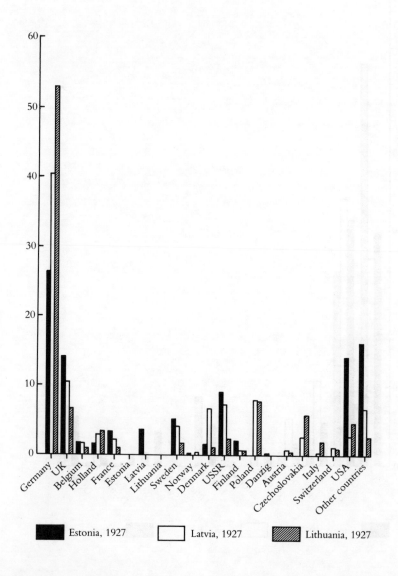

Estonia, 1927   Latvia, 1927   Lithuania, 1927

Chart 4 Distribution of the foreign trade of the Baltic countries: imports as percentage of the total value

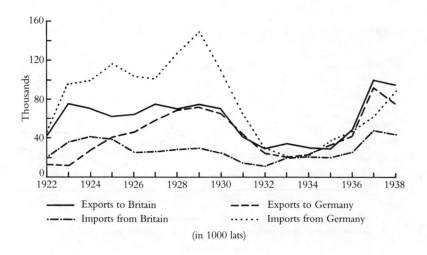

(in 1000 lats)

Chart 5 Value of British and German trade with Latvia, 1922–38

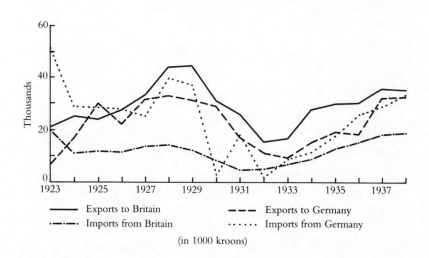

(in 1000 kroons)

Chart 6 Value of British and German trade with Estonia, 1923–38

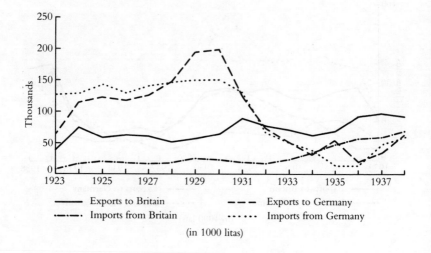

Chart 7 Value of British and German trade with Lithuania, 1923–38

Index